WANTA BET?

A Study of the Pari-Mutuels System in the United States How It Works— And the Sports Involved

BOB and BARBARA FREEMAN
with
JIM McKINLEY

Published by Freeman Mutuels Management

Manufactured in the U.S.A.

Printer—Moran Industries, Inc.

Binder—Becktold Book Binding.

ISBN 0-9608022-0-7
ISBN 0-9608022-1-5

Library of Congress Catalogue Card No. 82-90023

Cover photography courtesy of:
    SCI Photography
    Neal Studio
    USTA
    Dania Jai Alai
    United Totalisator Co.

To Judi, Don, Dave, Dina and Gina
And to John and Shirley Bogle
and Dedicated to the memory of
Curt and Verna Freeman.

TABLE OF CONTENTS

Foreword

Pari-mutuels wagering on five major sports in the United States, thoroughbred horse racing, quarter horse racing, harness horse racing, greyhound dog racing, and jai alai is one of the most controversial subjects on the American scene at the present time. Its importance is reflected in several ways. The controversy over its benefits or harm is accentuated for the same reasons that other social and business items are being studied in order to be placed in their proper priority. It has a much bigger impact on the problems of economy, taxation, and energy than first comes to mind. In 1980 the total amount of monies wagered during the year was about 13½ billion dollars, of which more than 800 million dollars was returned to different branches of government in the form of revenue.

At the present time there are over half a million people employed at the tracks and frontons presently operating in conformance with legislation permitting their operation. This includes owners and stockholders of tracks and frontons, employees to carry on their operation, breeders, owners, and trainers necessary to furnish the animals involved in all sports except jai alai, jai alai players, supervisory personnel representing the state permitting these operations, fringe companies who are manufacturing equipment, supplies, and services necessary to carry on the business of the sports involved.

It affects the fans and customers who attend these events. It is estimated that in 1980, over 105 million fans passed through the gates of these five sources of entertainment. The Daily Racing Form puts out a pamphlet each year listing the order of popularity of spectator sports. Horse racing is number one. That is, if you include at least two of the three categories in one group. Regardless of your personal preference, the unbiased figures in 1978 looked something like this: thoroughbred plus harness horse racing fans totaled more than 79 million. Actually, this was necessary since if all categories were separated, automobile racing drew 50,750,500 fans as opposed to 50,587,804 paid admissions to thoroughbred tracks. Greyhound racing, although legal in only 13 states, totaled 20,046,298 and quarter horse tracks and jai alai frontons totaled many millions more.

At any rate, the bottom line comes down to the fact that more people pay to attend the five sports subsidized by pari-mutuels wagering than any other combined group of sports.

The next group that is indirectly affected by pari-mutuels wagering is the merchants that derive different portions of their business from fans coming to, or leaving these facilities. This is an intangible figure. There is no concrete way to estimate this number, but it is considerable.

Another group that is affected is those who benefit from the tax revenue generated from all of the above, whether or not they approve or disapprove of the pari-mutuels systems. It indirectly affects the tax structure of states who do not permit legalized wagering, but whose constituents cross their own state borders to contribute to the sports' success in a neighboring state.

Thirty one of the fifty states permit wagering on one or more of the five sports. Thoroughbred racing is permitted in twenty four states, quarter horse racing, harness horse racing and greyhound racing each have legal approval in fourteen states, and jai alai is limited to four states. Florida is alone with legislation permitting all five sports. The other thirty permit one or more of the categories, but exclude others. Betting on these events at locations other than track or fronton premises is limited to four states. New York and Connecticut have off track betting facilities, while Nevada and New Jersey conduct these activities in conjunction with legalized gambling casinos.

The statistics listed above raise many important questions.

Will more states legalize betting on one or more of these sports?

Is this system a good way to raise needed revenue?

Would the added revenue from this source be worth the price of alienating the segment of society who are opposed to betting in any form on moral grounds?

Is it possible to control these sports to a degree where the public will be protected if they participate in this revenue raising industry?

What does pari-mutuels wagering really mean and how does it work?

Who are the people connected with these sports, what are their actual duties, and how do they go about participating if they so desire?

How did these sports originate?

Are they worth the time to understand, to a degree, how they work?

How did they become connected with wagering?

How did they grow to a multi-billion dollar per year industry?

Which of the five sports would be the best to consider for future legislation?

Is it possible to still call these five events "sports" or do these statistics place them in the realm of "big business"?

Most of the answers to the above questions are certainly debatable to say the least. We will try to answer them as fairly and accurately as possible throughout the book, from the standpoint of thirty five years of experience working in the industry. I'm sure the answers that each individual comes up with will vary from one end of the spectrum to the other. The purpose of the book is for everyone to have accurate reasons to either favor the pari-mutuels system or disagree with it.

Acknowledgements

To list each person to whom we owe a debt of gratitude would take several pages, and even then, we would probably miss someone or probably several someones, who have contributed not only time and research material, but needed encouragement as well. The co-operation from the Racing Commissions of the many states, who furnished us statistics and other necessary information was fantastic. The same is true of the various organizations connected with racing and jai alai. We will list these organizations by their trade name only as we're sure several people were probably involved with assembling the material we requested.

The Jockey Club, Thoroughbred Racing Protective Bureau, Horseman's Benovolent and Protective Association, Thoroughbred Racing Association, Jockey Guild, Daily Racing Form, American Quarter Horse Association, United States Trotting Association, Greyhound Racing Record, National Greyhound Association, Greyhound Hall of Fame, American Greyhound Track Operators Association, National Association of Jai Alai Frontons, Inc., Newport Jai Alai, American Mule Association, National Association of Racing Commissioners, Southern Technology, United Totalisator, American Totalisator, Automatic Totalisator, Turf Photo Supply, Eye in the Sky, Photo Trackmaster, Puett Starting Gates, Louisville Downs, New York OTB, Teletrack, SCI Photography and Moran Industries.

A few names from the organizations listed above that were especially helpful come to mind.

Jack DeFee, Al Papara, Don Essary, Ken Guenthner, LaVerne Ordway, Jesus Sandoval, John Shelhamer, Bob North, Juanita Gordon, Dick Hairgrove, Ned Gutierrez, Dave Mendelson, Clay Puett, Bill King, Bill Drew, Glen and Frenchy Thibodeaux, Beth Smith and Teresa Wynne.

Others who willingly gave their time and information and deserve a vote of thanks are Dan Shimeall, Dave Freeman, Rafe Sagalyn, Polo Terrazas, Jesus Cuaron, Howie Nodurft, Vern Falde, Paul and John Hartwell, Pat Kelly, Jerry Porterfield, Jeff Johnson, Bernardo Cocio, Pat Kierens, Jim and Marge Bindner, Ep and Ginny Hall, Ray Johnson, Joe Gonzales, and Mike Snyder.

An extra special "thank you" to our friend, Steve Nodurft, one of the few Americans to become a successful jai alai professional for help concerning everything having to do with jai alai. To Dan Moldea, author of "The Hoffa Wars" for giving the necessary encouragement to finish the book when the issue was in doubt. And to Mary Ann McKinley for help in many different ways.

PART ONE

Sports Used for Pari-Mutuels Wagering

Chapter One
Thoroughbreds: "The Sport of Kings"

Sometimes a knowledge of the mechanics of pari-mutuel wagering, and the inevitable emphasis on money, obscures the fact that the sports themselves are ancient. And that people have been betting on them for centuries without benefit of modern pari-mutuels operations.

Probably the best-known of these sports is thoroughbred horse racing, nicknamed "The Sport of Kings". Although quarter horses, harness racing, greyhound racing and jai alai have made serious challenges to it's dominance in the past few decades, thoroughbred racing still draws more spectators than any other single sport in the nation, drawing fans from twenty-four states to more than ninety recognized tracks.

Volumes have been written about its origin and history. The documented records in colonial days were contemporary, and since travel was limited and news items were of a local nature, thoroughbred breeding and racing advanced in many different sections of the country—each almost entirely independent from the other.

Historians generally agree on certain facts and theories however, and we will try to give a brief resume on the development and popularity of the sport. Most experts maintain that the thoroughbred breed results mostly from crossing native English mares with imported "Arabian" stallions. The term "Arabian" was used rather loosely by the English, and many of these stallions may have been either Barbs or Turks. At any rate, three sires from these imports stood out. They were Byerly Turk, Darley Arabian, and the Godolphin Arabian.

Byerly Turk was imported in 1689, Darley Arabian in 1703 or 1704, and Godolphin Arabian in 1730. Horses were small at that time in comparison with the ones of today. Most were about 14 hands high, (a hand being about 4 inches). The Darley Arabian was said to have been about 15 hands high, a giant in those days. Regardless of size, every thoroughbred has descended from one or more of these stallions.

Three seems to be the magic number, as the crossing of the Arabians with English mares resulted in the second big three: Herod, Matchem, and Eclipse, known as the "Pillars of the Stud Book". All three contained blood lines from the original imports in varying degrees. Eclipse is often called the first truly great racehorse and today approximately 90% of thoroughbreds descend from this famous stallion. The Darley Arabian was the predominate ancestor of Eclipse. He was foaled in 1764, a fourth generation offspring. An interesting sidelight to Eclipse is that he proved almost untrainable. He was a very vicious animal, described by jockeys of that day as "bull-headed", "savage-tempered", "unmanageable", and "not altogether sane". The idea of gelding him was entertained more than once, so the world almost lost its most important stallion.

The long workouts given him to break his spirit somewhat, probably was instrumental in building him up for the long races, popular during this period. It was not uncommon for a race to be decided in three heats of four miles each. Eclipse raced only two years, at the ages of five and six. He was invincible during these two years. He won easily, even when they required him to carry as much as 168 pounds.

Meanwhile, in North America, there had existed an early ancestor of the horse, but the species vanished for unknown reasons. Only fossils remained as proof that this was true. The first North American horses of modern times was imported from Europe. On Christopher Columbus's second trip to the new continent, he brought some horses with him, which he left behind in the West. In the 1500's the Spaniards brought horses, so by the time the English colonists arrived in Jamestown in 1607, there were already quite a few horses on the continent. They were located mostly in Mexico, in what is now the Southwestern States, and around the Caribbean. They were horses of Spanish Barb descent, the same as were being imported by England at that time. The settlers brought some horses with them in 1607, but they were forced to eat them the following winter during a famine. The next record of horses in the colonies was in 1620, at which time the colonies' sponsors sent them twenty mares. These twenty, and those sent in subsequent years, fared better than those they had brought originally. It was recorded that "the woods were full of horses". A favorite past-time of the children was trying to catch them. They were small horses, most being thirteen to fourteen hands tall and were of mixed English, Scottish, and Irish stock. When domesticated, most were trained to the pacing gait.

At first the settlers had neither time nor a place to race their horses, but soon they began racing them in the short, narrow streets between cabins. These races were known as "street drags". This was dangerous to the inhabitants and some of the first laws on record were in regards to street racing. The next step was to clear straight, narrow paths in the wilderness on which to conduct their racing. Because of the work involved in building these paths, most were only a quarter of a mile long. So while the English horses were running at a distance of four miles, the settlers were limiting their races to a quarter of a mile. They called this "quarter-pathing". There was room for only two horses to race at a time, so they concentrated on training their horses to start fast and run full out for the quarter mile distance. This type racing is still popular in some areas of the country at the small bush tracks and is now called "match races".

As the colonies prospered, the wealthy began importing English race-horses and racing them at longer distances. The new aristocracy looked down on the "quarter-pathers". In time the native stock, combined with the Chicasaw horse of the Indians (a Barb descendant), moved West and South.

With the help of an imported thoroughbred named Janus, they were to become the fore runner of the quarter horse of today.

The Virginians, South Carolinians, Marylanders, and New Yorkers meanwhile were using much of their wealth to bring over thoroughbreds. The thoroughbreds weren't officially established until around 1880, but these imports called "breds", "bloods", or simply "racehorses", were of the same stock that was evolving into the new breed in England. Some probably had forged pedigrees, but the effect was to speed up the old Irish-English-Scottish mix. It also tended to gradually eliminate their tendancy to pace. The South became the breeding center of blood stock and remained so until the Civil War.

The North was also importing horses from England but because they were building more roads, their need was greater for harness horses to pull their buggies, while the South was faced with mud most of the year and continued to travel mostly by riding horseback. The need for road horses in the North, meant trotters and pacers, exactly what England was sending over. So the two sections of the country ended up with horses of two distinctly different types.

Religion also played a part in the type of horses that evolved. Most of the Southerners belonged to the Church of England, which was not at all opposed to racing horses. The New Englanders' religious views were stricter. Horse racing was considered a vice. However it wasn't long before they rationalized that horse racing was interpreted to mean running races and did not include trotters and pacers, pulling a conveyance. Road races became common, but they were not official nor recorded. As the decades passed, New England's trotters and pacers became larger and faster. The Narragansett pacer, developed in Rhode Island, became especially well known.

When England took over New Amsterdam from the Dutch, one of the first official acts of the new English governor of New York in 1665 was to order a racetrack built on Long Island. It was named New Market in honor of King Charles II who made New Market in England his home away from home. The track was an instant success. Soon many tracks sprang up around New York City and on Long Island. One Long Island track, called the Union Course, became famous for it's "North-South" races and competition became strong between the two sections of the country.

During the 1700's all the colonies had racetracks at one time or another, but their popularity ran hot and cold. They would be accepted, then abolished, only to be brought back again. During the popular periods, if one wanted to see the most famous men of that time all together at the same time, he need only go to an extremely fashionable race track. The tracks became the center of the social circle for the rich and famous. Records show that among the owners of horses racing during this period, George Washington and Thomas Jefferson were included.

The Revolution had a tremendous effect on racing as it did on everything else. It halted racing completely for a time. While the British officers were here, they confiscated and took back to England most of the good race-horses. Others were killed while being used by the cavalry. When the war was over they were not easily replaced, since bad feelings resulted in a standstill in the importing of English horses. Also the break with the Church of England, which approved of horse races, brought about a more puritani-cal religious attitude in the new country and racing lost favor.

After a brief cooling off period, however, the importing of thoroughbreds reached a higher point than before the war. As the flood of imports went on, the American stock increased greatly in number and quality. The records of most of these imports no longer exist, if they ever did, but two stallions secured during this period were to play a dominant part in the quality of American thoroughbreds that exist today. They were Diomed and Mes-senger.

Messenger was born in 1780 and raced for two years in England as a three and four year old. His record was fairly good but not outstanding. He was more successful at races up to two miles than at the longer distances of up to four miles, (four miles being the most popular distance during this period). He then disappeared from the records until 1788. Messenger's name next appeared in a Philadelphia paper on May 27th of that year, advertising him as a newly imported stallion. He was later moved to the New York City area, where he stood at stud for the rest of his life. He became known as the founder of the standard-bred horse and for this reason, his importance to the American thoroughbred is sometimes overlooked. Most of the mares brought to him were of the trotting and pacing variety, but the few running horses that he sired became outstanding.

Diomed did not arrive in America until 1798 at the advanced age of twenty-one. He had won the English Derby as a three year old and raced brilliantly for a time before breaking down. After that he was used as a stallion, but he was not considered a good sire in England and was sold for a modest price to a Virginia breeder. The new world seemed to agree with Diomed. For the next decade he produced outstanding racehorses up until his death at thirty-one years of age. Diomed's offspring became so superior that new blood had to be imported to keep the sport competitive.

Racing is most notable from the 1820's to the Civil War for the intense rivalries that sprang up between different sections of the country. The popu-larity of horse racing had spread west to Kentucky and south to New Or-leans, as well as to all points in between. Soon there would be race meetings in St. Louis and Chicago, as well as a winter meeting out of the new country in Havana, Cuba, with some of the leading stables sending their horses there. Again, as before the Revolutionary War, many areas would be a hot bed of racing for awhile and then die out, only to become popular again in a few years. However, in other places it would shut down permanently.

Up to this point we've ignored the background of racing in the West. The migration of large numbers of settlers across the prairies and mountains to California was accomplished almost entirely by use of the horse as transportation. When they arrived they found horsemanship in a correspondingly high state of development. The Spanish explorers usually took horses with them for use on their expeditions. Records show that in 1769 Captain Rivera y Moncado's group was accompanied by 140 horses on his trip from Lower California toward San Diego for a rendezvous with Gaspar de Portola. Racing of a sort probably began shortly after this group settled at San Diego. Unlike the forests of the East, California had suitable terrain for tracks, most notably the beaches. Visitors to the West Coast returned home in the late 1820's and early 1830's with reports of racing. One such visitor described the beach at Santa Barbara as a "favorite place for running horses". He described the sport as being quite advanced compared to Eastern racing. Grounds were specially set aside for the purpose, with judges, rules, and stakes. Up until 1848 the racing stock was almost entirely made up of descendents of the Spanish horses brought over by the explorers. The famous gold rush of that year created a greater need for horses and Eastern dealers began rounding up large numbers to be shipped to California. The gap between Eastern and Western racing was quickly bridged, although the first thoroughbred to be introduced was a mare "Black Swan", imported from Australia in 1851. Distance racing was popular, the Pony Express probably having a big influence on this form of racing. The first mention of heat racing was recorded in 1853.

The broad aspects of American racing had been gradually changing during this period also. English styles were being adopted. The North was becoming industrialized, which created a common bond with England. Wealthy Northern boys were attending schools abroad and brought home British ideas. Dash races were the vogue in England and becoming increasingly popular in America. The first set of organized statistics in 1836 showed that there were 62 races at four mile heats, and 247 at one mile. By 1860, the last complete season before the war, the number of four mile races had dropped to 24 and those at one mile had increased to 313. Races for two and three year olds had also become more common.

Then came the Civil War. The horse became a tool of war. Most of the great Southern racing and breeding centers were completely devastated. Some were able to send their stock north to Ohio, Illinois, and even to Canada. Paintings, records, and trophies were also lost. Kentucky maintained a policy of neutrality as much as possible, and came out of the upheavel in better shape than the states which had actually joined the Confederacy. When the war ended, Kentucky became the undisputed capitol of breeding, if not of racing. Some cities in the South tried to continue racing even during the war, but on a catch-as-catch-can basis only. Control of racing passed to the victorious North, and it became apparent that a new era of American racing was underway.

Dash racing instead of deciding races by heats became the standard American form. Although the South hung on to the old custom of horses' birthdays being May 1st for many years, the rest of the country changed the date to January 1st, a practice still followed today. The stepped up program of more and larger purses dictated the necessity of depending on patrons to foot part of the bill. The pure concept of sport for sport's sake had to be tempered with the realities of economic necessity. Gambling became the tool to generate revenue. California had explored the possibilities of obtaining revenues from racing as early as 1841. In Los Angeles, in this year, a new law provided that the winner of each race pay a tax of 20 reales for every $25 bet, $5 for every $50 and 6% of all sums of $100 or more. This law was abolished in 1846.

Pool betting was outlawed in New York in 1877, so the pool sellers moved across the river to New Jersey where it was also prohibited after a short time. Gambling as well as the nature of thoroughbred racing became very controversial subjects. The backers of running races and harness races came into sharp conflict with each other. The running horse eventually won the battle for popularity but today the two interests co-exist in a fairly amicable fashion.

The necessity for gambling to foot the bill for the expenses involved in conducting a race meeting, changed the whole concept of structuring races. A system had to be implemented that would encourage the public to wager. Before the Civil War the "conditions" for a typical race was very simple. An example would be "Purse $300, for all ages. Two mile heats". This would result in very one-sided races, and very few would wager on the outcome. Races were now made up to conform to past performances, and the types of races we are familiar with today became a reality—Handicaps, Allowances, Futurities, etc. The most effective device implemented to draw large fields, and encourage more wagering was the "Selling Race", which today is called a "Claiming Race". The systems of dash racing and bookmakers was imported from England. Different stipulations, in all the categories, went through periods of experiment, but the basic principles as set up in the beginning still exist.

The auction pool method of wagering had become quite common before the Civil War. It is still used today at small "bush" tracks where pari-mutuels wagering is not permitted, especially at quarter horse meets. Auction pools are identical to "Calcutta" pools, popular in golf tournaments today. Each contestant was "sold" to the highest bidder and the money thus collected went to the person buying the winning horse, after deducting a percentage for the auctioneer's fees. In return, the auctioneer paid the association holding the races a flat fee for the privilege of operating on its premises. Even when conducted honestly, this method had obvious disadvantages. First, the odds against an individual horse could not be determined until all the entries had been sold. Secondly, the bettor with the greatest amount of capital could monopolize the most logical choice. Those frozen out by this method, had either to buy an entry he didn't particularly like, or not bet at all.

Increased public interest in racing led to a demand for a system whereby the small investor could participate. Enter the bookmaker. Now everybody could become involved. The bookmaker would quote his odds on each horse. A bet was binding at the time it was made, at the odds quoted, but the bookmaker could change the odds as betting progressed. In essence, the bookmaker was also a gambler. He could win or lose, according to his handicapping and balancing of the books at odds of his own making.

When bookmaking actually started is not definitely known. Many believe it started in England during the reign of King George IV, but others maintain this practice was used as far back as the chariot races in Rome. According to the New York Herald, the first bookmaking in America was performed about 1866 by the Philadelphia firm of Sanford, Sykes, and Evans whose business was conducted primarily on cricket, regattas, and trotting races, but who would accept wagers on competition of any kind. The "American Racing Manual" lists James E. Kelley of New York, who opened a winter book on the 1871 Belmont Stakes as the pioneer bookmaking specialist in horse racing. The "Herald" published an article in 1894, estimating that at Brighton Beach about sixty bookmakers were handling over $1,000,000 on a typical racing day, consisting of six races. The bookmaker usually paid the Metropolitan tracks $100 per day for his permit to operate. The bookmakers would often bet with each other, "lay off bets", to balance their books. They also had the option to refuse to accept bets on certain horses when the chances of a horse winning would create a loss to their operation. Thus, they had the best of two worlds. They would often employ personnel to work in the barn area to get information advantageous to their operation. You can see that the options open to the bookmakers put the patron at a decided disadvantage. Again, a better system was needed to promote the growth of the racing industry.

THE INAUGURATION OF PARI-MUTUELS

In view of its ultimate significance, by far the most important development during the period between the Civil War and World War I, was the advent of the pari-mutuels system. Unlike most features of American racing, which were copied from England, this system originated in France and was a long time being accepted. It was introduced by Pierre Oller, owner of a perfume shop in Paris. While losing heavily to bookmakers, he hit upon a scheme whereby the betting public could bet against each other, and not have to go through the bookmakers. He sold tickets from his perfume shop at a standard price on the different horses in each race. From the money collected, he deducted 5% as commission for his services, then distributed the remaining money among holders of winning tickets in proportion to the number of such tickets that had been sold. His system became so popular that it was introduced within the grounds of the Parisian tracks. It soon replaced bookmaking entirely, and became the only legal form of wagering at French tracks. The percentage deducted was soon raised to 8%.

Literally translated, pari-mutuels means "mutual bet", and when it was first introduced in America, it was referred to as the "mutuals". The French spelling, however, eventually became the accepted form.

Despite its obvious advantages, the system did not immediately catch on at American tracks. Naturally the bookmakers were violently opposed to it. The big bettors didn't like it either, since large bets would depress the odds on their choice. Some small bettors also opposed it for the reason that a bookmaker would accept a bet of any size, whereas the "mutuals" required a minimum bet of $5.00.

In the 1870's and 1880's, the system received numerous tryouts at various tracks in New York, New Jersey, Kentucky, Maryland, Chicago and Washington D.C. It got a big boost in popularity on October 12, 1872 when a horse won at Jerome Park, paying off at odds of 234 to 1 in the "mutuals", but at only 5 to 1 to 20 to 1 from the bookmakers. Even so, the tracks only used the system on a sporadic basis. It is believed that if a large number of tracks had given the pari-mutuels an extended trial, the public would have accepted it at a much earlier date than they did. A big set back occured in 1908 when the Kentucky State Racing Commission issued a "mutuels betting only" edict in the middle of the Latonia spring meeting. The operator, Louis A. Cella, complained that he could not afford to continue operations without bookmaking. The records showed that the previous year, with bookmakers operating exclusively, the legitimate income to the track was $53,700 compared to the $74,632.80 income from the corresponding thirty days with a pari-mutuels system. Maybe the fact that Cella controlled the books as well as the track had something to do with his decision, but at any rate, he closed down operations.

Latonia re-opened that fall with books; the Racing Commission revoked it's license, the track filed suit against the commission, and finished out the meeting while litigation was in progress. In 1909 the books were on again, but did not survive for long.

Another reason the public was not overly enthusiastic about pari-mutuels was that they suspected that sometimes the system was not being carried out honestly. Undoubtedly, their suspicions were justified in some cases. The system was a far cry from the sophisticated electronic system of today, and ways to control malpractices had not yet been perfected, and would not be perfected for several more decades.

Still another scheme emerged to negate the positive aspect of the pari-mutuels. The big bettors of the time would find an almost certain winner at a small track, bet large amounts on the other horses in the race at the track, pushing the odds up on their favorite, and then bet him with the bookies, who were paying off at track odds. Many bookmakers were put out of business before this problem was solved. Finally the bookies simply refused bets on horses racing at small tracks and the scheme was no longer profitable.

Immediately after the Civil War, the emphasis shifted to more spacious facilities for racing. Racing resumed its popularity in many sections of the country. Some of the tracks built during this period are still flourishing today. The most famous are Saratoga, N.Y. (1864), Pimlico in Maryland and Monmouth in New Jersey (1870), the Fairgrounds in New Orleans (1872), Churchill Downs, Louisville, Ky. (1875), Timonium in Maryland (1887), Hawthorne, Chicago, Illinois (1891), Aqueduct in New York (1894), Oaklawn Park, Hot Springs, Ark. (1904), Belmont Park, N.Y. (1905), Rockingham Park, New Hampshire (1906), Laurel Raceway in Maryland (1911), and Bowie and Marlboro also in Maryland (1914). The triple crown for three year olds which include the "Kentucky Derby", the "Preakness" and the "Belmont Stakes" were all inaugurated during this racing boom.

The major tracks in California today were also built during this period, but have changed names, owners and locations through the years, and cannot claim the continuity of those listed above. The famed Santa Anita Park is one which fits this category. Eastern and Western competition was limited during this period because of transportation problems.

World War I did not greatly influence racing. There was a slight drop in the number of races held in 1917 and 1918 but not enough to stop the growth of the sport in general. Man of War was born in 1917 and he would do much to publicize racing for the next three decades. Even today, those who know little of racing, will recognize his name as the greatest horse of his time and maybe even of the entire history of racing in America.

The middle 1920's is often characterized as the golden age of sports. Racing grew rapidly during this period. In Ohio, Ascot Park opened near

Akron; Beaulah Park near Columbus followed suit in 1923 and two years later, Thistle Downs near Cleveland, and Coney Island (now River Downs), near Cincinnati joined the parade.

Dade Park (now James C. Ellis Park), built in Kentucky across the river from Evansville, Indiana started in 1922.

In Illinois, Hawthorne opened it's doors in 1922, Aurora Downs in 1923, Fairmont Park, across the river from St. Louis, Missouri in 1925, Peoria in 1926, Arlington Park and Lincoln Fields the following year.

Aksarben (Nebraska spelled backwards) began their operation in Omaha, Nebraska in 1921.

Florida joined the bandwagon in 1925 with a 51 day meet at Hialeah, near Miami. The next year, Seminole Park, Pompano and Tampa joined the ranks.

With few exceptions, the tracks above are still going strong.

In 1927, Bowie and the Fairgrounds set the pace with public address systems, giving a running description of the races. This soon became a standard practice at all the tracks.

An eleven day meet was held at Arlington Downs between Fort Worth and Dallas in 1929 to promote racing in Texas. The experiment worked as racing was legalized in Texas in 1933, but it did not survive long.

Pari-mutuels systems were being upgraded but still hadn't reached any degree of sophistication.

A lot of these gains got a temporary set back when the Depression hit in 1929, but in a round about way it was to help racing over the long haul. As states became pressed for money, they turned to pari-mutuels revenues as a painless form of taxation, the theory being that those who could afford to go to the track, could afford to pay more taxes. Some new tracks went out of business and others tottered on the brink, but of the tracks still in operation, 34 were in existence on "Black Tuesday" in 1929. Between this day and the start of World War II, 24 new tracks came into being, an increase of 70% in numbers during America's blackest economic period.

Another big turning point in racing came in 1930. The Preakness of that year became the first Classic race started from the *starting gate* or "machine" as they called it at that time. Such starts had been made in lesser events before, and experiments to build a workable gate had been going on for many years. As early as 1894, races had been started from a gate at Maspeth, N.Y. A gate with separate stalls for each horse was tried at Bowie in the early 1920's. Experiments with a movable gate, later in the decade, were made by Marshall Cassidy. The Jarvis-Waggoner gate was sampled in Lexington in 1927, and the Bradley-Stewart gates were used at the Fairgrounds in New Orleans in 1928. Of the early gates, those developed by John Bahr and W. C. Waite were the ones that survived. The use of the Bahr gate at the 1929 Hawthorne fall meeting is generally accepted as the origination of the gates on a permanent basis. 1930 was the first season in which starting gates of one kind or another were in general use throughout the country. The New York tracks were exceptions. They waited another year, until the gate had been thoroughly tested elsewhere. In some of the early models, the doors were opened electrically. A circuit failure resulted in an uneven start and caused much controversy. Later they perfected the system to work in a better manner. The stall gates are now held closed by electromagnets working against a spring, hence an absence of current is apparent at the time a horse is loaded into his stall. The stalls are opened by shutting off the electricity rather than turning it on, and a power failure subsequent to loading, will cause a start rather than prevent one.

The biggest problem remaining, is that the gates somewhat obscures the view of the start, one of the most important parts of the race. But on the positive side, the gates have almost eliminated long delays at the post and have made for more even starts. Some trainers still maintain that the sudden acceleration from a standing start puts too great a strain on a horse's legs. At any rate, this method of starting is a standard part of the American racing scene today.

By the 1930's, the "Sport of Kings" which had begun as a sport, primarily for the wealthy, had evolved to the point where the support of the common man was necessary to keep racing alive. During the lean years of the early 30's, the shortage of money required large crowds to keep the betting volume high enough to meet the track overhead. Racing not only held its own during this period, but grew rapidly. No less than seventeen tracks still operating today, made their start in this decade. Sportsman Park in Cicero, Illinois in 1932; Charlestown Turf Club in Charlestown, West Virginia; Long Acres in Seattle, Washington; and Pomona in California, all in 1933. Narragansett in Pawtucket, Rhode Island; Santa Anita near Los Angeles, California; and Bay Meadows in San Mateo, California in 1934. Fresno, California; Playfair in Spokane, Washington; and Suffolk Downs near Boston, Massachusetts in 1935. Santa Rosa, California; and Keeneland, in Lexington, Kentucky in 1936. Delaware Park near Wilmington, Delaware; and Del Mar near San Diego, California in 1937. Hollywood Park in Inglewood, California in 1938. And finally, Pleasanton, California; and Gulfstream Park in Hollywood, Florida in 1939.

Deciding the official order of finish in races where the horses were closely bunched caused much controversy during this period. Use of the pari-mutuels system, the fact that races were of a shorter distance, and that larger fields were involved, made this problem more acute. Judges had a great responsibility, sometimes even a dangerous one. The fans always thought their particular horse had won, and the losers felt cheated when the official order of close finishes was posted. The photo finish was the final solution to this problem, but it, like the pari-mutuels and the starting gates went through different stages of development to improve its accuracy. On Christmas Day in 1934, Santa Anita made use of a camera above the press box to take pictures of the finish and aid the judges in their decisions. They were able to print these pictures in a matter of only three minutes. Another step to gain the public's confidence had been accomplished. We will go into detail of how the photo finish camera operates a little later on, as even today, many people still question the results of a race after the photos are posted.

The thoroughbred industry had leveled off by 1936. The number of races conducted had dropped off slightly from the 1933-1934 level, but the purses had increased substantially, and the overall business of racing maintained a gentle upward trend until the next boom following World War II.

It was also during this period that horses from other countries were brought in to challenge the best horses in America and to vie for a share of the larger purses being offered. They met with only varying success, but the real impact to the sport was that the better ones remained here for breeding purposes and added some new blood lines to the American thoroughbreds.

Contrary to what might have been expected, the effect on racing by World War II was to increase its prosperity. The shortage of materials delayed construction of new tracks and the expansion of those already in operation, but overall the trend was still upward. When the war ended we were to see another boom, even greater than the one in the early 1930's. During the war years, thoroughbred racing went all out in the war effort. The Turf Committee of America was formed in 1942. It announced a goal of two million dollars, as the sport's contribution to war relief. This figure had been greatly surpassed by the end of the year, and more than sixteen and a half million dollars was collected within the next three seasons. This was accomplished by contributing the total receipts from special days of racing, setting aside certain percentages of regular purses and race track profits, and by outright donations.

Another so called "war baby", which became a permanent part of the racing structure, was the Thoroughbred Racing Association, Inc., an organization of tracks originally designed primarily to foster co-operation in the war effort. The TRA continued after the war as a trade association to promote harmony and to enforce ethics, in all phases of race track operations.

Spencer J. Drayton, a former FBI agent, was hired after the war to organize the Thoroughbred Racing Protective Bureau (TRPB) whose duties were to provide services to racing analogous to that performed by the FBI for the Federal Government. This organization is still a dominant part of racing, and it's contributions to the sport will be covered in detail a little later in the book.

Still another organization developed during this period was the Horseman's Benevolent and Protective Association (HBPA). In essence, it acts as a trade union for the horsemen. Its services will also be detailed later.

At the height of the war, some tracks had to shut down temporarily, others had to adapt its operations to wartime conditions. Rubber and gasoline were the big items in 1943, so racing dates were often granted with contingencies such as parking lots being closed, horse drawn vehicles being used in place of those powered by gasoline for track maintenance, and meets being held at facilities other than their own that were located more centrally to population centers. Most of these locations were accessible by transportation other than automobiles. The infields of some idle facilities were converted for use as victory gardens. Other track properties were used as defense plants.

Many new racing fans were created during these times. The swing shift workers, having their daytimes free, often used racing as their means of recreation. Many would become regular customers after things had returned to normal after the war.

The big upsurge in the 1940's after the war is reflected, not so much in the new tracks being built, but by the fact that many tracks that had closed down during the war were re-opened, and by the longer racing seasons and the number of races per day being increased by practically every track in existence. Actually, the tracks still operating today that held their first meets during the 1940's, number only ten. They are Great Barrington in Massachusetts in 1940; Golden Gate Field near San Francisco, California in 1941; Garden State in New Jersey in 1942; Northampton, Massachusetts in 1943; Atlantic City, New Jersey; Monmouth Park, New Jersey; and Portland Meadows in Oregon in 1946; Lincoln Downs in Rhode Island; and Ruidoso Downs in Ruidoso, New Mexico in 1947; and Hazel Park, near Detroit, Michigan in 1949.

Nevertheless, the number of actual races held, the number of racing days allotted, and the volume of business increased drastically. The bubble was to burst again in a few years before thoroughbred racing was to settle down to a normal growth that is enjoyed at the present time.

This period, however, is remembered mostly by the fact that racing was finally recognized for what it had actually become. Not only a sport, but a major national industry, representing enormous investments, not only in racetracks and horseflesh, but also in such allied businesses as feed companies, van lines, veterinary service, farming, totalisator companies, photo finish and video patrol companies, specialists in the news medias and publications, as well as the diversified personnel needed for the operation of the tracks themselves. Revenue from thoroughbred racing had grown to 94 million dollars in 1946, and has continued to grow in volume ever since.

As in every other business, this rapid growth created numerous problems. Tighter controls had to be implemented to insure honesty, both in the areas of the pari-mutuels system and in racing itself. The TRPB was to be a large factor during this period, especially in regards to procedures for identifying horses and ridding the business of the undesirable elements trying to infiltrate the industry; also in finding ways to stop trainers from using drugs on their horses to influence their performance. All in all, racing did a remarkable job of housecleaning during the post war era, to the extent that racing became by far the most thoroughly supervised of all sports. The peculiar nature of this industry requires that strict vigilance be maintained and kept up to date for it to survive and prosper.

Photo Patrol and Telefilm (moving pictures taken from different angles during the race) became a standard procedure during this period of time. It has helped greatly to protect the public from malpractices as well as to increase the safety of the jockeys.

By 1948 it was evident that some areas had been over-saturated with tracks. Fifty-seven of seventy-seven tracks operating during this year showed a decrease in daily mutuels handles. Whereas the tracks alone had borne the brunt of the financial squeeze during the depression of the 1930's, the aggregate revenue to the states was down also, for the first time since the depression.

This trend was to continue for two more years before it was to recuperate in 1951. In 1949, fifty-five tracks showed another decrease, while only eighteen reported a gain. A little satisfaction was derived from the fact that decreases were smaller than in 1948, and 1950 again showed a smaller decline. Forty-one tracks showed a decline, although percentages were not so great, while thirty-six had shown an increase.

A drastic reversal of this trend occured in 1951. Seventy-eight meetings reported a higher figure than the proceeding year while only three showed a further decline. Even these three reported that their decreases were very mild. 1952 and 1953 produced similar results.

From that point up to the present, racing has had its up and down years. Some tracks faltered, but new ones were built to replace them in the overall picture. Improvements have been made in regards to better security and controls, better equipment and more sophisticated pari-mutuels systems. Revenue to states is still on the upward swing. Tracks built in the 1950's, 1960's and 1970's and are still operating include: Centennial Race Course in Denver, Colorado, and Detroit Race Course in Detroit, Michigan (1950); Solano in Vallejo, California (1951); Rillito Park in Tucson, Arizona (1953); Cahokia Downs across the river from St. Louis, Missouri in Illinois, and Fonner Park in Grand Isle, Nebraska (1954); Atokad (near Sioux City, Iowa) in Nebraska, Turf Paradise outside Phoenix, Arizona, and Commonwealth (formerly Miles Park) in Louisville, Kentucky (1956); Waterford Park in West Virginia (1957); Park Jefferson (also near Sioux City, Iowa) in South Dakota (1958); Latonia (near Cincinnati) in Kentucky, Sunland Park (near El Paso, Texas) in New Mexico, and Shenandoah Downs in West Virginia (1959); Prescott Downs, Prescott, Arizona (1960); Yakima Meadows, Yakima, Washington (1961); Finger Lakes in New York (1962); Green Mountain in Vermont (1963); Evangeline Downs, Lafayette, Louisiana (1966); Sacramento, California (1968); Dover Downs, Dover, Delaware, Liberty Bell in Philadelphia, Pennsylvania, and Pocono Downs in Wilkes Barre, Pennsylvania (1969); Les Bois Park, Boise, Idaho (1970); Calder Raceway near Miami, Florida, Jefferson Downs in Metairie, Louisiana, and Santa Fe

Downs, Santa Fe, New Mexico (1971); Penn National in Pennsylvania (1972); Commodore Downs, Erie, Pennsylvania and Delta Downs in Louisiana (1973); Keystone, Philadelphia, Pennsylvania and Louisiana Downs near Shreveport, Louisiana (1974).

It is obvious that such a complex industry, with operations in all different parts of the country and subject to each particular states' laws and rules, must have some central body to co-ordinate the business in its entirety. Also, since it is such a mobile business, and in lots of cases, a seasonal one, it is necessary to have some national organizations to work in certain phases of the operations. I think it would be appropriate to explain more fully at this time, the part that these organizations play in the overall picture of racing.

CURTIS FREEMAN, OWNER
VICTOR BOLDREY, TRAINER
J.C. ELLIS PARK

JUDONDA

D. SHIREY, JOCKEY
7 furs. 1:28
Aug. 8, 1963

Judonda, owned by the father and mother of the author and named after his three children, Judi, Don and Dave.

Courtesy of SCI Photography

Courtesy of SCI Photography

THE JOCKEY CLUB

The Jockey Club was established in 1894 as racing's central ruling body. It was organized because the industry needed to standardize the rules and customs, that at the time, varied from one track to the next. As a result of it's work, today's racing in America closely follows the rules and regulations set down by the club.

Although thoroughbred racing constitutes an important part of the Jockey Club's work, the Club is equally involved with preserving the breeding integrity of these thoroughbreds. (The Club's name derives from England's racing turf authority of the same name.) Its members are chosen from among those who have proven to be dedicated to the advancement of the sport and the breed.

The huge growth of thoroughbred racing in this country has increased the Club's responsibilities a hundred fold since its inception. Its purpose is not only to encourage the development of the thoroughbred horse, but to establish racing on a footing that will command the interest, as well as the confidence and favorable opinion, of the public.

Every thoroughbred foaled in this country must be registered in the Stud Book before it may race. No thoroughbred is admitted unless its parentage has been properly verified. Through its records, the Club can keep a close watch over each thoroughbred throughout the course of its career. Documentation is primarily established through breeding records and identification submitted by owners of both stallion and mare. In case of doubt, blood tests of sire, dam and foal may also be required.

The integrity of the Stud Book is insured by an elaborate system of horse identification that the Jockey Club has developed and refined throughout the years. The system begins with the foal's birth. A complete description of its markings, submitted with its owner's application for registration, forms the basis of the horses's permanent record. When the animal arrives at the track, additional identification is established by means of a lip tattoo and the classification of the "chestnuts" (night eyes) on the horse's legs.

Upon returning to the breeding farm and entry into the stud, each thoroughbred must again be fully identified, before the Club will accept its offspring as legitimate progeny. Horses that are bred abroad, and imported into this country can be registered in the Club's Stud Book only if their owners supply proof of lineage that has been authenticated by the Stud Book of the country of origin. Imported horses must undergo the same rigid identification procedures as native born animals.

Integral to the problem of thoroughbred identification is the matter of the registration of names. The Jockey Club also supervises this procedure, which is a monumental task of its own. Over 28,000 foals are born each year. In 1979 alone, this number had reached 32,368 at this writing, and the Club estimates that 300 to 400 more will be added before the year is finished. The

he division secretary-treasurer is appointed by the president, with the
and consent of his fellow directors.

regional division has an elected committee, composed of members
Association, which oversees the operation of the division, including
ncial records and benevolence payments.

HBPA holds semi-annual Board of Directors meetings, at which the
nal President, and respective division presidents, each give progress
s. During the meetings all issues of primary importance are reviewed
the vantage point of State Racing Commissioners, and representatives
her segments of the industry, as well as federal legislators, and other
ps which directly or indirectly affect the growth of racing. There are
en standing committees on the national level overseeing the interests of
emen.

he Purse Committee is dedicated to three goals: that horsemen are paid
highest purses possible to help offset their sizeable investments; that
k owners make a reasonable profit; and that track owners and horsemen
rk together with state legislatures to achieve the first two principles.

The Backstretch Insurance Committee reviews and keeps in force insur-
ce policies for backstretch personnel.

The Budget Committee keeps a watchful eye over the Association's fi-
ances.

The Executive Committee, between meetings of the National Board of
Directors, manages the affairs of the Association.

The Hall of Fame and Meritorious Service Committee recognize individuals for superior contributions to the HBPA and the thoroughbred industry.

The Advisory Board is an honorary consulting committee, comprised of
past national HBPA presidents.

The Assistance Committee is empowered to approve benevolent assistance to regional divisions upon request, in the case of disasters not covered
by insurance and related protective programs. Since 1966, the HBPA National Assistance Fund has distributed hundreds of thousands of dollars to
distressed horsemen.

The Off-Track Betting Committee reviews problems posed by off-track
betting—interstate and intrastate—throughout the nation. It also considers
ways to make OTB a benefit to horsemen.

The Planning Committee considers new proposals and the preferred future
policies of the Association.

The Public Relations Committee serves to familiarize the thoroughbred
racing industry and the general public with the goals and accomplishments
of the HBPA.

The HBPA's National Headquarters, located in the Washington, D.C.
suburb of Rockville, Maryland, serves as a clearing house in the HBPA
structure. The National Office is available to all divisions for advisory and
practical assistance on a day to day basis.

This office's specific duties are: to maintain a close liason with elected

Club also estimates the total number of thoroughbreds alive today to be
about 200,000. Each new name must not only be approved, but checked to
avoid duplication in spelling, or sound, of a name previously registered.

The paper work involved in these registrations is handled by the Club's
offices in New York City and in Lexington, Kentucky. Increased numbers of
new registrations have resulted in the increased use of computers. These
computers are now being used to maintain breeding and racing statistics, as
well as to store additional information which will aid in the processing of
new registration applications. The Jockey Club Statistical Bureau in Lexington also provides pedigree services and prepares thousands of catalogue
pages for sales companies and breeders each year.

Another duty of the Club is to register racing colors, stable names, partner-
ships and apprentice jockey contracts. Although the Club has jurisdiction of
these matters only in the State of New York, many other states recognize and
honor the colors and stable names of New York, with the Club's approval.

During the course of the Club's eighty odd years of service, it has introduced or promoted ideas and procedures which have significantly improved
thoroughbred racing in America. One of its major innovations, for example,
was to establish a school for racing officials. Through its facilities, aspiring
racing officials may obtain a thorough education in all aspects of thoroughbred racing, ranging from foal registration through learning the functions of a
Steward. Students from racing associations throughout the world have come
to America to attend these courses. Other major contributions include: participation in the perfection of the photo finish camera and the starting gate;
introduction of film patrol; transference of stewards and placing judges
stands from ground level to the roof; and aid in the establishment of the
Thoroughbred Racing Protective Bureau (TRPB).

Another successful venture was the initiation of the "Jockey Club Round
Table Conference" on matters pertaining to racing. Established over a score
of years ago, this conference, held annually at Saratoga Springs, New York,
during the month of August, attracts people from all segments of thoroughbred racing and breeding. At this forum, people can freely discuss mutual
problems and exchange new ideas. Guests and guest speakers from abroad
are also invited. In this way, American thoroughbred breeders and owners
can learn how their colleagues in England, France, Ireland, and other countries have coped with problems similar to those that exist in this country.

Other activities include the production of the film, "Thoroughbred", a
slow motion study of the thoroughbred in action, and the supervision of the
Jockey Club Foundation and the Cavanaugh Fund. Both of these organizations help to sustain indigent persons connected with thoroughbred racing.

Although the Club has always worked with foreign racing authorities and
groups, these activities have increased in recent years. The advent of better
horses and safer methods of transportation have resulted in an increased

exchange between countries of thoroughbreds for the purpose of racing and breeding. In consequence, the need for international co-operation has grown significantly.

Examples of the international co-operation are many. For instance, each horse must be accompanied on its travel by a passport, issued at the country of origin, which bears its complete physical description as well as its record of races run. In order to insure that the name of a great thoroughbred of one country will not be issued to the foal of another country, a list of internationally protected names is maintained. In a similar vein, a reciprocal agreement exists between countries whereby the owner, trainer, or jockey can not be licensed in another, before his credentials are cleared with the country of origin.

The Jockey Club is involved in all of the activities above, both at home and abroad as innovator, supervisor, and guardian of thoroughbred racing and breeding.

HBPA

The Horseman's Benovolent and Protective
1940. Its purpose was to give owners and tra
authorative and unified voice in horse racing. Ni
ers and trainers now belong to this organization.

The principle objectives of the HBPA are: to p
gaged in racing, employers and employees alike, w
times of illness, adversity or sudden disaster; to impr
the backstretch (barn area); to insure adequate accor
ings; to mediate, on behalf of individual members of
problems arise with track management or State Ra
protect individuals in the industry against the impo
taxes by federal, state, or local governments; to neg
reasonable share in the distribution of purses at tracks
bers race; to provide funding for backstretch health, we
ance programs; to co-ordinate with Racing Association
sions, and other racing organizations, the procedures fo
rules and conditions which affect the interests of horseme
establishment of recreation centers and related programs
and to monitor state and federal legislative developmen
horsemen have every possible legislative advantage.

HBPA membership has grown rapidly, and presently repre
50,000 owners and trainers of thoroughbred race horses at e
nearly all minor tracks in the United States, Canada, and Pue
membership consists of approximately 37,500 owners, 7
trainers, and 5,000 trainers. A horseman who meets the eligib
ments normally becomes a member of the Association when
horse in a race, either as an owner or a trainer.

In Florida, an individual is not considered a member unles
signed card to that effect on file with the horseman's bookkeepe

Any person who has performed some distinguished servi
thoroughbred racing industry and who is not already a member of
ciation, may be elected as an honorary member. HBPA membershi
with it the right to vote and participate in the activities of any div
which the member may be eligible.

The Organization has 26 regional divisions, as well as a National
quarters, which assists the divisions in carrying out the HBPA's goals.
the exception of employees, the HBPA Constitution and By-Laws pro
officers and directors of the Association, or of any regional division
receiving compensation for their services to the Association. The presid
of all divisions serve as a National Board from which they elect a Natio
President.

The division's presidential and vice-presidential positions are elected representatives in Congress, in order that the divisions are kept informed, and involved in federal legislation; to serve as a coordinator for legal, legislative, financial, and other activities; to regulate the Association's affairs, assuring fair and honest elections, and communicating racing news; to keep records and statistics; administer insurance and hospitalization programs, and to visit various divisions to provide consultations and other services; to provide a check-and-balance system on the financial integrity of the Association, by requiring annual audits of each division, and corporation statements in each state where the HBPA exists; to maintain a membership roster, updated monthly, by the various divisions; and to provide information and instructional material to divisions on a regular basis.

One of HBPA's first successful endeavors was the establishment of a benevolent fund for its members and their employees. Assistance is provided to help individuals meet medical and hospital bills, defray funeral expenses, and aid those who, due to advanced age or circumstances beyond their control, find themselves in need.

In 1956, the HBPA put its benevolence program on a permanent basis by establishing the HBPA Foundation, Inc. In 1959, the Foundation received a charity rating from the Internal Revenue Service. Donor's contributions to the Foundation are tax deductible. The HBPA Foundation has distributed more than 12 million dollars for charitable purposes since that time. Since 1973, the Association has paid out over one million dollars each year to the thousands of members and their employees. About thirty percent of all benevolence disbursed goes to owners and trainers, with the balance going to the stable-employees of members.

The concepts of assistance and protection moved the HBPA in 1955, to protect its members against the losses of horses and equipment as a result of fires, natural disasters and transportation accidents. Under the terms of the Fire Insurance Disaster Policy, carried by the National Association, every HBPA member is covered up to $10,000 per animal against the loss of horses while they are stabled on, or about the premises of recognized tracks, while at approved farms or training centers, and while in transit from one to the other. Equipment (tack) is similarly covered up to a maximum of $3,000 per owner or stable. Since the inception of the Fire Insurance and Disaster Policy, the HBPA has paid over two million dollars in claims.

In 1967, the HBPA began to make progress in establishing a national backstretch insurance policy. The Association called for a plan of medical insurance and a pension plan for stable employees at all major tracks. This insurance has subsequently been adopted by individual divisions and tailored to the social and regional demands unique to their areas. A number of HBPA divisions operate on a self-insured basis, providing a full schedule of benefits for their members. Other divisions have enrolled their members in insurance plans with major insurance companies, such as Prudential and Blue Cross.

The Public Liability and Property Damage Policy is a recent addition to the HBPA's membership services program. Owners and trainers who are members of the Association are covered. The maximum limits of coverage are $1 million bodily injury for each accident and $50,000 in property damage per accident. The coverage provides protection and defense of legal suits arising from the business operations of owning and training thoroughbred race horses, and as a result of accidents covered under the policy form. Coverage is provided for bodily injury or property damage occuring on the premises of any racetrack or training center approved by the insurer.

The HBPA provides further insurance protection for horsemen by making available a group term life insurance program. Qualified members can obtain up to $50,000 of inexpensive life insurance through this program, which offers an annual enrollment period.

In certain HBPA divisions, full mortality claiming insurance for horses is available at a cost of one percent of the horse's value. The insurance provides protection for an individual who claimed a horse which had to be destroyed as a result of an injury occuring during the race from which he was claimed.

Annually, over 6,000 backstretch personnel receive some sort of benefit. In recent years, this has amounted to well over one million dollars per year. This figure does not include millions of dollars in other coverage, available through various HBPA insurance programs.

The HBPA's concern for backstretch workers is not limited to their time spent in employment at the racetrack. In 1962, the Association founded Las Casitas, a home for elderly and needy backstretchers. The first home was established near the Del Mar track in Southern California. Since that time, the HBPA has purchased property for construction of a modern rest home, midway between Los Angeles and San Diego. In California, the HBPA stages an annual charity basketball game at Del Mar, which has raised considerable revenue for Las Casitas. Many entertainment and sports celebrities have contributed to the success of the charity event.

Several divisions offer retirement plans for their members.

Improvements in working conditions for backstretch personnel not only improve the quality of their lives, but also upgrade the caliber of individuals who seek employment on the backstretch. The HBPA has applied both planning and financial resources in many general and educational programs.

In 1970, the HBPA instituted one of the first racehorse education courses in the country at vocational high schools on Long Island, New York. Humber College in Toronto, Canada has a similar course sponsored by the HBPA. HBPA also gives an annual college scholarship grant and makes funds available for students who wish to attend courses of this nature at trade schools.

The Association offers courses in English and Spanish for backstretch employees. At different times, the HBPA has employed individuals to assist Spanish-speaking workers at the racetracks. In California, an HBPA interpreter works in the Racing Commission office to assist Spanish speaking employees in acquiring licenses. At New York Racing Association tracks, the HBPA has established English classes for Spanish speaking employees and an art school for all backstretch employees. It also sponsors art exhibitions at Saratoga, New York.

The HBPA endorsed, and contributed financially to a racetrack program, developed at the University of Arizona.

Various divisions sponsor boxing and bowling tournaments, celebrity tennis matches, softball and hockey leagues. Many divisions sponsor some form of fund raising activity for senior citizens, crippled children, cancer research, hospitals and for the HBPA Benevolence Fund. Free dinners and other festivities are often furnished the backstretch workers on holidays such as Christmas and Thanksgiving. Several HBPA divisions have, in cooperation with state welfare agencies, initiated mobile medical and dental care clinics for backstretch personnel at a minimal cost. An organization called "The Race Track Chaplaincy of America" offers church services on many track grounds for those who wish to attend. The HBPA has morally and financially supported this plan.

Finally, there are specific HBPA programs that benefit owners and trainers, like urging tracks to provide equine hospitals and on-track surgical facilities for injured horses (some are already established); setting up feed co-ops on a cost basis; bargaining with the tracks to secure a larger purse structure; obtaining interest on monies held in the Horsemen's Bookkeeper's account; bargaining for charity racing days, the proceeds going to the HBPA; publishing magazines and reports, and making films which will keep the owners and trainers better informed in their particular fields; providing the "HBPA National Counsel" to assist members in legal matters pertaining to racetrack matters; bargaining for a fair share of the Off Track Betting revenues; and lobbying at the State and Federal Legislatures for enactment of laws that will benefit the horsemen.

TRA

Another important thoroughbred organization is the Thoroughbred Racing Association, formed in 1942, by several tracks. The incorporators intended to provide a sounding-board for industry problems, as well as promote public interest in thoroughbred racing. In 1978, at their 36th annual meeting in Miami, Florida, the TRA members, representing approximately one-half of the thoroughbred tracks in the United States, issued a re-statement of the Association's role and services. These roles and services are listed below.

1. To serve as a strong and unified voice of the Thoroughbred racing industry and as such should include as many Thoroughbred tracks as possible, provided each track adheres to the TRA Code of Standards and By-Laws.
2. To place the maximum emphasis on the integrity of racing.
3. To insure the greatest participation by all members by enlarging the Board of Directors to include a representative of all associations or tracks, with an Executive Committee with powers to handle matters between Directors' meetings.
4. To represent the TRA in the area of Federal legislation, by sponsoring and/or performing activities connected therewith; to act in cooperation with other pari mutuel industries, when common Federal legislative problems exist; and to recognize that TRA expenditures for these purposes are to be borne only by the TRA tracks in the United States.
5. To provide assistance to the tracks in their relationships with State or Provincial legislatures through the TRA Legislative Task Force.
6. To provide statistical and informational services and reports to all members in the areas of: (a) Trend of Racing; (b) Stakes Schedules (Quarterly); (c) Executive Vice President's Newsletter (Monthly); and (d) Operational and Management Surveys (Periodically).
7. To emphasize the need of solving problems on a regional basis by conducting regional workshops or seminars.
8. To serve as a clearing house for information, statistical data, ideas, promotions, problem areas, etc., which would benefit the entire membership.
9. To assist in the promotion of racing, by continually seeking means of securing greater exposure on television.
10. To co-sponsor annually, with the National Turf Writers Association and the Daily Racing Form, the Eclipse Awards Program, designed to insure a unanimity in the industry as to the Horse of the Year and the Divisional Champions; to identify the most outstanding Owner, Trainer, Jockey, Apprentice Jockey, Breeder; and to cite exemplary performances in the field of Journalism, Broadcasting, and Telecasting.

11. To provide Racing Officials' Retirement and Health and Welfare Plans to TRA and non-TRA tracks.
12. To create, promote, publicize, advertise, and supervise various programs, activities, ventures, and enterprises related to Thoroughbred racing.
13. To recommend to the member tracks their support of those organizations and institutions which (a) engage in equine research, (b) provide formal educational programs designed to produce race track management personnel, and (c) are dedicated to the protection and promotion of the entire horse industry.
14. To maintain liason with (a) organizations and associations representing other segments of the Thoroughbred industry, and (b) with organizations and associations of other horse breeds.
15. To explore possibilities of group purchase in such areas as insurance, printing, generic TV commercials, etc.
16. Maintain a register of available part-time personnel such as officials, management, publicity, etc.

TRPB

In 1945, TRA established a sub-agency named the Thoroughbred Racing Protective Bureau. This sub-agency works within the framework of the TRA as a private investigative agency and to set up a Code of Standards representing a statement of basic ethical principles with which TRA member tracks should operate.

The TRPB operates on a round-the-clock, round-the-calendar basis at all of the TRA member tracks. At approximately 75% of these tracks, the TRPB agent also heads the track's individual security department.

Frequently non-member tracks employ this agency to aid in investigations of suspected racing irregularities. One of the Agency's major accomplishments has been to lip tattoo nearly 400,000 thoroughbreds for positive identification. Another service has been to fingerprint over 350,000 persons connected with racing in different capacities at member tracks. At the TRPB's nerve center in Lake Success, New York, more than 100,000 investigative cases are on file.

The figures listed above reflects the period from the Agency's inception through October of 1978.

The Department was headed by Spencer J. Drayton, a former Administrative Assistant to the head of the FBI from the formation of the Agency in 1945 until his retirement on December 31, 1977. His replacement at that time was Clifford W. Wickman, also a former employee of the Federal Bureau of Investigation.

JOCKEY GUILD

The last important organization in thoroughbred racing is the Jockey Guild.

Jockeys are probably the least understood and most underestimated athletes in the sports world. The few who are very successful are envied for the big money they make. The many who struggle to make a decent living are, for the most part, unappreciated for their skills and hard work. Jockeys must keep themselves in excellent physical condition if they are to be competitive. This in itself is a constant challenge. Besides having to compete in all sorts of adverse weather conditions—rain, snow, heat, mud, or whatever—most jockeys constantly fight a weight problem. Unless blessed with exceptional ability, a jockey must be able to ride at about 112 pounds in order to get enough rides to do well. Strict diets and sweat boxes are normal for all but a few. Those who can eat as much, and whatever, they want without creating a weight problem have a decided advantage over those who can't. Few spectators realize the amount of strength and stamina required for this skilled and dangerous profession. Most forget or don't realize that a jockey's work is not limited to a few rides during the official races, but also includes morning workouts. A jockey's day begins around daybreak, which makes it hard on them at tracks where racing is held at night. Since race horses don't have weekends off, and are in training seven days per week, this means the jockeys have to keep the same schedule, rain or shine, cold or warm. They need to ride to make a living. Lots of jockeys, for instance, ride hurt to some degree most of their careers.

Jockeys are professional athletes, but they differ in the way in which they learn their trade and the options they have once their active careers are finished because of age or injuries. In football, basketball and baseball, athletic scholarships carry most future pros through college. They are usually given special privileges in high school if they have the potential to play professionally. Not so with the future jockey. He's out in the barn area of a track, hustling mounts to exercise, cleaning out stalls, learning his trade the hard way. If he's interested in continuing his education, he has to figure a way to do it on his own. Although there are exceptions, most jockeys have a limited formal education. They're locked into a future of the horse racing business. Some may become racing officials. Most become trainers, valets, assistant starters or jockey agents. Some are fortunate enough to retire with enough money to own a racing stable or breeding farm. Very few get into other fields, since their experience from an early age was limited to horse racing.

The average person overestimates the earning power of a jockey. The top echelon, as is true with the superstars of other sports can become quite wealthy. But for the rest, a good living is about all they can hope for. Their gross earnings are usually substantial, but expenses are greater than in most other lines of work. Most have an agent, who contracts rides for them, and these agents receive a substantial percentage of their earnings. A lesser amount goes to their valets, who take care of their equipment during racing hours. The equipment itself is costly. Periods of inactivity caused by suspensions or injury are inevitable. Even the better jockeys can't escape slumps, the same as hitters in baseball.

Approximately 98% of the 1550 to 1600 jockeys now riding in the United States belong to this organization. Eight dollars is deducted from the money earned from each mount the jockey rides. This may seem a large bite from their paychecks, but the benefits are numerous and important. Most riders feel it is quite worthwhile. Formed in 1940, the national headquarters is in New York City. The organizational structure consists of a President, a Vice-President representing each section of the country (Eastern, Central, and Western), a National Managing Director-Secretary, a Treasurer and three Assistant Secretaries. There are also six managers plus an office manager, a five-person advisory council, and six to eleven directors for each of the Eastern, Central and Western sections. Most of the officers are either active or retired riders, and in many cases the same person doubles up in two categories (for instance, as an assistant secretary and manager).

Of the $8.00 per mount deduction, $4.50 goes into a savings account for the member and $3.50 is used for specific benefits. These include Group Blue Cross Insurance, hospital and medical bills resulting from track accidents, and $50.00 per week while recuperating from these accidents and until the member is able to resume riding. They receive representation during appeals of fines and suspensions which the guild and the member feel are excessive. Legal representation is limited to cases that involve the entire membership of the Guild. Many of these benefits are extremely important, especially those involving accidents at the track. Because of the high risk of injuries, accident insurance for a jockey would involve extremely high premiums, if coverage could be had at all.

The Guild also acts as a body to achieve better working conditions and equitable pay for the jockey's services. One ongoing effort is to establish a standard national rate for riding services. As with unions and guilds in other industries, there are many problems remaining to be solved to the satisfaction of both the guild and management. I believe that, on the whole, both jockeys and track management can be better served by a cooperative attitude toward each other.

A final note on jockeys: not too long ago, the prospect of female jockeys caused much controversy. From my observation, the women received as much or more opposition from the male jockeys as from track management. Most of the problems proved to be much less serious than either group anticipated, so it isn't much of an issue any more. Some female riders have done well. There seems to be little, if any, difference in courage and ability. Physical strength is another matter. Many female jockeys hold their own quite well in the shorter races, but only a few do well in the longer races. At any event, it seems likely that a bigger percentage of women will join the jockey ranks in the future.

Chapter Two
Quarter Horses: "The World's Fastest Horse"

Quarter horse historians agree that today's quarter horses can trace their ancestry to Spanish horses on their dams' side, and to English imports on the side of most sires. The Spanish strain apparently started when the Moors invaded Spain in the early 700s. It developed into the type of horse brought to America by the early Spanish explorers. The prototype colonial quarter horse owed an important debt to the ponies of the Cherokee and Chickasaw Indians, which in turn are believed to have been acquired from these same Spanish explorers. These early quarter horses (the "quarter-pathers") were described as general utility horses, short and heavily muscled, quick to action but not distance runners. The same words describe the quarter horse of today.

The earliest imports from England were probably "Galloways", brought over by the Virginia Cavaliers. They were described in much the same way as the horses of Spanish origin. In 1752, a grandson of Godolphin Barb, named Janus, was brought to Virginia from England. He played an extremely important, if not the leading, role in the breed of horse now known as the quarter horse. Although Janus's pedigree contained every cross calculated for a distance horse, his stock was more remarkable for speed than for endurance. From his shoulders back, he had outstanding characteristics of what would later become a thoroughbred. However, his front quarters were compact and heavily muscled, characteristic of the modern quarter horse. All but two of the earliest quarter horse families trace back to Janus (there are thirteen modern quarter horse families, the best known is probably that of Peter McCue).

Janus influenced thoroughbreds, too. When you trace blood lines of all kinds of race horses back far enough, many of the same names appear. Through selective breeding to acquire certain characteristics and conformation, peculiar to the needs of certain areas and periods of history, three distinct breeds have evolved: the thoroughbred, the quarter horse, and the standardbred.

Quarter horses have not changed much from their early days. The need of a horse for all around use by the average man was one that was fast and rugged and that could be used on farms, ranches, and racetracks.

That kind of horse played an important part in the Revolutionary War. Likewise the Revolution played an important part in quarter horse breeding.

Before the war, there were many places where this kind of horse was bred, but perhaps the best were developed in Virginia and the Carolinas. The first recorded quarter horse races were held in Enrico County, Virginia in 1674.

By 1690, large purses were being offered for these races. Large plantations often changed hands on the outcome of one of these sprints down a straight-away course. Any cleared field or dirt road served as a racetrack, which probably accounts for the dirt racing surface prevalent at American tracks today.

Racing was at a standstill during the war in most areas, but immediately after, racing was resumed in the middle and southern states, and west into Tennessee and Kentucky. Quarter racing thrived when men such as Andrew Jackson gave their support.

As America became more settled, the popularity of quarter racing waned and the practice of four mile races in the more developed areas replaced it. Quarter racing, however, simply moved to the new western frontiers.

So, quarter racing developed differently from the thoroughbred racing at large tracks in the East. It remained on an informal basis of matched races and weekend affairs at hundreds of small tracks that sprang up along the way, as the western movement carried pioneers into the Midwest, South-west, and Western areas of the present United States.

At the county fairs, in the agricultural communities, and on the half-mile tracks of the frontier, thoroughbreds and quarter horses occasionally competed against each other. More importantly, selected thoroughbred stallions were being used to improve the size and speed of the quarter horse. The most important stallion to influence this trend was Sir Archy, the thorough-bred son of Diomed. His importance in quarter horse blood lines is some-what surprising because he was a large horse, standing 16 hands high, and because his best efforts were recorded at four miles.

Organized quarter horse racing actually got its start in Tucson, Arizona, at a track called Haciedo Moltacqua. This track boasted a card of races that included not only quarter horses, but trotters, thoroughbreds and even some steeplechasers. Eventually quarter racing became the only type of race held at the track and, in 1943, a new race track was built, named Rillito Park. From 1900 to 1945, Rillito was joined by tracks at King City and Corona, California; Albuquerque, New Mexico; Del Rio, El Paso, Eagle Pass, and Bandera, Texas. Together they represented the birth of modern day quarter horse racing.

Louisiana is the home of the modern short horse, if racing is the criterion. The state produced more fast short-horses between 1900 to 1940 than any other single area in the country. Della Moore is probably the most famous of all the good horses produced during this period. An interesting sidelight in her racing career is that she ran her first race while she was still suckling her mother. The Cajuns initiated a practice of running "milk races". These races became common in the area around Lafayette. They served a dual purpose: they gave breeders an early line on their foals, and at the same time gave them a chance to bet money, furniture, wagons or whatever else wasn't tied down. The colts were taken to the race track and then not allowed to nurse their mothers for awhile. They were then held at the starting chute by two men while the mothers were led up the track, generally 156 yards. At a given signal, the colts were turned loose, and away they sprinted, looking for milk. Della Moore was an easy winner in her first start, so her feed and board was paid in advance. By the time she was a two year old, she was too well-known to find competition in the parishes around Lafayette, so she was transferred to another horseman who traveled all over the Southeastern areas racing short-horses.

Down through the years, there have been inumerable arguments about whether thoroughbreds or quarter horses are faster. It will probably never be decided, if only because of the difference in distance each breed has been trained to run best. Nevertheless, in August of 1947, a match race was arranged at Hollywood Park in Inglewood, California, between Fair Truckle, the thoroughbred record holder for ¾ of a mile, and Barbara B, the holder of the quarter horse record for ¼ of a mile. A stake of $50,000 was put up by the owners of the horses.

Because the distance (¼ mile) was supposedly best suited to the quarter horse, the start was designed to equalize the two by giving Fair Truckle a running start, to which he was accustomed. The gates were set 45 feet behind the starting line, and arrangements were made to time the race in two ways. From the gate to finish, and from the gate to 45 feet short of the finish line. This arrangement was to serve as an accurate check on the controversial difference between the standing start of the quarter horse and the running start of the thoroughbred.

Fair Truckle was the first from the gates, but Barbara B was even with him after 10 yards; fifty yards from the gates, she had managed a substantial lead and continued to widen her margin to a two-length advantage at the finish line. Officially clocked by four watches, the times were 22.5 seconds from the standing start and 21.6 from the running start. This race gave added ammunition to the backers of quarter horses who maintained their quarter horses were the world's fastest breed of horses. They may be correct, as the better class of quarter horses average in excess of 45 miles per hour from a standing start, at a distance of ¼ mile.

The quarter horse division of horse racing also boasts the richest purse in the world. The All American Futurity is held annually on Labor Day at Ruidoso Downs, New Mexico. The Futurity was the first horse race in history to offer a purse of over $500,000 and later the first to offer one over $1 million.

Quarter horse racing has come a long way from Colonial days. In 1978 there were 68 pari-mutuels tracks in 14 states, and 22 recognized bush tracks operating in the United States. (A recognized track is one which is accredited by the American Quarter Horse Association, by meeting certain standards of this Association, whether or not there is pari-mutuels wagering on races at that track.) The attendance for these ninety tracks was 6,597,496.

The public wagered $267,767,730 at those having pari-mutuels, while the purses for all the recognized tracks was $30,294,392. The number of new quarter horse foals registered in 1978 totaled 119,287.

In addition to the 12,768 races run at the recognized tracks in 1978, hundreds of bush tracks not recognized by the Association ran several thousand undocumented races. When you then add the quarter horses being used for purposes other than racing, such as on cattle ranches and at rodeos, the enormous size of the quarter horse industry is clear.

AMERICAN QUARTER HORSE ASSOCIATION

The American Quarter Horse Association, founded in 1940, has its head-quarters in Amarillo, Texas. The AQHA oversees and regulates the business of quarter horses in all its complex categories. It is a non-profit organization, which collects, records, and preserves the pedigrees of American quarter horses. It also publishes a Stud Book, and promotes any and all other matters such as may pertain to the history, breeding, exhibition, publicity, sale, and improvement of the breed and racing.

The Association has a membership in excess of 117,000. Many thousands more own and race quarter horses but are not members of the Association. The AQHA's Board of Directors is composed of representatives from the fifty states, Canada, and Mexico. The Board of Directors elects the Executive Board, the direct governing body of the Association. The Executive Board consists of the President, two Vice-Presidents, and two members who work with the Executive Secretary and General Manager concerning Association policy. In turn, the Executive Secretary works directly with department heads and the various committees of the Association.

Racing activities are guided by the Association's Racing Department, headed by the Director of Racing. The external governing body is the Racing Committee, a non-salaried group, whose duties are to cultivate the best interests in quarter horse racing, both for the participants and the public. The Association's Director of Racing is charged with executing the will of the Racing Committee, and to regulate all matters which pertain to racing and its best interests.

The Racing Department collects the results and maintains permanent records and past performances on all approved quarter horse races and the horses which participate in them throughout North America. The results are published by the Racing Department in its monthly publication, the *Quarter Running Horse Chart Book*. Past performance lines on all quarter horses are furnished by the Racing Department to any race track, *The Daily Racing Form*, or any association that might request them.

The Racing Department can supply these past performances lines and other information at a moment's notice through its complete on-line data-processing system. This ultra-modern system also allows anyone to tie directly into and communicate directly with the computer to obtain past performance lines at anytime; day or night, free of charge.

The procedures for conducting a quarter horse pari-mutuels operation are identical to that of the thoroughbred meets in regards to rules of racing. The conditions book, methods of identification, jurisdictions of racing officials, the starting method, the pari-mutuels system, the horseman's bookkeeper, the jockey's regulations—in fact almost every department of the track's operations are the same. The difference is the breed of horses, the distances raced, and the supporting associations with which the horses and horsemen are associated.

Chapter Three
Standardbreds: "Harness Racing"

Harness racing goes back to the dawn of recorded history. Horses racing while pulling two wheeled carts long preceded horses racing with jockeys.

According to John Hervey, an eminant horse historian, the horse originated as a small, dwarflike animal and gradually evolved to it's present size, partly through environment, and partly through concentrated breeding.

About forty years ago, baked clay tablets were unearthed in Asia Minor in a country known as Mitanni, later known as Cappadocia, and for many ages was part of the Assyro-Babylonian empire. These tablets, dated at 1350 B.C., contained more than nine hundred lines of script, describing the preparation of the horse for training, his diet and grooming, and methods for training him for speed at the trot. At the end of one hundred and forty-four days, he was ready either for racing, the hunting field, or the battle field.

We know that trotting races were held at the Grecian Olympics in around 1000 B.C., some two hundred years before races with riders on the horses backs were inaugurated.

It is assumed that since the Olympic participants of that era was limited to kings, princes, and persons of great wealth, horses had not been bred to the size and strength so as to be able to carry persons of this weight on their backs during competition.

The trotter then disappeared from recorded history for more than 2000 years. Perhaps warfare, plus the extensive care necessary to train a trotter may have been the major reason. However, about two hundred years ago, the so-called Norfolk Trotter became prominent as a road-horse, although not as a race horse (there was probably competition among neighbors along the country roads).

In 1788, a grey thoroughbred stallion named Messenger, a distinguished racer in England, was imported to this country. As we've seen, Messenger was a successful sire of running horses in America, one of the founders of the thoroughbred lineage. But as time went by, it became apparent that he had also sired a separate and distinct breed of trotters which far surpassed all other trotting horses, up to that time, in speed and quality. His progeny became widely known as superior performers.

Their gait was, of course, the result of training a speedy horse to harness. Both trotting and pacing gaits are acquired, not natural gaits. The natural fast gait of a horse is a gallop, and when urged farther, it is normal for him to run, an extension of the gallop. When trotting, the left front and right rear legs go forward together. When pacing, the left front and left rear legs move forward simultaneously, then the right front and right rear legs, giving the horse a sort of rolling motion (pacers are thus often referred to as "side-wheelers").

In racing, the trotter or pacer must stay on the same gait throughout the race, and all horses must use the same gait. Trotters do not compete with pacers. If the horse breaks this gait, goes offstride and breaks into a gallop, he must be pulled up and gotten back into the gait designated. He is not disqualified for breaking stride, so long as he does not improve his position while galloping.

Trotting races of the early nineteenth century were mainly conducted with riders rather than with a sulky, with the riders sitting in an upright position. The high-wheeled sulky was used from the 1850s until 1892 when the bicycle-wheel sulky was introduced.

Harness racing has its share of distinguished horses. The first recorded mile in less than three minutes while trotting was registered in 1806, by a gelding named Yankee, at Harlem, New York, where a trotting track flourished for many years. (Nothing is known of the breeding of Yankee) By 1839, this mark had been lowered to 2:32 by a horse named Dutchman. In 1845, a grey mare named Lady Suffolk became the first horse in harness to trot a mile in less than two and a half minutes. Her time was recorded as 2:29½ at Hoboken, New Jersey.

This record was still standing when a bay colt named Hambletonian was foaled at Chester, New York. He was destined to become the "Great Father" of the modern standardbred horse. "Standardbred" became the name used to distinguish the horse trained to harness from the thoroughbred and came from the breeding goal of developing horses who could trot or pace in standard time (2:20 or better). Hambletonian's reputation as a sire was such that his stud fee soon rose to $500, an unheard of price before his time. Hambletonian himself was rarely raced, yet almost 99% of standardbred horses today can trace their bloodlines to him. The classic trotting race today, called the "Hambletonian" is held yearly.

The "Hall of Fame" for the standardbreds is located at Goshen, New York, a small city which a hundred years ago was the main seat of harness racing and standardbred breeding in the nation. There are many colorful exhibits on display there at the present.

In the fifty years from when Lady Suffolk trotted the mile in under two and a half minutes until the use of the new sulky in 1892, the trotting record had been lowered to 2:08¼. In the first year after the introduction of the lighter, pneumatic-tired sulky, the record had been lowered another four seconds. By 1903, a horse named Lou Dillon was timed trotting the mile in two minutes at Readville, Massachusetts. Meanwhile, the pacers were doing a little better. In 1897, the pacer, Star Pointer was clocked in 1:59¼.

Next, came the pacer, Dan Patch, often called the greatest harness horse of all time. In the early nineteen hundreds, with equipment considered crude by modern standards, Dan Patch climaxed his brilliant career by pacing a mile in 1:55¼, a record that held up until 1938, when Billy Direct lowered the pacing record to 1:55 at Lexington, Kentucky. The following day, a trotter named Greyhound, lowered the trotting mark to 1:55¼, at the same track. Coincidentally, the same year saw the formation of the United States Trotting Association.

Billy Direct's pacing record was not broken for twenty-two more years, until, on the one-mile oval at Lexington, Adios Butler paced a mile in 1:54 ³/₅. A year later, he cut more than two seconds from the records at one-half mile tracks by pacing in 1:55 ³/₅ at Delaware, Ohio. This half-mile track record was finally equaled by Albatross in 1972.

At the mile-long ovals, Brett Hanover lowered the pacing record to 1:53 ³/₅ in 1966 and Steady Star set the new record of 1:52 in 1971 at Lexington. Nevele Pride finally broke Greyhound's thirty-one year record in 1969 at Indianapolis, Indiana by trotting a mile in 1:54 ⁴/₅.

The standardbred trotter and pacer of today are much stronger, faster specimens than their ancestors of the foundation period. The best of them are among the world's finest road horses, in the horse show world. A height of from 15½ to 16 hands prevails—despite the old idea that, in order to allow free play of the limbs, the harness horse should have unusual body length, sometimes as much as four inches longer than he is tall. This idea no longer prevails. Greyhound, for example, is taller than he is long. He was also taller than the average trotter, measuring almost 16½ hands high. Billy Direct was a much smaller horse, more than a hand shorter than Greyhound. The average standardbred weighs between 900 and 1000 pounds.

In the early days of harness racing, it was necessary for the horses competing to be mature, well seasoned, durable animals because of the rigorous conditions and the long distances involved. Now, two-year-olds are used extensively in racing programs, and have raced a mile in less than two minutes at both the trot and the pace.

Interestingly, it is possible to train a horse for both gaits. Those that are trained for both are called "double gaited". Most are faster at one gait than at the other, but there are exceptions. The World's Champion double-gaited horse is Steamin' Demon who paced a mile in 1:58 ⁴/₅ and trotted the same distance in 1:59 ¹/₅. The fastest double-gaited mare was Calumet Evelyn, who paced in 1:59 ¹/₄ and trotted in 1:59 ½. Some bloodlines (or "families") produce mainly pacers, the offspring going to this gait naturally. Among these are the families of The Abbe, Abbedale, Grattan, and Billy Direct. Pacers now far outnumber the trotters, and there is some concern that the trotting gait might die out in the future. Many colts from other families are first tried as trotters. If they show no trotting aptitude, or are more inclined to pace, they are switched over to pacing. Much of the change is accomplished by shoeing and by the use of hopples.

Harness horses are numerous, if not plentiful. In 1978, 13,991 horses were registered by 43,362 members of the U.S. Trotting Association. They raced at 486 tracks before about 30 million spectators. These 486 tracks include pari-mutuels operations, the Grand Circuit, and state and county fairs. Purses totaled $204,578,607.

Adios is often considered the greatest stallion of any breed. Although he died in 1965, by 1972 the lifetime earnings of his get had reached more than 19½ million dollars.

In the formative years of harness racing, the races were long and run under severe conditions. But, gradually, there evolved a system of the best three heats in five (a heat being one competitive mile in a race which requires two or more mile-dashes to decide the winner of a single race). This system was universal until the early 1900s. With the marked increase in horses' speed, a movement began to shorten the racing distance and cut down on the number of heats. At the present time, where pari-mutuels wagering is a part of the program, the races consist of a single dash at distances from three-fourths of a mile up to two miles. The vast majority of races are still over the one mile distance.

However, on the Grand Circuit, and the state and county fair circuits, most races are still decided by the best two out of three heats. If tracks in these two fair circuits include pari-mutuels wagering, they usually revert to the single- dash system. Most tracks are either one-half mile, or a full mile in circumference, but some are five-eights, or three-quarters of a mile in length.

The training of standardbreds is unique. Like thoroughbred and quarter horses, a standardbred colt is considered a weanling from the time it is born until January first of the following year. (All horses' birthdays are on January first, so on his first birthday he becomes a yearling.) During his yearling year, he gets some basic training. He gets used to being groomed, to the feel of the harness, to the bit in his mouth, and to being guided by the reins without being hitched to a "bike". He'll probably get some light track training in the fall months of his yearling year. A colt usually requires about nine months of schooling and serious training before making his first start. An older horse will round into shape with about five months training before starting his annual racing campaign.

The illustrations shown in this chapter details the different equipment that is possible to use on both pacers and trotters. It's possible to use almost all of these items on a horse, but usually a combination of only some of these will be used at one time, depending on the individual need of each horse. A fan needs to know about those of greatest importance to the horse's performance. In the illustration, the pacer is pulling a training cart, while the trotter is pulling a sulky used in actual races. A training cart, also called a jog cart, is longer and heavier than the racing sulky. It is used in training and early warm-ups, primarily because it is much more comfortable for the driver. Note that the driver's legs are not parallel with the shafts, but are in a more normal position. The average training cart weighs about 60 pounds. The racing sulky is much lighter, about 39 pounds. The sulky or "bike", normally used in the final pre-race warm-up as well as in the race itself, is made so that a driver's legs are alongside the shafts. With the driver in this position, the sulky and the wheels are in almost perfect balance. The result is a

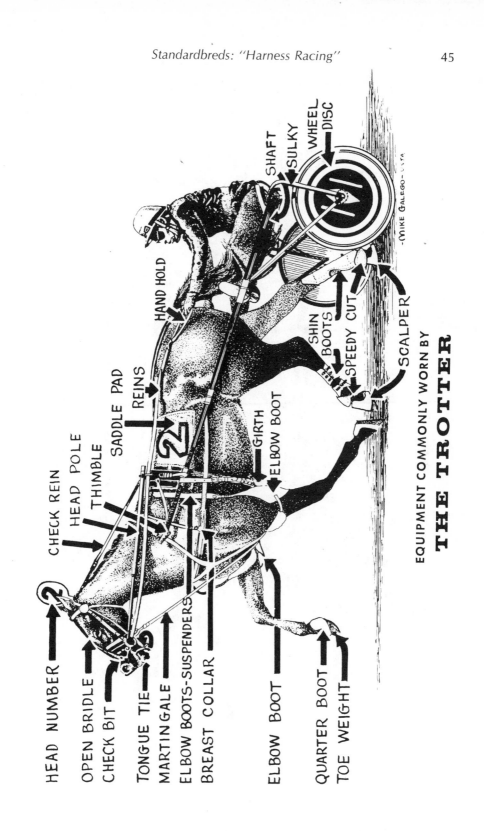

EQUIPMENT COMMONLY WORN BY

THE TROTTER

CHECK REIN

HEAD POLE

THIMBLE

SADDLE PAD

REINS

HAND HOLD

SHAFT

SULKY

WHEEL

DISC

SHIN BOOTS

SPEEDY CUT

SCALPER

GIRTH

ELBOW BOOT

HEAD NUMBER

OPEN BRIDLE

CHECK BIT

TONGUE TIE

MARTINGALE

ELBOW BOOTS-SUSPENDERS

BREAST COLLAR

ELBOW BOOT

QUARTER BOOT

TOE WEIGHT

-MIKE GALEGO - USTA

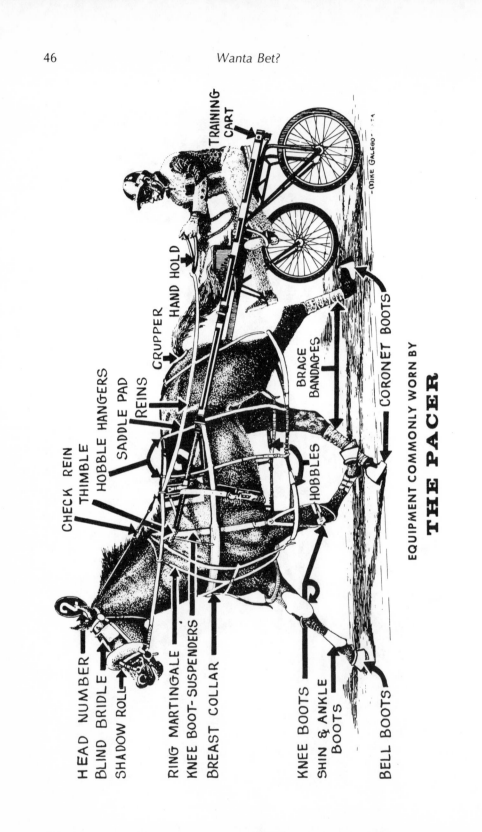

EQUIPMENT COMMONLY WORN BY

THE PACER

TRAINING CART

CRUPPER

HAND HOLD

CHECK REIN
THIMBLE
HOBBLE HANGERS
SADDLE PAD
REINS

BRACE BANDAGES

CORONET BOOTS

HOBBLES

HEAD NUMBER
BLIND BRIDLE
SHADOW ROLL

RING MARTINGALE
KNEE BOOT-SUSPENDERS
BREAST COLLAR

KNEE BOOTS
SHIN & ANKLE BOOTS

BELL BOOTS

—MIKE GALEGO

free-wheeling action, which makes the driver's weight of little importance, because the force of forward momentum provided by a heavier driver will compensate for any drag that additional weight might produce. Some people, though, feel the additional weight may make a slight difference on a muddy track. The cost of the racing sulky in 1978 averaged about $450. Inflation has increased this cost since that time.

The hopples or hobbles (either term is accepted) are used only on pacers and are made from either leather or plastic. These straps encircle the front and hind legs on the same side of the horse to keep those legs moving in unison while pacing. Occasionally, a pacer races without hopples, but these "free-legged pacers" are rare. Their trainers believe that the horse will give a better performance without the hopples. Trotters and free-legged pacers are more likely to break stride than pacers wearing the hopples.

Shoeing is crucial to harness horses. The trotter usually wears a heavier shoe—about 8 ounces—than the pacer, who takes about a 5-ounce shoe.

Some standardbreds race with the "shadow roll," a large sheepskin type roll, worn across the face just below the eyes. It cuts off the horse's view of the track, so that he won't shy at shadows, pieces of paper or other objects.

The check rein, running from the bit in the horse's mouth to the top of his head and then back, to hook on the harness keeps the horse's head high, enabling him to maintain a more even gait, with a balanced, reaching stride. It also helps control his speed and direction. During training, the horses' heads are gradually raised until they become accustomed to the check rein.

A head pole is used on some horses to keep them from turning their heads to the opposite side on the turns.

The U.S. Trotting Association registers the colors of racing jackets and caps worn by a driver. The particular pattern and combinations of colors chosen by a driver may not be used by anyone else in an official race. A driver may ask for a change during his career. If the new pattern is available, the Association usually will grant the request. These requests are rare and usually the same colors will be used by the driver throughout his career.

Harness races are usually contested at speeds averaging twenty-five to thirty miles per hour. When leaving the starting point, and during the final stages of the race, speeds of close to thirty-five miles per hour are attained by the best trotters and pacers. A pacer is generally considered to have slightly better speed, and is usually able to leave the gate at a slightly faster pace, although less than a second separates the world's record for each.

We have discussed several times what constitutes a break, but not the reasons why it occurs. A few reasons are: coming up to the starting gate at a speed uncomfortable to a horse, either too fast or too slow; by overextending himself to try to reach a speed beyond his capabilities; when he becomes tired; by hitting a hoof against a leg; or when he becomes frightened by sounds, or by an unnatural object on the track, such as water or a piece of paper.

The terms used to describe standardbreds of different sex or age are like those used for thoroughbreds and quarter horses. A newly born horse is a foal or a suckling, as long as he remains with his mother. His father is the sire and his mother, the dam. When weaned, he is known as a weanling until January first, at which time he becomes a yearling, regardless of his calendar age. On the next January first, he becomes a two-year-old. A male is called a colt until he becomes a four year old. At four, he becomes a "horse" or "stallion", unless he's been neutered. Males are often gelded to induce them to race more willingly and consistently. In this case he is called a gelding. A female is a "filly" until the age of four. Then she's called a mare.

The comparison of jockeys and harness horse drivers is interesting. Although they must meet the same basic requirements for licensing, and their participation in racing procedures are almost identical, there are some key differences. A person of almost any weight can drive trotters or pacers without changing the results of a race to any great degree, while the jockey must be quite small to compete. Age is also less of a factor in being able to compete as a driver. Jockeys are highly trained athletes, and must be strong and in excellent physical condition to perform well. They retire much earlier on the average than drivers, since driving is much less strenuous. With notable exceptions like Johnny Longden, most jockeys give up this occupation in their early forties. By contrast, the most recent survey by the U.S. Trotting Association, covering the 35 top-ranking drivers in each of the past ten years, showed the successful driver's average age to be 39. Bi Shively won the Hambletonian when in his seventies. It is quite common for an owner in harness racing to also be the trainer and driver. Most drivers are professionals, but the U.S. Trotting Association recognizes "amateurs" and defines them as persons who have not accepted any valuable consideration by way of or in lieu of compensation as drivers during the past ten years. In other words, they drive their own horses and accept no pay if they drive someone else's horses. Ordinarily, these amateurs limit their driving to the "fair circuits".

A winning driver ordinarily receives 10% of the winning purse, although "catch drivers" (those who make driving their primary occupation) often share part of the 10% with the trainer who engages them to drive his horses. This corresponds closely to the relationship of the jockey and the jockey's agent.

Usually the "catch drivers" limit their activities to the last pre-race warm-up and the race itself, while the trainer drives in the rest of the training procedure, and usually uses a training bike.

Just as electric totalisator equipment revolutionized the pari-mutuels operation, the mobile starting gate, which moves ahead of the moving horses changed harness racing. Prior to its use, the field was started by a method known as "scoring." With no barrier to keep the horses even at the start, the drivers would jockey for a better position, and the starter who was positioned at the starting point would, through vocal instruction only, try to get as even a start as possible. Numerous false starts and claims of not getting a fair shake resulted when he did allow the race to start by yelling "Go!" When he was dissatisfied with the alignment he'd yell "Recall," and the procedure would start again. A series of these recalls often became very boring to the patrons.

Harness horse training and pre-race preparations are quite different from that of the thoroughbreds and quarter horses. In training, they are jogged several miles a day. The weight of shoes, the harness, and other equipment is constantly changed to determine each horse's maximum potential. He is trained to normal starting speeds, an important procedure. Ordinarily the horses first line up about ¼ of a mile from the starting point. The starting gate then moves not less than 11 miles per hour for the first ⅛ of a mile, increases the speed to 18 miles per hour for the next ¹/₁₆ of a mile, and then gradually accelerates to a maximum speed of 35 miles per hour at the starting point.

Different horses need varying amounts of training and limbering-up before their performances, so there is no set procedure for pre-race warmups. But the following approximates what happens on race days. The first warmup is for about two to three miles of jogging clockwise, and a leisurely mile counter clockwise, timed at about 2:45. Then the horse is taken back to the paddock, sponged off and covered with a blanket. In about thirty minutes, he comes back on the track for a second warmup for one mile at about 2:30. The sponging is repeated, and he again gets a short rest. The training cart has been used for all of the above workouts. Now the racing sulky is put on. Depending on the trainer, from one half hour to one hour before the race, a final workout is given. The time for this last workout is usually from five to seven seconds slower than the anticipated race time. He is now sponged off for the final time before the race. (A thorough sponging and walking procedure is followed after the race itself, called cooling out, to prevent soreness later.)

During these warmups, some between actual races, a horse has designated saddle cloths of different colors to allow the spectators to identify and watch the horse's performance. This is necessary, since horses from several races might be warming up simultaneously. This amount of pre-race activity, sometimes as much as ten miles, might seem excessive to those not familiar with training methods, but it consists of no more than a limbering up excercise. The trainer soon learns the best procedure to enable his horse to race at his best. Horses do the early workouts, going clockwise, or the "wrong way of the track" to help with traffic control, since at this time the horse is going at a much slower speed.

As for competition, most trainers feel that one race a week is ideal, with a minimum of four days rest between starts.

Many patrons who do not thoroughly understand the sport have misconceptions about driving practices during the races. Drivers are sometimes suspected of not trying, when actually they are getting the maximum effort from their horse. Most drivers are meticulous race-planners and analysts. They carry stop watches, both during training and in the actual race. A driver checks the time at least every quarter of a mile, to determine the pace being set. He knows how fast his horse needs to go in each part of the race in order to cover the entire mile in the fastest time possible. Sometimes, of course, a driver and horse are boxed in or forced to the outside. The driver adjusts as best he can. Post position is a big factor. A horse racing five feet out from the inside point at which a half-mile track is measured, travels 62 feet farther than a mile in the course of the race. A horse ten feet out travels 126½ feet farther, and one 30 feet out, 376 feet farther. The difference on a track with a mile circumference is, of course, less. Many drivers feel that a spot in second or third place on the rail is the ideal position, since he is close to the front, but still has the leader breaking the wind for him. Of course, he risks getting boxed in and not everyone can be second or third in an eight horse race. Some horses will do better when urged with a whip, others will sulk from it and decrease his speed. Sometimes it appears that a driver is pulling back hard on the lines to slow the horse. Sometimes this is true, but it's because the driver feels the pace is too fast for his particular animal and he needs to save him for the finish. At other times he is trying to keep the horse's head up to assure a faster stride and oftentimes reining-in is necessary to keep a tired horse from breaking stride.

U.S. TROTTING ASSOCIATION

As mentioned earlier, the U.S. Trotting Association was formed in 1938. It is harness racing's equivalent to the thoroughbred's Jockey Club and the quarter horse's AQHA. "A plan for the creation and establishment of one central governing body to have exclusive control and authority over harness racing in the United States, which shall supercede and replace all parent or governing bodies now existing" was the resolution of standardbred owners, breeders, and racing officials who met in Indianapolis on November 13, 1938. "One central governing body" was the key phrase, since before that time, three different groups regulated the sport in different sections of the country. They were the National Trotting Association, the American Trotting Association, and the United Trotting Association. The Trotting Horse Club of America and the American Trotting Register Association also were active. Confusion caused by varied and sometimes conflicting rules of the different groups was the biggest problem. It was decided in Indianapolis that all associations would cease their official functions on January 1, 1939. Former representatives from these three groups met formally in Columbus, Ohio on January 6th and 7th, 1939, to finalize the merger and officially create the U.S. Trotting Association.

E. Roland Harriman was probably more instrumental in bringing about this merger than any other one person. With others, he agreed to underwrite the USTA until it became firmly established financially. His home town of Goshen, New York was the site of one of the three USTA offices upon its formation. The other two were located in Hartford, Connecticut and Bellefontaine, Ohio. By 1945, the offices in Goshen and Bellefontaine were closed and their records consolidated with the office in Hartford. In 1948, the headquarters were moved from Hartford to 750 Michigan Ave., Columbus, Ohio, where they are located at this time. This location was chosen largely to give the USTA a more central location geographically.

Upon formation, the USTA was divided into eleven districts, ten in the United States and one in Canada. This provided full representation and alleviated any unequal distribution of power to any one section of the country. Only about 6,000 standardbreds were racing in 1939, but now over 45,000 compete each season. Because of the large increase in the number of horses racing and because the sport has expanded into new areas of the nation, there are now fourteen districts.

Each of the districts has from one to seven directors, depending upon population. In all cases, directors are owners, breeders, officials, drivers, or racetrack operators who are elected by district members. There are currently just under 50,000 USTA members, represented by 55 directors from the fourteen districts.

In March of each year, a national meeting of all district directors is held in Columbus, Ohio. At that time, problems confronting the sport and proposed rule changes are acted upon. Fiscal reports are analyzed and executive officers are elected. Day-to-day operations are carried out by the Executive Vice-President from the Columbus office.

The basic function of the USTA is to be the rules-making and record-keeping body for the sport of harness racing. Specific responsibilities are divided among several different departments of this non profit organization which employs 120 people.

A. Membership Department: processes membership applications and renewals; registers stable and corporate names; and handles orders for USTA publications.

B. Legal Department: drafts and interprets USTA rules; cares for legal matters arising in connection with the conduct of USTA business; conducts officials' schools and seminars; schedules appeals of fines and penalties to the District Board, executive committee and Board of Appeals; prepares lists of suspensions, fines and denials of membership.

C. Driver License Department: conducts tests for those interested in obtaining licenses to train or drive standardbreds; handles applications and renewals for licenses of the approximately 12,000 drivers and 9,000 trainers currently active in harness racing.

D. Publicity Department: provides information, research and photographic services to racetracks and the various media; publishes the monthly magazine *Hoof Beats;* conducts promotions designed to attract interest in harness racing; prepares books *Trotting and Pacing Guide, Harness Handbook,* etc; prepares a daily message service, "The Harness Racing Hotline"; provides results of major stakes and feature events from racetracks nationwide to the media; and provides harness racing films.

E. Data Processing Department: provides timely and accurate information used by other USTA departments, members of the USTA, breeders, etc.

F. Program Department: prepares and issues eligibility and validation certificates for each harness horse; maintains a current file of race programs and charts; provides program information on stakes horses; handles inquiries concerning horses' earnings.

G. Color Registration Department: regulates the life-time registration of drivers' colors.

H. Registration Department: documents new standardbred foals and oversees their naming; records changes in ownership of all harness horses; is involved with the exchange of records when horses are imported or exported; keeps records of which mares are bred to which stallions.

I. Identification Department: co-ordinates the lip-tattooing of each horse that races in the United States, usually when they are yearlings.

J. Treasury Department: oversees the financial dealings such as budgets, cash flow, etc.
K. Track Department: licenses all fairs and pari-mutuels meetings where harness racing is conducted; supplies these groups with necessary information; keeps records of and handles applications for all stakes and futurities; oversees the blood-typing of all standardbred stallions.
L. Security Department: investigates violations of USTA rules; handles complaints relative to financial responsibility; co-ordinates with State Racing Commissions; has the power to reject membership applications because of rules infractions.

Every person who breeds, owns, drives or trains standardbreds is a member of the USTA. So, too, are harness track owners and officials. In 1978, there were 43,362 members of the USTA. There were 13,991 new registrations of foals. There were 48,177 starters at 486 different tracks racing for $204,578,607 in purses. Pari-mutuel racing was conducted in fourteen states, handling $2,733,382,632 and attended by 25,431,195 racing fans. The states' share of the revenue was $150,321,429.

In closing the chapter, I'd like to add that from my observations, while harness racing is one of the oldest sports in the country, it is one that for those who did not grow up with it, find hard to understand. Hopefully, the above information will answer some questions and make the sport more enjoyable for those who attend.

Courtesy of USTA

LEBANON, OHIO
NOV. 4, 1978
1 MILE
FAST

HI DOS KNIGHT
OWNER-SURREY HILL FARM   K. PHILLIANS-TRNR.
PACE   ROBERT ROBERTS-DRVR.
0:31:4   1:04:1   1:36:1   2:07:1

Chapter Four

Greyhounds: "The Sport of Queens"

Greyhound racing, as we know it today, is a relatively new sport. However, the greyhound itself has had an impact on the lives of men for many centuries. The greyhound may be the oldest known pure breed in the world. By nature, the greyhounds are domesticated and docile animals, but many centuries ago, when mankind was faced with the continual daily problems of survival, this breed was invaluable because of his natural instincts to chase a quarry to use for food. Records have been found describing his use for this purpose by the Medes, Assyrians and Egyptians. By the time of Britian's King Canute, a decree prohibited any person below the rank of Gentleman from owning these valuable animals.

There have been numerous stories as to where the Greyhound came by his name. One of the most accepted reasons is attributed to the early Greeks. Since the greyhound chases by sight, and has little or no sense of smell, the Greeks called them "Gazehounds". Other names given them in ancient times were "Gazelhounds" and "Greihounds".

Ancient art has depicted the greyhound. Somewhere between 3100-2780 B.C. the Egyptians possessed Tjisems (a breed of canine) which were considered domesticated. Egyptian art on monuments shows dogs with pointed muzzles, long pointed ears, thin lean bodies, long slender paws, and short curly tails held high. Egyptologists call him a Saluki, apparently a decendant of the jackal.

Assyrians and Greek sculptures and paintings depict a dog very much like the Greyhound chasing and hunting gazelles. A lamp in a British museum, dating from 400 B.C. shows a similar animal holding a hare in his mouth.

Tomb reliefs from 2280-2052 B.C. show the North African Soverign, Antef II, flanked by dogs as he strode into battle. The name of one of his dogs, Abiquor, in the Berger language, means "Greyhound".

As early as the 1st Dynasty (3200-2700 B.C.), a curved disc showing two gazelles being attacked by greyhounds was discovered. While archaeologists were exploring the tomb of Egyptian King Amten, three carvings of greyhounds were found. On Ptaheptep's sepulcher at Sakkra (2500 B.C.), greyhounds are shown at the start of a coursing race.

One of paintings of the funerary chest of Tatankhamun (18th Dynasty, (1361-1340 B.C.) shows King Tut attacking the Nubians with a pack of greyhounds at his side.

The greyhounds belonging to the Pharoahs and Arabian sheiks were highly regarded as the treasured companions of men of royal blood.

The whelping of these animals was an event that transcended all else, except the birth of a son in his master's household.

As time continued, the greyhound began to appear in Egypt, north to Judea, Persia, and through the valleys of the Tigris and Euphrates, and into Babylon. From there the greyhound spread into Bractria from Parthia to Afghanistan; and into the Russias. Greyhounds found themselves in Thrace, Macedonia, and in Greece, Rome, and the British Isles.

Cleopatra is said to have owned and raced a kennel of greyhounds. The Hebrews also kept racing kennels, with the Israelites picking up their interest in greyhounds from the Mesopotamians.

When the first greyhound reached Britain has been disputed by many historians. Some believe that the greyhound was introduced into Britian by the Phoenicians during the early trading voyages or by the Cretans about 500 B.C.

As man became an agriculturist, hunting with greyhounds was no longer needed. But, as a sporting breed, the dog gained unusual esteem everywhere because of his fantastic physical attributes. He became the source of pleasurable recreation. Historically, mankind has always admired fleet footed animals, and the greyhound met this qualification. Greyhounds have been timed at speeds of more than 40 miles per hour. They will run as hard as they can for as long as they can, and have been known to drop from exhaustion.

Greyhound coursing gained prestige under Queen Elizabeth I of England. She raised coursing to the status of a sport, by having a code of rules to insure complete fairness to the quarry and the greyhounds. Because of these efforts, greyhound racing became known as the "Sport of Queens". In the early period of English history, the killing of a greyhound was punishable by death. It is generally accepted that todays greyhound breed was actually developed in England, as the English were the first to establish a greyhound stud book in 1882. From there the breed spread to other countries.

Late in 1776 the first greyhound coursing club was founded at Swaffham. This club's success encouraged the advent of coursing clubs throughout England. In 1780 the Ashdown Club opened, followed by the Malton Club in 1781, the Newmarket Society in 1805, the Amesbury in 1822, and the world famous Altcar Club in 1825.

Greyhounds became popular as hunters in frontier America in the early 1800's. They were brought to the New World by English and Irish settlers. The first mention of greyhounds in the United States can be found in the book entitled "Oregon and California in 1848", where a greyhound-antelope race was described. As the settlers moved west they were confronted with an over abundance of wild game, especially the hares and jack rabbits. These animals were a serious threat to the farmers and a solution had to be found to control their numbers. Greyhounds proved to be the answer to this problem. The areas where they were used most extensively were in the Plain States in the Midwest and Southwest. Thus, the states of Kansas, Texas, Oklahoma, and Arizona became the leaders in breeding and raising greyhounds. Private coursing meets were held as early as 1849, but public coursing was first introduced in California. The sport met with indifferent success at that time. The first public meeting with any real value was held at Great Bend, Kansas in 1886. After a few years of inactivity, California revived the sport and held annual meetings at Merced. Greyhound coursing clubs soon sprang up in many other states, most notably in Colorado, Kansas, the Dakotas, Montana, and Minnesota.

Breeders and club officials soon recognized the necessity of a governing board and The American Coursing Board was organized in October, 1893. Their rules, for the most part, followed those of the National Coursing Board in Great Britain. As coursing grew in the 19th century, a stronger authority was needed. The National Coursing Association, known today as the National Greyhound Association was founded in 1896 in Abilene, Kansas. This association, administers and controls all coursing in the United States and maintains the American Stud Book.

In early 1900's coursing gained a firm footing as a spectator sport in some parts of the country.

In 1905, Owen Patrick Smith promoted a coursing meet in Hot Springs, South Dakota, in hopes of increasing the town's tourist trade. The first meet was such a success that Smith quit his job as secretary of the Hot Springs Chamber of Commerce and devoted the rest of his life to the greyhound industry.

During the planning stages of the coursing meet in Hot Springs, Smith enlisted the services of George Sawyer, an expert on greyhound racing. The two men again met in Salt Lake City in 1907 during the Intermountain Coursing Association meeting. Smith told Sawyer that the general public was condemning the use of live hares to train greyhounds. By this time the rabbit "pest problem" had been controlled, and the greyhound was no longer needed for this purpose. It was at this time that Smith proposed a plan to substitute an artificial lure for the live hare.

In 1907 Smith raised enough money to build a small circular track near Salt Lake City. He stuffed a rabbit skin, mounted it on a motorcycle, and rode it around the track, with the greyhounds in close pursuit.

In 1912, Smith obtained a patent on his mechanical lure and a track was opened in Houston, Texas, but did not prove successful. In 1919, Smith and Sawyer joined forces to found the Blue Star Amusement Company, and built a track in Emeryville, California. From there they went to Tulsa, Oklahoma and formed the International Greyhound Racing Association. Their next stop was Riverside Park in Chicago. Here they met with protests against daytime racing, which eventually led to the introduction of night racing.

From Chicago, Smith moved to Hialeah, Florida, where a greyhound track was built on the grounds of the Hialeah Thoroughbred Racetrack. The first Miami Greyhound Derby was held there in 1922.

By this time, the 1912 patented Smith Lure had been improved to a great extent. The new system consisted of a motor mounted on four wheels, which ran on a track for ³/₁₆th of a mile, carrying an artifical rabbit on the end of a long arm that extended into the racing area. Although greatly improved, there were still imperfections in his lure. At times it would slam into the brakehouse and fall off the track before the race was finished. Or it would stop too quickly. An Emeryville stockbroker, George Heintz, solved some of the problems by designing a folding arm which made the lure disappear after each race, while allowing the motor mounted vehicle to continue around the track.

On January 3, 1925, the St. Petersburg Kennel Club opened it's doors. Later to be known as Derby Lane, it is the oldest greyhound racing track still in operation in the United States. In 1926, Biscayne (located in Miami Shores); Jacksonville; Sarasota; and Tampa built racing facilities, and by the middle of the 1930's, greyhound racing was firmly established as a recognized sport.

Several factors made greyhound racing late getting accepted as a pari-mutuels sport in comparison with horse racing. Greyhound promoters were inclined to regard the sport as merely ancillary to horse racing. In many cases, the dog track was within the confines of a horse track, or in near proximity. In some instances, dog races were held between horse races.

Unfortunately, several promoters of this period had questionable morals. They would move into an area, run a meet and skip out with the profits, leaving debts and bad impressions with the local citizens. Although these practices are impossible today because of strict supervision of the sport, the memories of these events are still in the minds of many, and has made it difficult to legislate dog racing in many areas of our country. At one time or another, there were tracks in New York, New Jersey, Ohio, Illinois, North Carolina, Missouri, Texas, California, and Oklahoma. None of these states permit dog racing at this writing, although there are on-going attempts to revive the sport in many of these states.

At the present time, there are thirteen (13) states in which dog tracks are operating, with the fourteenth (Nevada), scheduled to begin racing in 1981. Several other states are planning to introduce legislation to legalize greyhound racing in the near future. Fifty two (52) race meetings at forty seven (47) tracks were in operation in 1978 in these thirteen states and reported a total attendance of almost 21 million patrons. This makes dog racing one of the top ten spectator sports in the United States; quite impressive since there were thirty seven (37) states including most of the more populous ones, which still banned greyhound racing. Almost two billion dollars were wagered at these fifty two tracks. It seems likely that the volume will go over the two billion mark in 1980.

Florida was the first of the thirteen states to legalize dog racing, in 1931, and still has almost one third of the tracks now in operation. Racing was held at 18 different Florida tracks in 1978 and were responsible for almost half of the money bet on greyhounds in the United States for that year. Oregon was the second state to legalize the sport in 1933. There is still only one track in operation in Oregon. It is located on the outskirts of Portland and operates only during the summer months for less than 100 days. Massachusetts inaugurated dog racing in 1935 and for many years was successful with only limited exotic wagering. They finally joined the other states in using quinellas, exactas, and other forms of exotic wagering and are doing very well using these additional pools. Arizona was the fourth state to join the ranks in 1942. For many years, the only tracks in operation were located in Phoenix and Tucson, but gradually four more were added as the population grew, and now there is year around racing in the state. South Dakota opened a track in Rapid City in 1949, soon followed by a second one located in South Dakota but really on the outskirts of Sioux City, Iowa.

Colorado also began their greyhound program in 1949. At first, racing was held solely during the summer months but gradually new tracks were built, and at this time five are in operation and dates spread out, so that at least one track is operating each month of the year.

In these formative years, greyhound racing was seasonal. Winter racing was held in Florida and Arizona and summer racing in Oregon, Massachusetts, Colorado and South Dakota. For the most part, the same kennels provided the dogs for both seasons, making the long trip south for the winter and going back north in the spring. Gradually, racing seasons became longer, the racing plants were enclosed, and heating and cooling systems were installed. These factors, in addition to new tracks being built in states already permitting greyhound racing, has allowed kennels to operate, for the most part, in one general area.

Arkansas was the only state during the twenty four year period from 1949 to 1973 to be successful in passing legislation for dog racing. This came about in 1955. There is only one track in Arkansas, but it has become the largest in the country, both in yearly volume and in average daily handle. It is located in West Memphis, across the river from Memphis, Tennessee. (Racing was held at different times in North Carolina and Montana, but was discontinued after a few years of operation.)

It was to be eighteen years after the successful venture in Arkansas before more states were able to pass legislation permitting greyhound racing. In 1973 Alabama and New Hampshire both opened new tracks. Alabama now has two tracks, one in Mobile and the other in Green County, thirty miles south of Tuscaloosa. New Hampshire has three locations: Seabrook, Hinsdale, and Belmont.

Three years later, in 1976, Connecticut, West Virginia, and Vermont joined the ranks. The one track in Connecticut is located at Plainfield. West Virginia and Vermont started a trend that could be a large factor in the future. Horse tracks that were having financial difficulties converted their facilities to dog racing. Wheeling Downs, at Wheeling, West Virginia, and Green Mountain at Pownal, Vermont were the tracks involved in this conversion. In 1977, this same concept was applied to Lincoln Downs in Rhode Island. Two horse tracks in Florida have also converted to dogs. 1981 will see the fourteenth state added to the list. A track is now under construction at Henderson, Nevada, near Las Vegas. This will be a combination facility for both dogs and horses. Several states considering legalizing pari-mutuels betting may follow this example.

The betting procedures are identical in horse and dog racing. However, the rules of racing, the method of providing dogs for racing at each track, and the procedures used to organize and regulate racing at greyhound tracks are quite different from horse tracks.

To begin with, one person can care for and train more dogs at one time than he can horses. Whereas the owners, trainers and grooms necessary to furnish enough horses for a race meeting number in the hundreds, the personnel required to serve the same purpose at a dog track is minimal.

Dog tracks issue what is known as "bookings", simplified to mean a contract to furnish a specified number of dogs qualified to race for a specified period of time. The number of "bookings" issued varies from track to track, according to the policies of each individual track, and is determined largely by the volume of money being wagered at a particular track as well as the number of allotted racing days. The purses in dog racing is determined entirely by a percentage (usually between 2% and 3%) of the mutuels handle. Therefore a small track usually issues less bookings than a large one, due simply to economics. The number of bookings issued by a track might vary from as few as twelve at a small track to as many as forty at a large one. It takes as many dogs to fill races at a small track as at a large one, so each contractee where a small number of bookings is the practice, must maintain a larger number of dogs eligible to race at all times.

When a "booking" has been issued to an owner or a trainer, he must turn the registration papers of the dogs in his possession over to the Racing Secretary for screening. The dogs accepted by the Racing Secretary are then in his hands to use for racing at his discretion. Owners and trainers do not enter their dogs for certain races as in the case of horses, although the trainer may specify that they are to be used only for certain distances. Almost all dog tracks are built in two sizes, either 440 yards, or 495 yards in circumference. The 495 yard tracks are known as Futurity tracks. The most common distances raced are $5/16$ and $3/8$ of a mile. Some tracks have used, and are using, $3/16$, $7/16$, and $9/16$ distances. The longer races are called marathons and some tracks are increasing the number of races at these distances. The merits of these marathon races are quite controversial at this time. Whether or not this trend will continue is uncertain. Whereas the number of entries vary greatly in horse racing, governed by the number of horses entered in each race by their trainers, most dog races consists of eight entries.

A few dog tracks use or have used nine entries but this is not common practice.

It would seem that there would be no problem in maintaining an ample supply of greyhounds to race at the limited number of tracks now in operation in the United States, but such is not the case. This problem is not as great as that confronting the horse industry, since it takes much less time to prepare a greyhound for racing, the gestation period is much shorter for dogs than horses, and puppies are born in litters as opposed to the single birth of a colt. However, the rapid increase in the number of racing days per year has created a demand for the addition of a large number of qualified racing stock of all varieties. Most of the puppies that will eventually reach the track are produced on regular breeding farms, and is an independant operation from that of the racing kennels.

An average brood bitch will have at least one litter per year and sometimes two. A litter usually consists of from five to eight puppies, but occasionally as many as twelve are born in one litter. Greyhound puppies are very affectionate and playful animals and are usually allowed to run free in their pens until they are about twelve months old. They are watched closely from the time they are born. A diet, high in vitamin and mineral content is essential for their future success in racing. They are handled regularly to get them accustomed to obedience and to the extensive grooming which will be their daily routine when they reach racing age. Care of the eyes is especially important since greyhounds chase principally by sight and cannot race well with any trace of astigmatism or short sightedness.

When a puppy is approximately twelve months old, his preliminary track training begins. He is now individually kenneled inside a building. Attention is paid to nail trimming, cuticle care, bathing and worming. He begins morning and evening workouts in a large field. He is turned out three or four times daily into a large, clean paddock area for short periods. The amount of exercise he gets is controlled. Too much excerise before he is completely matured can hamper or even ruin his racing capabilities in the future. During this training period he must learn balance in his running, to get in stride quickly, to run straight, and how to maneuver the turns with maximum speed. Once an average greyhound gets into full stride, (between 100 and 400 yards), he is traveling at about 20 yards per second. This is equivalent to about 40 miles per hour. After 400 yards his speed decreases. These figures reflect running in a straight line and cannot be maintained while negotiating the turns on a circular track. It can be assumed from these figures that a greyhound will lead a racehorse up to 700 yards, providing both start together and are running under ideal conditions, best suited to each. The stride of a greyhound will be from 12 to 20 feet, depending on his size, as compared to the horse's stride of 23 to 27 feet.

The size of a full grown greyhound will vary according to his bloodlines, diet in his formative period, etc. Size varies from 45 to 70 pounds in females and from 55 to 90 pounds in males. It is generally agreed that an average female will weigh approximately 60 pounds and a male approximately 68 pounds.

There are 14 basic greyhound colors: brindle, dark brindle, black brindle, blue, black, red, dark red, fawn, red fawn, black and white, white and black, red and white, white and brindle, and white and brindle ticked.

Proper education and training is very important in developing a racing greyhound. New circumstances and surroundings are frightening to a young dog, so he must be handled gently. On the other hand, he must be brought to the peak of his physical and mental condition for his racing career as soon as possible. Most trainers like to have their dogs make their first start when they are between 16 and 18 months of age. Some develop faster than others, and start at an earlier age, but they are exceptions. Most reach their racing peak when they are about two years old, but again this depends on each individual dog. Most have completed their racing careers at the age of four years, but some continue to race until they reach the maximum age at which they are permitted to compete. (A dog may finish the meet in which he is competing when he reaches his fifth birthday, but is not allowed to start in any subsequent meets.)

Most successful racers will start from 200 to 250 times during their careers, barring any permanent injuries.

Specific training methods at a pre-racing age will vary according to the philosophies of the trainer, and the rate at which each dog matures. A general outline of training procedures is as follows: first, he must be familiarized with the collar and taught to lead. Next, he must be introduced to strangers to prepare him for the crowds and noise when he finally goes to the track to race. When this has been accomplished, he is taken to a small circular track. He is released by hand and allowed to run about 100 yards around the track and then to seize an artificial quarry. This is repeated until he is taught to run hard to seize this quarry. Next, he is allowed to chase the artificial lure. Again, he is released by hand and the lure is kept fairly close in front of him so that he can see it well. This encourages him to give it a hard chase. Gradually the distances are increased to about 300 yards.

By the second month of training, most dogs are ready to break from a starting box. Hopefully, he will learn to crouch down in the starting box, remain still but alert, and jump out cleanly and fast when the lid lifts. The back of the boxes are closed, allowing only frontal vision. This keeps him from turning in the box. The lid is then lifted, and the dog is allowed to jump out and grab the lure. He is next taught to crouch down by using a cover in the starting box, leaving approximately nine inches at the bottom so that he must stay low and thus keep his head down in order to see the mechanical lure. The final phase of his education teaches him to distinguish the noise of the mechanical lure and to co-ordinate his reflexes of sight and sound. The lure is brought past the box slowly at first. The speed is gradually increased until it is traveling at the speed used in competitive conditions. This phase of his training ordinarily takes about a month.

Now the greyhound is ready for the training track where he can apply what he has learned, in the company of other dogs with similar experience. The procedures at the training track are carried out under simulated racing conditions. These schooling races are watched closely and attempts are made to match dogs with others of comparable ability. Those who pass this test are ready to be officially schooled in preparation for actual racing. Official schooling usually takes place at night in order to get the young dog used to the lights and spectators. Those who fail this test are taken back for more preliminary training until they are again ready for official schoolings.

Before a dog can be officially schooled, a permanent record must be made for identification purposes. In addition to a tattoo number, which he will carry throughout his racing career, he is examined thoroughly and all of his physical characteristics are recorded on what is known as a Bertillion Card. This information includes his name, age, breeding, sex, weight, coloring, and all other distinguishing markings in detail. One of the most differentiating characteristics of the greyhound is his toenails. The color and appearance of each nail is detailed on the Bertillion Card. Also scars by which he can be accurately identified are recorded. This card will be used at each and every racetrack where he performs during his lifetime.

Greyhound tracks conduct schooling races, actually practice races under actual racing conditions, including the weighing-in procedures. These races are open to the public. Young dogs who have completed their basic training period are placed in these races. They must perform to the satisfaction of the Officials, as well as to meet a minimum qualifying time before they are eligible to compete in official races. If they qualify, they are ready to compete in Maiden Races with other dogs who have never won an official race. After winning one of these maiden races, they are placed in a grade according to the grading system used at the particular track where they are competing. Experienced dogs are also subject to schooling races. There are several circumstances governing when they must school. Examples are: when a dog arrives from another track and did not have an official start within a specified period of time, usually ten days; when a dog has been sidelined because of injuries for more than ten days, or has not raced for any other reason in the same period of time; when he has raced poorly in his last start; or when he has interfered with another dog in his last start. Interference (commonly called a strike) is when a dog deliberately fights or interferes with another dog during a race. Continued practice of interfering results in a dog being barred from further competition.

It is interesting to note that many, many greyhounds go through the above described training and never qualify for a single official race. Some believe the ratio is less than half of those whelped. It is hard to determine the actual cost of raising and training a greyhound to racing age during this period of inflation. This figure will vary greatly due to the facilities available, the size of the breeding farm, as well as many other factors. A conservative estimate at this time would probably be in excess of $1,000 for each racing dog.

There are two distinct types of racing kennels. Those who maintain their own breeding farms and own all the dogs racing under their name, and those who lease their racing stock from operators of breeding farms. Some kennels are a combination of both systems. When leasing is involved, the breeder usually receives 35% of the purse money, and the lessee 65%. The lessee must feed and maintain other expenses involved in a racing operation. When the dog's racing career is finished, he is returned to the original owner.

Training procedures of racing dogs vary slightly with each trainer, but in general are as follows. Each dog is confined to a small crate within a small kennel, ordinarily housing about forty dogs. Each such facility has two small turnout pens, one for the males and the other for the females. The dogs must be turned out into these pens several times in each 24 hour period, usually four or five times. Dogs must be muzzled at all times when they are outside their crates. While affectionate and lovable to humans, they are prone to fighting with each other, and even with muzzles, must be supervised during "turnouts". There are two types of muzzles. The ones used in the pens are made of wire, while the muzzles used during actual racing are plastic and leather. The racing muzzles are much lighter, and must fit well to keep them from flopping during the race, yet leave enough room for freedom of action and breathing.

An interesting sidelight is that all greyhounds have two names. One is their official racing name and the other their kennel name. The chief reason for dual-naming is to prevent the dogs from becoming distracted by spectators who call out their program name during the post parade and the race.

Normal procedure for dogs in training is an early morning turnout, another at mid-morning, still another before the dogs which are racing that day or night are taken to the track, and finally the turnout after the night's races are completed. The crates must be cleaned, either at the early or mid-morning turnout, and fresh bedding added when necessary. The bedding is usually shredded paper. All dogs must be groomed daily and special attention paid to the dogs who will be competing on that particular day. The greyhounds are watched closely each day for physical ailments, especially during the turnouts. The amount of excerise each dog gets depends on what kind of racing rotation he is currently in. If he is racing every few days, he needs very little exercise between races, possibly only a brief walk on the morning of the day he is scheduled to race. The others need regular exercise, mostly on the sprint paths which are provided by the facilities where the dogs are quartered or by the track itself. A dog being prepared to resume racing in the near future, usually will be unofficially schooled occasionally. (Many states require that the tracks licensed to hold race meetings provide kennel facilities on track property. Others permit the trainers to quarter their dogs elsewhere.)

On the day a dog is scheduled to race, he is taken to the paddock area at least one hour before post time for the first race. After his initial weigh-in, he is turned over to the Kennel Master. (He will be under his supervision until he is blanketed, weighed again immediately before entering the track for the post parade, and the race itself.) At this time, he is turned over to one of the licensed leadout personnel. Post weights are announced to the public at this time. During the post parade, the Patrol Judge rechecks the muzzle to see that it fits properly. He also checks to see that the blanket is securely and accurately tied. A blanket that is either too loose or too tight, or that becomes untied during the race will hamper a dog's performance. Immediately following the race, the dog is returned to his trainer. At this time, he checks his physical condition, making sure he has not been injured during the running of the race. He also washes the dog's feet, and pays special attention to his toes. Particles of sand sometimes work their way under the skin around the toenails. If not cleaned properly, it may become infected and cause lameness. Finally, he is cooled out by whatever method his particular trainer uses, returned to the kennel and given his meal for the day. Music is usually played in the kennels at all times. It is not only soothing to the dogs, but shuts out the outside noises. This helps the dogs get their much needed rest.

Contrary to what is believed by many who have never been close to racing greyhounds, they enjoy their work very much, and get very excited when they realize that it's their turn to go to the track to race.

We have mentioned several times the act of weighing the dogs. Dogs must conform to an official racing weight. The set racing weight of each dog is submitted by the trainer to the Racing Officials at the start of each racing meet. When a dog is weighed in by the Kennel Master prior to a race, he must weigh within 1½ pounds from his "set weight" or he cannot race. He must also weigh within 2 pounds of the weight at which he raced in his last previous start. The dogs are weighed immediately prior to the race in which they are competing, because some dogs lose considerable weight while in the paddock through nervousness. Dogs in this category are known as "weight losers". A record is kept of these particular dogs and they are watched carefully by the Racing Officials and the Veterinarian. If, in the opinion of the Presiding Steward and the Veterinarian, the weight loss is not too great to impair his racing potential, he is allowed to race. A list of these chronic "weight losers" is posted for the betting public's information. The amount of weight lost by dogs in this category is influenced by whether he races in the early or late races on the program.

Greyhounds are fed different amounts of food, according to their particular needs. A fairly accurate average figure is 2½ pounds per day for a dog during the periods he is in competition. A trainer will learn his needs as his training continues and the food is carefully weighed for each individual dog. Horse meat or beef, along with dog meal is the basic food. This is mixed with various kinds of vegetables and fruits, such as spinach, green beans, peaches, etc. Cereal (All Bran or similar brands) is sometimes added, as is small amounts of pumpernickel bread. Karo syrup, in small quantities may also be added periodically. All these items are mixed together thoroughly in a large tub. Vitamin and mineral supplements are added to each dog's serving according to his individual needs. Occasionally the trainer may cook up a good beef stew, both to supplement the diet, and as a treat. Dogs scheduled to compete during a current day or night are sometimes fed a very light meal in the morning to prevent any lethargy that might occur during racing hours, and then receives his ordinary meal at night after the race.

A close study of the training procedures shows that greyhound trainers have a very exacting and confining life. Their work goes on seven days a week, fifty-two weeks a year. Visits to the kennels must be made every few hours. It is impossible to sleep regularly, unless duties are divided between the trainer in charge and his assistants. Frequently greyhound training is a family affair, so that each member can have some free time. Trainers are usually paid a base salary, plus a percentage of the purses earned. This system will vary according to circumstances and to the individual kennel involved. A rough estimate of earnings is from $300 to $500 per week, plus living expenses. The kennel owner furnishes all necessary equipment, including the trucks and trailers for hauling the dogs, refrigerators for keeping the feed, muzzles, collars, lead straps, blankets, feed pans, etc. Inflation constantly affects the cost of keeping a dog in training. A rough estimate would be $5.00 per dog per day at this time. Since purses are based almost entirely upon from 2½ to 3½ per cent of the track handle, it is obvious that the better dogs usually race at the larger tracks. Of course, the smaller kennels will have some exceptional dogs and do not have bookings at the larger tracks. New pups breaking in are unknown quantities, until they become experienced racers, so there are usually several top notch animals from these categories. Thus there are always some excellent dogs racing at even the smallest tracks.

It is generally agreed that a dog will race better for a trainer that he likes than for one that he doesn't. This is especially true in the case of very timid dogs. A very small percentage are extremely timid, even to the extent that they are classified as "spooks". They are actually afraid of people and end up responding to a very few trainers, and in some cases, only one person. Some of these "spooks" have proven to be very capable racers, but only when they are with a trainer that they like and trust. Many trainers are convinced that dogs realize when they have won, and will come off the track happy when they do well, and depressed when they have not. Some trainers repaint the interior of the kennels, change the location of crates in the kennel, or do various other things to stimulate a dog's desire to perform better. These methods are often used when the entire kennel is not doing well for no apparent reason.

In the early days of greyhound racing, breeding farms were based, with few exceptions, in Texas, Oklahoma, Kansas and other states where jackrabbits were plentiful. These rabbits played a big part in the racing dog's early training, and in coursing meets. With the recent growth of dog racing, many farms have been built nearer the locations where racing has been legalized. This was done largely for convenience of shipping, and to be more accessible to the trainers who will be leasing or buying their young dogs. Some owners and trainers maintain their own breeding farms in order to make their business more profitable and to be better able to produce the types of racers best suited to their particular needs. In this way, they can better control the bloodlines of the type of dogs that they prefer. Without question, greyhound breeding is becoming more scientific all the time. Imported dogs from Australia, New Zealand, England, Ireland, and a few from other areas have played a big part in the improvement of the class of dogs now competing in this country.

Stud service fees vary greatly according to the success of different blood lines, as is true in the case of thoroughbred, quarter horses, and standardbred horses. Stud services range from $100 to more than $1000 according to the demand for certain blood lines at any given time.

Like horse racing, greyhound racing has contingent organizations which play important parts in the growth of the industry.

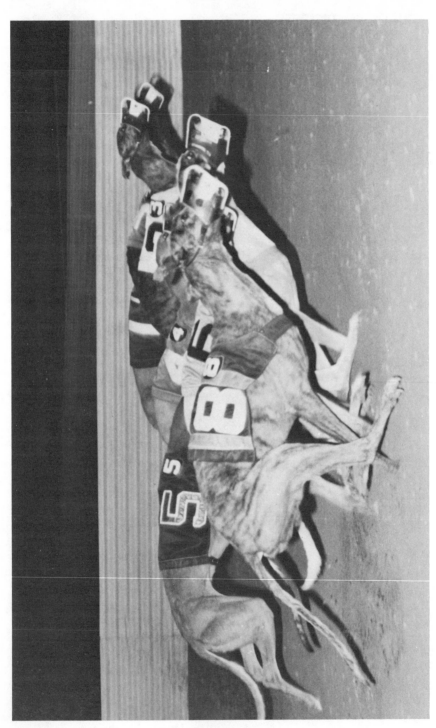

NATIONAL GREYHOUND ASSOCIATION

The National Greyhound Association has been in existence since 1894. At that time the organization was called the National Coursing Association. In 1972 it was officially changed to its present name by an amendment of the membership. In 1906, at Friend, Nebraska the NCA began publishing an annual Stud Book, along with a quarterly magazine called "The Coursing News". This name was changed to "The Greyhound Review" in 1972 at the same time the organization became known as the "National Greyhound Association".

This organization is under the active direction of a secretary-treasurer and keeper of the Stud Book. The staff consists of 13 full time employees, including the assistant secretary and the review editor. It was permanently located in Abilene, Kansas in 1944. The present site is located two miles west of Abilene and was built in 1961.

The organization has jurisdiction over all matters pertaining to the breeding and registration of greyhounds in North America and the Canal Zone. It maintains a registry which keeps records of the breeding, litters, and individual registrations of all greyhounds whelped or imported into these areas.

Membership exceeds 3000 and individual dog registrations numbered more than 22,000 in 1978. Both categories are growing rapidly.

The organization maintains a rigid identification system to keep the industry free from fraudulent breeding practices. The efficiency of the organization is enhanced because it is operated by, and under the jurisdiction, of the people closest to the greyhound—the owners and breeders themselves.

An official size track is maintained on the Association's grounds. Two meets are held here annually, usually the last week in April and the first week in October. Pari-mutuels wagering at the present time is not legal in Kansas, although attempts are under way at this time for legalization. However, as many as 10 stakes, plus their consolations, are offered each year, with emphasis on pups. Details of these stakes are published regularly in the "Greyhound Review" proceeding each meet. These stakes offer a dual purpose. Besides racing for the prizes, owners and trainers are able to observe dogs in action under official racing conditions, before the auction which is held after the stakes races. Other activities during these racing meets, include a formal banquet honoring veterans of the sport, a bar-be-que for all members attending the meeting, NGA business meetings, executive committee meetings, Greyhound Hall-of-Fame meetings, Hall-of-Fame inductions and programs, and various other events in conjuction with the organization. All of these activities make these events a huge convention, combining business with a social gathering of those connected with various aspects of the greyhound industry.

The Hall-of-Fame, inaugurated in 1963, is located in Abilene, adjacent to the Eisenhower Center. The displays include those covering the formative days of greyhound racing, those showing the nature and care necessary to maintain a racing dog, pictures and exhibits of famous people and dogs in the sport, (not only in the United States, but from foreign countries as well) and pictures of breeding farms. The highlight of the museum is a large model of a racetrack, complete with multi-slide projector display to illustrate all the facets of modern day greyhound racing. Three outstanding dogs were enshrined at the first ceremonies: Flashy Sir, Rural Rube, and Real Huntsman; names familiar to all those who have followed this sport through the years.

The American Greyhound Track Operators Association (AGTOA) is another organization instrumental in preserving and promoting greyhound racing. This is a non-profit corporation, composed of the owners and operators of the major greyhound tracks throughout the United States. The AGTOA was formed in 1946 and originally was made up only of tracks in the state of Florida. In 1947 tracks in New England asked to be affiliated, and subsequently, invitations were sent to tracks outside Florida to attend meetings. In 1957, the by-laws were amended to include associate members.

In 1959, following several meetings of members from tracks throughout the country, it was resolved to create an unincorporated association to be known as the National Conference of Greyhound Racetrack Operators. This national conference became a part of the AGTOA. Finally in 1961, 12 Florida tracks plus 12 more from other states voted unanimously to become one organization, known as the AGTOA. (The Florida tracks still maintain their own group, which is now known as the Florida division of the AGTOA.)

Originally the organization intended to provide uniformity among its member states regarding its racing rules. Its role has expanded to include all facets of operation and conformity. A good way to explain this involvement is to list the different committees formed at the 1978-1979 annual meeting. These committees include: budget; by-laws and legal; executive; government affairs; greyhound chemistry and health research; Greyhound Hall-of-Fame; greyhound racing information service; Greyhound Racing Record; National Association of State Racing Commissioners (NASRA)-AGTOA liason; public relations; totalisator evaluation; uniform rules; World Greyhound Racing Federation; and AGTOA Insurance Co., Ltd.

The AGTOA maintains a fulltime staff, headquartered in Miami, Florida, and annually holds a national conference to exchange ideas and to take care of general business. At these meetings, they concentrate on developing new techniques for the improvement and growth of the greyhound industry. The AGTOA is a founding member of the World Greyhound Racing Federation, which was formed to promote international greyhound racing throughout the world.

The organization also is the majority stockholder in Greyhound Publications, Inc., which publishes the weekly "Greyhound Racing Record". This publication is the voice of the industry and includes editorials, general news from various areas of the country, as well as charts of results of races from all member tracks. Semi-annually, a listing of all dogs racing in the United States is published, giving their national ratings, a condensed record of their accomplishments, and their general racing characteristics. The "Record" is also a medium for breeders to advertise their dogs for sale or lease, for dogs being offered for stud services, for job opportunities available, and for advertisement for equipment of all kinds connected with breeding and racing greyhounds. This weekly is also based in Miami, Florida.

Other companies connected with the industry include Totalisator, Video Patrol, Photo Finish, and similar operations which also service horse racing and jai alai operations. Companies whose operations are limited to greyhound racing only are those manufacturing and servicing lure systems, starting boxes, dog trailers, dog food, muzzles, collars, leads, blankets, etc.

Even though greyhound racing is still in the process of rapid growth, 1978 saw the operation of fifty-two tracks in thirteen states. They held racing a total of 5598 nights as well as holding 1255 daytime programs. Daytime racing (matinees) is relatively new in dog racing, but is growing rapidly by popular demand of the spectators. The total amount of money wagered at these 7353 programs in 1978 was $1,876,460,987. Paid attendance was reported to be 20,816,821. Revenue to state and local governments from these operations was listed as $135,554,038.68. Each performance handled an average of $255,297. Per capita betting averaged $90.14 throughout the country. These operations provided full or supplemental income to more than 3000 owners and breeders, trainers, track employees, as well as to those working for organizations and companies servicing this industry. Growing pains are apparent in these areas. The same general problems facing greyhound racing is being faced by the different horse racing groups and jai alai, but concentrated efforts are constantly being made to minimize these problems as rapidly as possible.

Chapter Five
Jai Alai: "The Merry Festival"

Jai Alai (pronounced "hi-li") is undoubtedly the least understood of the five categories of pari-mutuels contests, and the only one in which some kind of animal is not involved. At this writing, there are only four states which have legalized wagering on jai alai: Florida, Nevada, Connecticut, and Rhode Island.

But in these four states, the sport is making rapid progress. In 1978, Florida had 10 *frontons* (the official name for the facilities where jai alai is played), Connecticut had three, Nevada two, and Rhode Island one. The game's acceptance is clear from their business. At these sixteen locations, there were 2,256 night performances and 691 afternoon programs, playing before 8,214,365 spectators who bet an average $69.09 per performance. A total of $567,555,752 was wagered; the four states received a tidy $38,453,500 in revenue. Although many other parts of the world offer this sport—Spain, France, Italy, Mexico, Indonesia, Venezuela, Macao and the Phillipines (Cuba had extensive facilities before the revolution)—the sport's growth has been limited in the United States by the reluctance of legislatures to authorize pari-mutuel frontons.

It was in the Basque region of the picturesque Pyrenees (officially a part of Spain) that the game as we know it today had its beginning. As far back as the Roman Empire, around 200 B.C., the Basques stubbornly refused to be conquered, and retreated into their natural mountain fortress in the Pyrenees. They have preserved their heritage, racial integrity, and their own language to the present, although they number only about 2,000,000. As far as they are concerned, they are still a free and independent people, although nominally under the jurisdiction of Spain. The jai alai players, about 90% of whom are Basques, share these characteristics. The Basques originated their game by throwing a lively piece of rubber against a sheer, flat rock. It's hard to pinpoint the actual date that jai alai began, or when various rules of the game originated, but we know it was a long, long time ago. *Jai alai* means "merry festival." In these early days, the game was the culminating event in religious gatherings that drew thousands of spectators. The earliest documented fronton was in 1798 located at Marquina, Spain.

Then, as now, jai alai was a tempestuous game that typified the sturdy Basque character, requiring tremendous courage, stamina, agility, strategic cunning, and prolonged periods of practice. The game built a substantial following in Spanish-speaking countries. Indeed, for generations the game had international recognition but only as an amateur sport. Its professional debut in the United States in Miami, Florida, didn't come until 1904, but pari-mutuels were not yet authorized. In 1926, World Jai Alai, Inc. built a fronton in Miami for exhibitions. Finally, in 1935, the Florida legislature approved jai alai for pari-mutuels wagering at a site now known as Miami Jai Alai. Frontons began operating at Dania and Tampa in 1953, followed by West Palm Beach in 1955. Daytona Beach opened its doors in 1959. Orlando was the newcomer in 1962. Melbourne and Ocala built frontons in 1971 and 1973, respectively. In 1974, a fronton was built in a state other than Florida, when Metro Goldwyn Mayer's gambling casino in Las Vegas built facilities. Florida added another fronton at Fort Pierce in this same year. Frontons were built in Bridgeport and Hartford, Connecticut in 1976, as well as at Newport Beach, Rhode Island. Milford, Connecticut started operations in 1977. The list was completed in 1978, with the addition of operations at Quincy, Florida and at MGM's new casino in Reno, Nevada.

Several states have made unsuccessful attempts to legalize jai alai, notably California. Over objections from the state's horse-racing industry, an assembly bill for legalization passed but was later killed by the Ways and Means Committee. The bill would have placed jai alai under the jurisdiction of the California Horse Racing Board and allow frontons in areas where they wouldn't directly compete with horse-racing meets (e.g. San Bernardino and Riverside counties, as well as in the San Joaquin and Sacramento Valleys).

The game itself is difficult to describe. Perhaps the easiest way to visualize the game is to say that it is like a combination of hand-ball and racquet ball, played on a three-wall court.

The dimensions of the court (cancha) vary by location. The ten frontons operating in Florida vary in length from 170 feet to 180 feet, and from 33 to 55 feet in width, also from 40 to 73 feet from floor to ceiling. A reasonable average would be 175 feet in length, 50 feet in width (including a 15-foot apron), and 50 feet from floor to ceiling. The ceiling height is important because a ball deflecting from the ceiling is dead.

The front playing wall (frontis) is made of solid granite blocks, 12 to 18 inches thick, to withstand the repeated, powerful impact of the ball (pelota) travelling at approximately 150 miles per hour. The pelota's speed varies greatly, governed as it is by the conditions and angles from which the ball is thrown, and by the strengths of the players. The maximum recorded speed is 188 miles per hour, which justifies the nickname, "World's Fastest Game." Some frontons build the rear wall (rebote) from the same material used for the front wall. Others use high-grade gunite for this rear wall as well as for the side wall (lateral). A granite rear wall results in a slightly livelier court. The floor is made of specially hardened cement, approximately 12 inches thick, with a 15-foot wooden apron. A heavy screen mesh stands between the raised spectator stands and the court. This lets the spectators watch the game while protecting them from the pelotas. The screen isn't part of the playing area. A line on the court, inside the screen, designates whether a ball is in bounds or out of bounds. The pelota is the size of a tennis ball and harder than a golf ball. Skilled players can make it curve as much a three to four feet from the point where it is thrown to the front wall.

Jai alai balls are hand-made. A small round core of virgin para rubber is wound with strips of rubber until it weighs from 100 to 105 grams, followed by layers of nylon string until it weighs from 115 to 118 grams. Next, the ball is covered with goat-skin sewn together with thick seams. The final covering is another layer of goat-skin, sewn together with thin seams. The finished product is placed in a vise to ensure its continued resilience. Some balls are wound more tightly than others, which makes them more lively. In dry climates, finished balls are stored in humid temperature controlled areas, similar to tobacco storage rooms. Balls are taken out of play after a few games and returned to storage for needed repairs and for use at a future date, the procedure known as "resting the *pelotas*". The longer the "resting period" the better the performance the next time they are used. A resting period of at least one month is desirable. Most *pelotas* are made in Spain at a cost of more than $100 each, and are kept in repair by experienced "pelota makers" at the fronton site. Frequently these individuals are former jai alai players.

Players propel the balls with a *cesta*, a curved basket strapped to their right hands and wrists. The *cesta* is used to catch and throw the ball during the contest. Most of the *cestas* are also made in Spain. The rim *(arros)* is made of chestnut. This rim holds the ribs *(costillas)*, made of thin wood, reinforced with reeds. These reeds are mostly from Spain, but some are imported from Mexico and Argentina. The glove covering the player's hand, and attached to the basket portion of the *cesta*, is made of leather and contains five fingers and a tongue. Some tape is used to reinforce the reeds especially in dry climates. The size and shape of the baskets, as well as the glove, are tailored to meet the requirements of the individual players; for example, a player's size or speciality—such as whether he is a back-court or front-court specialist. Players usually keep six to eight *cestas* on hand. The life of each *cesta* is about one month. Players are obligated to order and pay for new ones from Spain as the need arises. Delivery of the new *cestas* usually takes about two months and costs approximately $130.00. *Cesta* (or "basket") makers are hired by the fronton to keep the cestas in repair, until they are no longer serviceable. All *cestas* are made for right-handed players. It's illegal to play jai alai left-handed.

All players are required to wear helmets like those used in American football except that they do not cover the ears. Hearing is very important for the safety of the players. The fronton furnishes the helmets.

Players provide their own shoes, similar to tennis or basketball shoes, and the white uniform pants. The fronton furnishes the colored shirts which designate the player's number: red for #1; blue for #2; white for #3; green for #4; black for #5; yellow for #6; brown for #7; and purple for #8. It is interesting to note the similarity of the color scheme with that of greyhound racing blankets. The frontons also furnish the traditional sash or belt, known as a *faja*.

The basic rules of jai alai have not changed to any extent down through the years. But scoring procedures have been adjusted to fit the pari-mutuels structure.

The rules are fairly simple and easy to follow. A point is gained when a ball in play is not returned by one of the opponents before it has struck the floor in fair territory a second time, or when a player is unable to keep the ball within the playing boundaries on his return shot. A player may also lose a point by holding the ball for too long between catching it and throwing it in return. Interference by a player results in the point being replayed. The ball is put into play by the server throwing the ball against the front wall to rebound into the designated serving area. Returns by the opponent may touch the back or side wall and/or the floor, so long as the *pelota* reaches the front wall in fair territory before it has touched the floor more than once. The same is true of all subsequent shots taken alternately by each player. There are singles and doubles matches as in tennis.

Scoring jai alai has changed. Prior to the pari-mutuels era, the *Partido System* was used. This means that a singles or a doubles match was a one-on-one affair. The same opponents competed until a specified number of points, one at a time, was reached. Young players usually played until one person or team had scored 25 points; mediocre players usually used 30 points as a game-winning total; the best players went to 35 points. This scoring is still used in parts of the world where pari-mutuels systems are not in effect, or even in places where the *partido* system is used as a promotional event. Professionals from all over the world return to Spain for special *partido* matches at certain times of the year. Winners of these special matches gain a great amount of prestige.

The *partido* system had to be adapted to the pari-mutuels system, where the betting pools are formed as in dog or horse racing.

In the pari-mutuels system, there are usually eight contestants in each game. They're numbered from one to eight regardless of whether a singles or doubles match is involved. Number one plays against number two. The winner of the point plays number three and the loser goes to the end of the line behind number eight and will play again when his turn comes. The winner stays on the floor until he has lost a point. A game is completed when one contestant or team has scored the designated number of points, i.e. *one less point than the number of contestants involved.* Thus, 7 points would conclude a game with eight players or teams. The entry (player) with the next largest number of points at that time would finish second and the entry with the third most points would finish third. In case of a tie, the entries involved play off the tie by competing for the tie-breaking points. There can be no ties or "dead heats."

Several years ago, an additional scoring rule was added at most frontons: after all eight contestants had played once during each game, each winning effort for the remainder of the game was worth two points instead of one. This shortened each game, and fronton managers wanted that for a good reason. Figure that a greyhound race is ordinarily over in less than one minute, and a horse race in less than three minutes. But a normal jai alai game takes ten to fifteen minutes. Betting is at a standstill while the game is in progress. It was impossible to offer as many games as management would like without *long* sessions at the fronton. Even with this innovation a 12-game program lasts about four hours (some frontons still offer one or two games a program that use the single-point system to provide some extra thrills).

Top-flight players make jai alai a fascinating sport, and they are in short supply. In recent years, efforts have been made to produce players of high quality in various parts of the world. But Basques still make up about 90% of the players. This figure is remarkable when you consider the fact that there are only about 2 million inhabitants in this area of the world from which to draw. Even priests scout prospects for the training schools, considering jai alai a calling second only to soccer, and certainly with status equal to that of doctors and lawyers. The principal training schools have always been at Gurenica and Marquina in Spain, but with the recent demand for more good players, there are now three additional schools in Spain, four in France, and two in the United States (one at Miami, Florida and one at Milford, Connecticut).

Potential professionals are recruited as young as eight years of age. At training schools, the recruits are started with modified *cestas,* and a soft *pelota.* Gradually they work their way up to the standard equipment. Recruits learn the fundamentals of the game and undergo rigid physical training. Many drop out, but those who stick and show promise are soon representing their towns, districts or even their country in national and international amateur contests. Once graduated, the players are assigned to frontons around the world. Often these students are sponsored and funded by jai alai companies. There are currently some amateur minor leagues in the United States. Most of the better players now end up in the United States because of the better pay. Eighteen is the average age for players to begin professionally. Their peak playing years usually comes between the ages of 28 and 32. Ordinarily, a player retires at 38 to 40, barring serious injury. Surprisingly, there are few serious injuries in this fast and strenuous game.

The fronton's matchmakers divide their players into three groups when making up games: rookies; mediocre players; and those with exceptional talent. Contracts for their services are negotiated with the players' manager. Contracts are usually from one to three years. Incentive bonuses are the rule in securing good players. Winners of singles games usually receive $25 for a win, $15 for finishing second, and $10 for third. Doubles winners usually receive $12.50 each for a win, $7.50 each for second, and $5 each for third. Special events, or at frontons handling a large amount of money, might pay as much as $100 for a win, $60 for finishing second, and $40 for third. Purses are currently getting larger. Ordinarily a contract includes a round-trip fare to and from Spain each year. (Many make this trip primarily to compete in prestigious *partido* matches.) Payment of their federal United States income taxes is often included in the contracts. Frontons maintain a state representative that watches the overall operation for procedure and honesty.

There are approximately 500 active players in the United States. A fronton usually needs at least 32 players if it has one program a day, and from 42 to 45 players if it has matinee and night games. Four games per day or night is a normal practice. Players usually specialize in either front or back court positions in doubles matches.

A player's integrity is guaranteed by the risk of his losing, not only money, but his honor. A dishonest player would lose his visa and be held in disgrace by his family and friends. As with other professional sports, strict rules are enforced by the players' manager, both on and off the court. Some places are "out-of-bounds" to the players. A player is required to keep himself in top-notch physical condition and report to the fronton ready to play to the best of his ability.

Jai alai at pari-mutuels frontons, with its combination of skilled athletes, a fascinating game, and the thrill of betting, is a sport that daily is attracting new fans in the states where it's legal. It's likely more places will legalize the sport before long, and the "world's fastest game" and the "oldest game now being played that involves a ball of any kind" will expand in the United States.

Courtesy MGM Grand Jai Alai

Chapter Six
Racing Oddities

Pari-mutuels wagering is limited to thoroughbreds, harness and quarter horses, greyhounds and jai alai, right? Almost! Appaloosa and Arabian Associations are constantly trying to make inroads into the racing scene. Occasionally they are able to stage a few races in conjunction with established thoroughbred or quarter horse operations. Up to now, they haven't succeeded in getting people to bet any large amounts on these races, but they have created added interest from the spectator's viewpoint. Attempts are still being made to increase the number of these races, and maybe some day in the future they will catch on. Their chances will be much better if a large number of new tracks come into being, creating too many racing dates for the available thoroughbreds and quarter horses.

And please don't laugh, mule racing is now a reality. One track at Bishop, California has a license to operate pari-mutuels wagering on mules. The Eastern Sierra Tri-County Fair conducts this short meet. Short because there aren't many racing mules. However, the meet's handle is increasing each year. The first year (1978), the total was $126,000. In 1979, it rose to $210,000, and in 1980, $244,512, almost double the 1978 totals. The original license was granted as a five-year pilot program. An ammendment to this legislation was introduced in February 1981, to open mule racing throughout California. Efforts are being made to pass legislation in other states as well. Arizona, New Mexico, and Colorado seem to be the most likely possibilities at the present time.

Mules aren't quite as fast as thoroughbreds or quarter horses, but their times from 200 yards to a half-mile are much better than one might expect. The better mules go 200 yards in a little over 13 seconds, 440 yards in a little over 28 seconds and 660 yards in a little over 38 seconds. These times will probably improve as better mares are bred to jacks. In fact, some fine quarter horse mares and thoroughbred winners are now being bred for mules.

Exhibition races at Ruidoso, New Mexico were recently shown on a special TV program. Many were quite favorably surprised by their performance.

A good racing mule could cost as much as $10,000 today. Most are highly-spirited, sensitive animals, and remarkably intelligent. Trainers maintain that mules are very much aware of what's going on near them, and that it takes more time and patience to train a racing mule than a race horse. Purses are naturally still small. The top racing mule in 1979, "Miss Hazard County" earned a total of only $15,000, but the earning potential will grow as futurities are established and, especially, if more legislation is passed to allow wagering on mule races.

The American Mule Association was formed in 1977, with it's headquarters in Fresno, California. There were approximately 300 racing mules nationwide in 1979, and the number is growing each year. Chart books are kept for mules in the same manner as for horses. It will be interesting to see how far this new sport will spread in the coming years.

If betting on mules doesn't seem odd, then neither will some of the gimmicks that have been tried in other pari-mutuels sports, with different degrees of success.

Through the years, greyhound tracks have tried several ideas in an attempt to creat interest in the sport. Monkey jockeys for the dogs re-appeared a few years ago at Caliente for a short time, but this was not a new idea. During almost all of the 1930s, when dog racing was trying to become established, monkey-jockeys were used in non-betting races as a promotion. They would have, for instance, two races a week in conjunction with the official races.

I have heard many stories from the veteran trainers who either furnished dogs for these races, or were on hand to watch them. These accounts lead me to believe that the monkey jockeys drew the interest of a large number of fans. The monkeys were strapped to a miniature saddle on the dog's back and were dressed in miniature jockey outfits. It took considerable patience and time to train both the dogs and monkeys to perform. Some of both species would never co-operate. I heard from several people about one monkey who stood out from the rest and won most of the races he participated in, no matter which dog he rode. In any event, the monkey business was discontinued because many people thought it was a form of mental cruelty for the dogs and monkeys who were unwilling participants.

Another popular gimmick used several decades ago was the "mutt races". The track would set aside a special day for these races when the track was not being used for pari-mutuels racing. Anyone could enter their pets of any breed to compete in an elimination process. Races were usually about 100 yards in length on the straightaway in front of the grandstand. The owners would release the pets by hand, rather than place them in a starting box. They did run the mechanical lure in front of them and some would actually chase the lure. There seemed to be no pattern of breed or size that predominated. The only breeds barred were greyhounds, whippets, and Italian Greyhounds. Actually in the early period of dog racing, some commercial meets were held, with registered whippets as the only competiters. Whippets closely resemble the greyhound in appearance and confirmation except that they are much smaller. Italian Greyhounds are miniature replicas of the greyhounds now competing. Most are in the ten to fifteen pound range. They are beautiful animals, and most make good pets. However, a big percentage are high-strung and usually quite nervous around a crowd of people.

I recall one "mutt derby" in particular, held in Rapid City, South Dakota, almost thirty years ago, since my own dog was a competitor. Competitor might be too strong a term, since he ran half way to the finish line and then darted off the track into the crowd, looking for the family. It wasn't too embarrasing, since many other dogs did the same thing.

At any rate almost one hundred dogs were involved in the countdown.

Winners were pitted against each other and the losers eliminated until there were eight still eligible for the big race. It was won handily by a little mongrel weighing no more than fifteen pounds. The field that he beat included German Shepherds, Great Danes and the like. The mutt probably wasn't the fastest, but he concentrated on trying to catch the mechanical lure and paid absolutely no attention to the other dogs. He was so good that a special exhibition race was held between races of an official program a few nights later. He was pitted against an Italian Greyhound at a distance of 200 yards, starting in the backstretch and continuing around the stretch turn, and down the stretch to the finish line. The Italian Greyhound easily outdistanced him, but he refused to quit when the race was over. He continued around the track a couple of times, still looking for the mechanical rabbit. He wouldn't even come to his owner until he was exhausted.

"Mutt races" weren't discontinued because of lack of interest, but rather because of too much interest. The confusion of trying to control a hundred pet owners, many of them young children, let alone having an excited dog on the end of his leash was too much. So were the inevitable dog fights plus the danger of someone getting hurt. Insurance rates were high and the chance of lawsuits, resulting from injuries, too great. But it was great publicity for the tracks while it lasted, and a lot of fun for the fans.

Another promotional item that lasted for some time was hurdle racing for the dogs. A few of the large horse tracks also had some hurdle and steeplechase races until very recently. The volume of betting on the hurdle races at the dog tracks was small compared with the regular races. But I believe that the practice would have been continued regardless of this factor, due to the extra publicity generated, if it hadn't been for the pressures from those who felt it was too dangerous for the dogs. There actually were many more spills and injuries to the dogs during these races.

Brush type hurdles were used for the dogs. It was interesting to watch some dogs figured out that they could do better by going through the brush area, rather than clearing the hurdle completely. It's rather obvious that brains was a more important factor than speed in many cases.

In the late 1940's, a match race between a quarter horse and a greyhound was held on a dog track, in Phoenix, Arizona. Actually, the quarter horse didn't stand a chance. The horse could more than hold his own on the straightaways but the turns were too sharp for him and the real contest was whether or not the jockey could keep the horse on the track coming out of the turns. The dog won by quite a margin.

Another interesting match race was held in 1938 at a track in Fowler, Ohio between a greyhound and the great olympic star, Jesse Owens. The greyhound started from the quarter mile box, while Jesse ran from a standing start at a point even with the $3/16$ mile starting box. According to witnesses, they crossed the finish line stride for stride.

There have been numerous other promotions such as ostriches pulling racing sulkies, and someone will probably come up with other ideas in the future, but it will probably be a long time before anything will challenge the five categories of sports detailed in this book as a basis for pari-mutuels wagering.

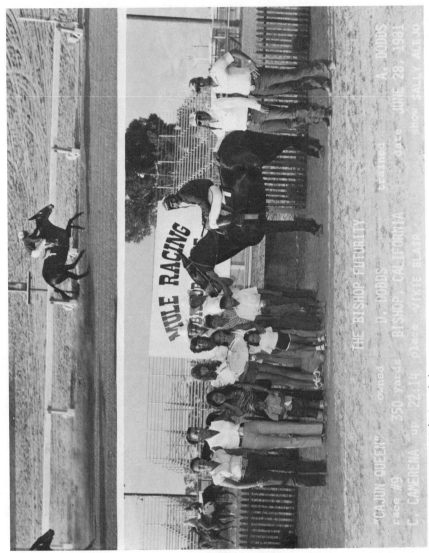

Courtesy of American Mule Association

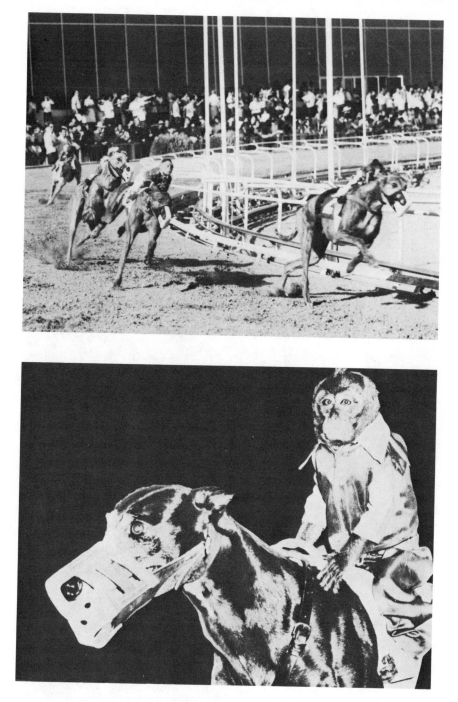

PART TWO

Sports or Big Business?

Chapter Seven
State Statistics (1978)

Charts and statistics on the following pages have been assembled to help the reader understand the actual status of the pari-mutuels system in the United States.

It may help to answer some of the questions asked in the "Foreward" of this book. The states or communities now studying the possibilities of using the pari-mutuels system as an added source of revenue may be able to find a comparable situation in another state to help them make a decision on this issue.

In states already using this medium for tax purposes, the situation is constantly changing. Additional days of racing are being granted or refused according to the judgement of officials responsible for making decisions which will benefit or harm their constituents. This also applies to requests for new facilities. These requests may be for either a different category of racing or jai alai, or it may be an additional site for the type of sport now being utilized.

The first chart will show exactly which sports are now being used in each state authorizing pari-mutuels wagering.

Comprehensive statistics follow (state-by-state) for the year 1978. These statistics include the number of racing programs, attendance, volume of business (handle), amount of revenue received by the state, average daily volume, and per capita wagering (average amount wagered per customer per program).

Charts are also included which show these same items on a national basis i.e.—broken down as to statistics on each category of racing and jai alai, nationwide.

Percentage of increase or decrease of attendance, volume and per capita wagering for the years 1979 and 1980, together with a personal assessment of the reasons for these increases or decreases, follow the state charts.

The (M) in number of racing days represents matinees, usually on the same day that night racing was held. Matinees were figured as separate days of racing to figure the daily average, even though night races were held on the same date.

Attendance was not documented on fairs since usually admission to other functions of the fair included entrance to racing without additional admittance fees.

Average daily handle and per capita figures nationally do not include the 613 fair dates.

Some of the 21,229 racing days were actually held at fairs but were included in yearly Racing Commission reports in the same manner as regular commercial tracks. These particular fairs are included in the national averages.

Some State's Commission reports include miscellaneous revenue in the pari-mutuels reports. Others list them separately. It is simply a difference in bookkeeping and statistical methods.

Although the charts show the figures for 1978, a few states use a fiscal year for their reports, running from July 1, 1978 to June 30, 1979. All figures are based on 12 months operation.

Attendance figures are not available for off track betting since there is no admission fees.

Some of the items included in the miscellaneous revenue figures include franchise fees, licences for employees, uncashed mutuels tickets, state admission taxes, track licence fees, and fines assessed for breaking rules of racing.

At the few tracks where thoroughbred and quarterhorses raced on the same card, handle and revenue, as well as daily average and attendance, were estimated as closely as possible.

The 613 fair dates are a small percentage of the actual number of days of racing at fairs nationally. Pari-mutuels wagering is not used at most and accurate statistics of attendance is not available.

STATES INCLUDED IN NATIONAL CHART

THOROUGHBREDS	QUARTERHORSES	HARNESS	GREYHOUNDS	JAI ALAI	O.T.B.	FAIRS
			Alabama			
Arizona			Arizona			Arizona
Arkansas			Arkansas			
California	California	California				California
Colorado	Colorado		Colorado			Colorado
			Connecticut	Connecticut	Connecticut	
Delaware		Delaware				
Florida	Florida	Florida	Florida	Florida		
Idaho	Idaho					
Illinois		Illinois				
Kentucky	Kentucky	Kentucky				
Louisiana	Louisiana					
		Maine				Maine
Maryland		Maryland				
Massachusetts		Massachusetts	Massachusetts			
Michigan	Michigan	Michigan				
						Montana
Nebraska	Nebraska					
	Nevada		Nevada	Nevada		
New Hampshire		New Hampshire	New Hampshire			
New Jersey		New Jersey				
New Mexico	New Mexico					
New York	New York	New York			New York	
Ohio	Ohio	Ohio				Ohio
Oregon	Oregon		Oregon			Oregon
Pennsylvania		Pennsylvania				
			Rhode Island	Rhode Island		
South Dakota	South Dakota		South Dakota			
			Vermont			Vermont
Washington						Washington
West Virginia			West Virginia			
						Wyoming
						*
(24)	(14)	(14)	(14)	(4)	(2)	

*States combining horse or dog racing with their other fair operations handle their bookkeeping in different ways. In states where pari-mutuels wagering is legalized, some include the fair statistics with the commercial tracks, some separate the two. There are extensive racing programs at fairs in states which prohibit pari-mutuels wagering. Therefore, the states listed under the category of fairs is not complete.

RECAP OF PARI MUTUELS WAGERING IN ALABAMA (1978)

TRACKS	NUMBER OF RACING DAYS		TOTAL ATTENDANCE	TOTAL PARI MUTUELS HANDLE	TOTAL REVENUE TO STATE	DAILY AVERAGE	PER CAPITA
Greyhounds							
Green Track	250	64(M)	530,528	49,158,602	2,040,802.82	156,556	92.66
Mobile Greyhound Park	120	44(M)	355,666	33,424,061	2,772,130.22	203,805	93.98
Azalea City Racing Club	120	46(M)	313,778	30,780,211	2,549,254.20	185,429	98.10
(At Mobile)							
STATE TOTALS	644		1,199,972	113,362,874	7,362,187.24	176,029	94.47

RECAP OF PARI MUTUELS WAGERING IN ARIZONA (1978)

TRACKS	NUMBER OF RACING DAYS		TOTAL ATTENDANCE	TOTAL PARI MUTUELS HANDLE	TOTAL REVENUE TO STATE	DAILY AVERAGE	PER CAPITA
Throughbreds							
Arizona Downs	61		246,849	24,708,016	1,113,537.30	405,049	100.09
Turf Paradise	59		310,870	29,902,379	1,377,118.95	506,820	96.19
Rillito	46		58,741	4,075,678	46,269.34	88,602	69.38
Prescott	27		42,465	3,528,718	48,768.87	130,477	83.10
Totals	193		658,925	62,214,791	2,585,694.46	332,356	94.42
Greyhounds							
Amado	64	48M	88,501	8,646,430	390,548.00	77,200	97.70
Apache	61	18M	147,770	13,543,642	709,918.52	171,439	91.65
Black Canyon	62	12M	107,584	12,000,750	627,049.88	162,172	111.55
Tucson	123	49M	261,178	23,017,898	1,381,073.88	133,825	88.13
Yuma	61	24M	114,544	7,099,800	322,884.84	83,527	61.98
Phoenix	63	—	258,814	22,493,176	1,349,590.56	357,035	86.91
Western	63	—	216,529	21,148,318	1,268,899.08	335,688	97.67
Totals	497	151M	1,194,920	107,950,014	6,049,964.76	166,590	90.34
Miscellaneous Revenue					46,336.15		
STATE TOTALS	739	151M	1,853,845	173,963,795	8,681,995.37	206,854	93.84
County Fairs Not Considered In Averages							
County Fairs							
Apache	4			142,293		35,573	
Cochise	4			171,969		42,992	
Coconino	4			306,442		76,611	
Gila	4			119,897		29,974	
Graham	4			114,936		28,734	
Greenlee	3			92,431		23,108	
Maricopa	4			1,495,066		498,355	
Mohave	4			138,422		34,606	
Navajo	4			170,041		42,510	
Pima	3			253,444		84,481	
Santa Cruz	4			231,624		57,906	
Yavapai	3			434,009		144,670	
Yuma	4			128,416		32,104	
Totals	49			3,798,990		77,530	

RECAP OF PARI MUTUELS WAGERING IN ARKANSAS (1978)

TRACKS	NUMBER OF RACING DAYS		TOTAL ATTENDANCE	TOTAL PARI MUTUELS HANDLE	TOTAL REVENUE TO STATE	DAILY AVERAGE	PER CAPITA
Thoroughbreds Oaklawn Park	49		1,037,037	114,431,968	7,392,487.50	2,335,346	110.35
Totals	49		1,037,037	114,431,968	7,392,487.50	2,335,346	110.35
Greyhounds Southland	112	29M	1,056,755	106,046,767	6,594,105.25	752,105	100.35
Totals	112	29M	1,056,755	106,046,767	6,594,105.25	752,105	100.35
STATE TOTALS	161	29M	2,093,792	220,478,735	13,986,592.75	1,160,414	105.30

RECAP OF PARI MUTUELS WAGERING IN CALIFORNIA (1978)

TRACKS	NUMBER OF RACING DAYS	TOTAL ATTENDANCE	TOTAL PARI MUTUELS HANDLE	TOTAL REVENUE TO STATE	DAILY AVERAGE	PER CAPITA
Thoroughbreds						
Santa Anita	78	2,062,072	306,591,435	25,858,899.00	3,930,659	148.68
Golden Gates (Pac. Assoc.)	59	556,318	85,097,900	6,116,813.00	1,442,337	152.97
Hollywood	78	1,886,285	315,741,616	26,192,652.00	4,047,969	167.39
Golden Gates (Tanforan)	39	356,759	58,127,686	3,911,104.00	1,490,453	162.93
Del Mar	43	712,306	100,052,821	7,306,451.00	2,326,810	140.46
Bay Meadows (Tanforan)	20	183,749	27,226,812	2,165,786.00	1,361,341	148.17
Oak Tree	24	524,019	75,565,591	5,344,876.00	3,148,566	144.20
Bay Meadows	59	538,506	90,007,221	6,354,053.00	1,525,546	167.14
Totals	400	6,820,014	1,058,411,082	83,250,634.00	2,646,028	155.19
Quarter Horses						
Los Alamitos (HQR Assoc.)	57	393,804	50,521,143	3,326,613.00	886,336	128.29
Bay Meadows	58	224,367	29,983,839	1,685,723.00	516,963	133.64
Los Alamitos	82	557,506	75,684,266	5,367,707.00	922,979	135.76
Sacramento	35	80,043	5,058,939	65,453.00	144,541	63.20
Totals	232	1,255,720	161,248,187	10,445,494.00	695,035	128.41
Harness Racing						
Bay Meadows	33	107,293	15,370,522	973,542.00	465,773	143.26
Los Alamitos	58	290,800	42,873,174	2,917,386.00	739,193	147.43
Sacramento	44	187,355	14,457,966	176,727.00	328,590	77.17
Golden Gates	28	124,143	8,449,950	316,550.00	301,784	68.07
Hollywood	79	667,401	95,049,362	6,758,867.00	1,203,156	142.42
Totals	242	1,376,992	176,200,974	11,143,072.00	728,103	127.96

Continued on next page

RECAP OF PARI MUTUELS WAGERING IN CALIFORNIA (1978)—Continued

TRACKS	NUMBER OF RACING DAYS	TOTAL ATTENDANCE	TOTAL PARI MUTUELS HANDLE	TOTAL REVENUE TO STATE	DAILY AVERAGE	PER CAPITA
Fairs						
Solano County	12	80,057	9,403,450	637,229.00	783,620	117.46
Alameda County	12	127,008	13,862,636	920,935.00	1,155,220	109.15
Sonoma County	12	92,779	10,102,695	673,686.00	841,891	108.89
San Mateo County	12	84,133	13,961,471	923,215.00	1,163,456	165.95
Humboldt County	9	17,338	1,426,948	35,466.00	158,550	82.30
San Joaquin County	12	60,444	7,177,497	219,029.00	598,125	118.75
California State	14	121,422	10,372,437	690,609.00	740,888	85.42
Los Angeles County	14	167,356	21,877,643	1,455,863.00	1,562,688	130.73
Fresno District	11	101,387	9,342,521	636,964.00	849,320	92.15
Orange County	14	150,171	22,918,082	1,510,036.00	1,637,005	152.61
Totals	122	1,002,095	120,445,380	7,703,032.00	987,257	120.19
STATE TOTALS	996	10,454,821	1,516,305,623	112,542,232.00	1,522,395	145.03

RECAP OF PARI MUTUELS WAGERING IN COLORADO (1978)

TRACKS	NUMBER OF RACING DAYS		TOTAL ATTENDANCE	TOTAL PARI MUTUELS HANDLE	TOTAL REVENUE TO STATE	DAILY AVERAGE	PER CAPITA
Thoroughbreds							
Centennial	96		360,829	31,458,755	1,426,170.10	327,695	87.18
Centennial (Mixed Meet)	12		25,860	2,368,128	96,048.00	197,344	91.57
Totals	108		386,689	33,826,883	1,522,218.10	313,212	87.48
Quarterhorses							
Rocky Mountain QH Assoc.	38		93,057	7,672,435	315,965.79	201,906	82.45
Centennial (Mixed Meet)	11		23,697	2,170,799	88,058.55	197,344	91.57
Totals	49		116,754	9,843,234	404,024.34	200,882	84.31
Greyhounds							
Interstate	71	7M	125,815	17,009,860	850,493.00	218,075	135.20
Cloverleaf	71	23M	266,101	27,002,374	1,350,118.70	287,259	101.47
Pueblo	71	11M	140,224	10,206,462	510,323.10	124,469	72.79
Mile High	71	14M	489,709	42,375,520	2,118,776.00	498,536	86.53
Rocky Mountain	71	15M	223,539	25,209,892	1,260,494.60	293,138	112.78
Totals	355	70M	1,245,388	121,804,108	6,090,205.40	286,598	97.80
Fairs							
Colorado State	6		26,000	340,550	13,622.00	56,758	13.10
Gateway	10		6,119	528,812	21,152.48	52,881	86.42
Moffat County	7		3,607	274,514	10,980.56	39,216	76.11
Western Slope	4		2,593	105,514	4,220.56	26,378	40.69
Ski-Hi Stampede	7		7,818	230,022	9,200.88	32,860	29.42
Navajo Trails Fiesta	6		7,306	226,296	9,051.84	37,716	30.97
Uranium	10		7,382	480,338	19,213.52	48,034	65.07
Totals	50		60,825	2,186,046	87,441.84	43,721	35.94
Miscellaneous Revenue					49,942.32		
STATE TOTALS	562	70M	1,809,656	167,660,271	8,153,832.00	265,285	92.65

RECAP OF PARI MUTUELS WAGERING IN CONNECTICUT (1978)

TRACKS	NUMBER OF RACING DAYS		TOTAL ATTENDANCE	TOTAL PARI MUTUELS HANDLE	TOTAL REVENUE TO STATE	DAILY AVERAGE	PER CAPITA
Greyhounds							
Plainfield	284	162M	1,011,690	100,421,789	8,882,948.00	225,161	99.26
Totals	284	162M	1,011,690	100,421,789	8,882,948.00	225,161	99.26
Jai Alai							
Hartford	203	38M	1,048,437	72,942,506	6,028,225.00	302,666	69.57
Bridgeport	148	75M	872,710	85,290,414	7,040,760.00	382,468	97.73
Milford	160	65M	687,954	78,605,961	6,536,373.00	349,360	114.26
Totals	511	178M	2,609,101	236,838,881	19,605,358.00	343,743	90.77
STATE TOTALS	795	340M	3,620,791	337,260,670	28,488,306.00	297,146	90.77
Off Track Betting (OTB)	310			114,731,495	8,100,282.00	370,102	93.15
TOTAL REVENUE					36,588,588.00		

RECAP OF PARI MUTUELS WAGERING IN DELAWARE (1978)

TRACKS	NUMBER OF RACING DAYS	TOTAL ATTENDANCE	TOTAL PARI MUTUELS HANDLE	TOTAL REVENUE TO STATE	DAILY AVERAGE	PER CAPITA
Thoroughbreds						
Delaware Park	50	340,209	39,681,444	678,197.00	793,629	116.64
Totals	50	340,209	39,681,444	678,197.00	793,629	116.64
Harness Racing						
Brandywine	136	695,966	56,476,654	1,514,143.51	415,270	81.15
Dover Downs	119	223,104	18,410,886	119,000.00	154,713	82.52
Harrington	39	74,570	4,924,169	73,862.43	126,261	66.03
Totals	294	993,640	79,811,709	1,707,005.94	271,468	80.32
Miscellaneous Revenue				961,243.80		
STATE TOTALS	344	1,333,849	119,493,153	3,346,446.74	347,364	89.59

RECAP OF PARI MUTUELS WAGERING IN FLORIDA (1978)

TRACKS	NUMBER OF RACING DAYS		TOTAL ATTENDANCE	TOTAL PARI MUTUELS HANDLE	TOTAL REVENUE TO STATE	DAILY AVERAGE	PER CAPITA
Thoroughbreds							
Calder	117		855,152	118,433,606	4,378,291.73	1,012,253	138.49
Florida Downs	68		240,251	23,287,745	433,124.27	342,467	96.93
Gulfstream	44		550,422	94,568,590	5,786,569.38	2,149,286	171.81
Hialeah	50		373,676	65,472,325	3,205,771.77	1,309,447	175.21
Tropical	50		407,442	61,275,390	2,981,735.01	1,225,508	150.39
Totals	329		2,426,943	363,037,656	16,785,492.16	1,103,458	149.59
Quarterhorses							
Gator Downs	45		109,549	8,537,195	121,871.49	189,715	77.93
Totals	45		109,549	8,537,195	121,871.49	189,715	77.93
Jai Alai							
Dania	105	54M	769,202	43,110,698	2,561,051.58	271,136	56.05
Florida	105	53M	394,488	22,999,806	1,353,552.83	145,568	58.30
Fort Pierce	100	56M	246,622	15,745,948	929,087.34	100,936	63.85
West Palm Beach	87	45M	438,646	27,635,823	1,628,724.13	209,362	63.00
Big Bend	99	16M	132,943	9,041,510	530,185.91	77,278	68.01
Miami	105	54M	976,739	68,003,504	3,993,964.78	427,695	69.62
Ocala	127	65M	279,626	16,269,466	966,840.73	84,737	58.18
Melbourne	105	56M	252,739	16,346,910	954,648.51	101,534	64.68
Tampa	105	54M	700,049	42,054,356	2,488,104.44	264,493	60.07
Daytona Beach	128	58M	415,631	26,560,653	1,554,862.90	142,799	63.90
Totals	1066	513M	4,606,685	287,768,674	16,961,023.15	182,247	62.47
Harness Racing							
Seminole Park	91		135,830	8,662,292	109,649.89	95,190	63.77
Pompano	105		530,920	46,166,382	2,245,665.53	439,680	86.96
Totals	196		666,750	54,828,674	2,355,315.42	279,738	82.23

RECAP OF PARI MUTUELS WAGERING IN FLORIDA (1978)—Continued

TRACKS	NUMBER OF RACING DAYS		TOTAL ATTENDANCE	TOTAL PARI MUTUELS HANDLE	TOTAL REVENUE TO STATE	DAILY AVERAGE	PER CAPITA
Greyhounds							
Tampa	101	54M	774,631	68,767,506	5,399,655.92	443,661	88.77
Bayard	42	16M	126,842	11,955,921	900,136.78	206,137	94.26
Biscayne	156	84M	1,424,425	150,013,792	11,821,836.29	625,057	105.32
Bonita Springs	105	54M	389,611	28,599,706	2,205,999.43	179,872	73.41
Daytona Beach	128	62M	499,723	38,627,078	2,950,329.60	203,300	77.30
West Palm Beach	105	50M	593,743	49,702,464	3,867,220.43	320,661	83.71
Hollywood	105	54M	995,719	86,961,497	6,863,393.51	546,928	87.34
Jacksonville	159	57M	694,829	58,892,431	4,518,332.62	272,650	84.76
Jefferson Co.	105	24M	197,354	15,262,138	1,129,152.65	118,311	77.33
Key West	105	20M	79,958	5,457,114	344,209.77	43,657	68.25
Miami Beach	98	—	389,437	33,334,242	2,592,910.83	340,145	85.60
Orange Park	102	35M	415,579	38,070,746	2,913,190.08	277,889	91.61
Pensacola	106	56M	228,359	17,418,315	1,280,751.30	107,521	76.28
St. Petersburg	101	53M	993,644	82,293,728	6,525,776.24	534,375	82.82
Sanford-Orlando	105	54M	545,280	44,326,336	3,419,457.65	278,782	81.29
Sarasota	100	55M	475,733	42,218,077	3,264,667.57	272,375	88.74
Ebro	105	36M	216,742	17,629,160	1,310,236.45	125,030	81.34
West Flagler	51	26M	422,618	43,370,314	3,449,659.04	563,251	102.62
Totals	1879	790M	9,464,227	832,900,565	64,756,916.16	312,065	88.01
Miscellaneous Revenue					2,848,788.17		
STATE TOTALS	3515	1303M	17,274,154	1,547,072,764	103,829,406.55	321,144	89.57

RECAP OF PARI MUTUELS WAGERING IN IDAHO (1978)

TRACKS	NUMBER OF RACING DAYS	TOTAL ATTENDANCE	TOTAL PARI MUTUELS HANDLE	TOTAL REVENUE TO STATE	DAILY AVERAGE	PER CAPITA
Thoroughbreds						
Les Bois	51	194,413	5,065,107	79,726.56	125,062	32.81
Gem County	6	3,987	36,508	1,968.69	26,249	39.50
Coeur D'Alene	26	44,688	2,616,806	39,359.11	121,105	70.46
Pocatello	22	19,804	58,701	8,009.16	29,124	32.35
Rupert-Minadoka	7	7,528	24,992	2,077.77	23,746	22.08
Cassia County	3	3,998	6,158	512.38	13,664	10.25
Jerome County	4	3,574	10,871	938.63	18,772	21.01
Oneida County	3	2,779	1,604	1,132.16	30,191	32.59
Eastern Idaho	5	8,631	96,478	2,537.45	40,592	23.52
Totals	127	289,402	7,917,225	136,261.91	85,834	37.67
Quarterhorses						
Les Bois	51		1,313,034		125,062	32.81
Gem County	6		120,986		26,249	39.50
Coeur D'Alene	26		531,919		121,105	70.46
Pocatello	22		582,033		29,124	32.35
Rupert-Minadoka	7		141,229		23,746	22.08
Cassia County	3		34,833		13,664	10.25
Jerome County	4		64,219		18,772	21.01
Oneida County	3		88,969		30,191	32.59
Eastern Idaho	5		106,518		40,592	23.52
Totals	127		2,983,740		85,834	37.67
STATE TOTALS	127	289,402	10,900,965	136,261.91	85,834	37.67

All tracks held mixed meetings. No breakdown of attendance and revenue between thoroughbreds and quarterhorses.

RECAP OF PARI MUTUELS WAGERING IN ILLINOIS (1978)

TRACKS	NUMBER OF RACING DAYS	TOTAL ATTENDANCE	TOTAL PARI MUTUELS HANDLE	TOTAL REVENUE TO STATE	DAILY AVERAGE	PER CAPITA
Thoroughbreds						
Washington Park	48	587,793	78,903,156	7,044,529.00	1,643,816	134.00
Sun Times Daily News Charity Trust (At Arlington)	5	51,943	6,882,131	651,372.00	1,376,426	132.00
Atheletes For Better Educ. (Arlington)	1	10,367	1,361,437	126,908.00	1,361,437	131.00
Balmoral Racing Club	72	253,331	30,804,021	2,159,090.00	427,834	122.00
East St. Louis Jockey Club (Cahokia)	79	368,789	35,975,761	2,516,545.00	455,389	98.00
Estate of Thomas Carey (Hawthorne)	54	509,718	78,943,003	6,868,900.00	1,461,907	155.00
HBPA (Arlington)	1	11,007	1,595,369	150,128.00	1,595,369	145.00
National Jockey Club (Sportsman)	66	623,032	87,639,730	7,524,474.00	1,327,875	141.00
Ogden Fairmont Jockey Club (Fairmont)	85	465,974	43,188,325	3,078,576.00	508,098	93.00
Arlington Park	48	552,775	71,937,225	6,323,666.00	1,498,692	130.00
Totals	459	3,434,729	437,230,158	36,444,188.00	952,571	127.30

Continued on next page

RECAP OF PARI MUTUELS WAGERING IN ILLINOIS (1978)—Continued

TRACKS	NUMBER OF RACING DAYS	TOTAL ATTENDANCE	TOTAL PARI MUTUELS HANDLE	TOTAL REVENUE TO STATE	DAILY AVERAGE	PER CAPITA
Harness Racing						
Woodlawn Comm. Del. Corp (Sportsmans)	2	32,961	3,661,856	345,625.00	1,830,928	111.00
Mississippi Valley Trotting Assoc. (Cahokia)	61	175,211	17,062,756	1,080,129.00	279,717	97.00
Pyramid Trotting Assoc. (Sportsmans)	24	282,416	34,522,718	3,015,323.00	1,438,447	122.00
Maywood Trotting Assoc.	50	379,267	56,262,804	4,627,582.00	1,125,256	148.00
Arlington-Washington Park	58	304,487	45,658,731	3,508,476.00	773,877	150.00
Associates Racing Assoc. (Maywood)	22	170,994	24,842,977	2,078,075.00	1,129,226	145.00
Atheletes For Better Education (Maywood)	1	11,911	2,098,159	196,424.00	2,098,159	176.00
Balmoral Park	41	205,720	24,839,571	1,856,739.00	605,843	121.00
Chicago Downs Assoc. (Sportsmans)	44	590,682	68,724,063	6,092,150.00	1,561,911	116.00
Crusade of Mercy (Sportsmans)	5	56,158	6,866,359	651,064.00	1,373,272	122.00
Duquoin State Fair	5	20,336	635,226	44,219.00	127,045	31.00
Egyptian Trotting Assoc. (Maywood)	16	130,352	21,079,886	1,739,786.00	1,317,493	162.00
Fox Valley Trotting Club (Sportsmans)	33	362,763	44,043,255	3,779,067.00	1,334,644	121.00
Quad City Downs (Moline)	75	186,054	14,131,052	849,213.00	188,414	76.00
Quad City Trotting Assoc. (Moline)	42	121,417	9,267,009	570,244.00	220,643	76.00
Suburban Downs Inc. (Hawthorne)	46	375,893	55,028,496	4,531,555.00	1,196,272	146.00
Southern Ill. Trotting Assoc. (Fairmont)	25	74,294	7,485,363	479,881.00	299,415	101.00
Sun Times Daily News Charity Trust (Maywood)	6	57,283	8,959,075	847,550.00	1,493,179	156.00
Totals	556	3,538,199	445,169,356	36,293,102.00	800,664	125.82
Miscellaneous Revenue				1,162,408.00		
GRAND TOTALS	1015	6,972,928	$ 882,399,514	$ 73,899,698.00	$ 869,359	$126.55

RECAP OF PARI MUTUELS WAGERING IN KENTUCKY (1978)

TRACKS	NUMBER OF RACING DAYS	TOTAL ATTENDANCE	TOTAL PARI MUTUELS HANDLE	TOTAL REVENUE TO STATE	DAILY AVERAGE	PER CAPITA
Thoroughbreds						
Latonia	105	410,908	53,590,307	2,545,539.48	510,384	130.42
Keeneland	31	354,745	32,048,185	1,522,288.79	1,033,812	90.34
Churchill Downs	79	956,231	99,109,485	4,707,700.54	1,254,550	103.65
Ellis Park	57	261,260	29,462,390	1,399,463.52	516,884	112.77
Totals	272	1,983,144	214,210,367	10,174,992.33	787,538	108.02
Quarterhorses						
Commonwealth	32	54,477	3,161,250	150,000.00	98,789	58.03
Totals	32	54,477	3,161,250	150,000.00	98,789	58.03
Harness Racing						
Latonia	62	105,762	8,376,806	421,282.00	135,110	79.20
Louisville Downs	129	385,037	30,057,426	1,522,905.00	233,003	78.06
Midwest	93	139,997	11,257,319	566,899.00	121,046	80.41
Red Mile	75	192,241	10,933,452	553,976.00	145,779	56.87
Totals	359	823,037	60,625,003	3,065,062.00	168,872	73.66
Miscellaneous Revenue				2,000,000.00		
STATE TOTALS	663	2,860,658	277,996,620	15,390,054.33	419,301	97.18

RECAP OF PARI MUTUELS WAGERING IN LOUISIANA (1978)

TRACKS	NUMBER OF RACING DAYS	TOTAL ATTENDANCE	TOTAL PARI MUTUELS HANDLE	TOTAL REVENUE TO STATE	DAILY AVERAGE	PER CAPITA
Thoroughbreds						
Fairgrounds	101	886,955	117,950,347	6,644,480.33	1,167,825	132.98
Evangeline	91	354,630	33,721,161	1,545,748.03	370,562	95.06
Jefferson (Lakefront)	32	117,159	13,492,694	541,189.51	421,647	115.17
Louisiana Downs	104	814,974	96,798,749	5,244,020.00	930,757	118.78
Jefferson	105	462,056	46,551,100	2,267,030.85	443,344	100.75
Delta (Mixed)	105	215,528	26,761,742	834,029.68	347,994	118.81
Totals	538	2,851,302	335,275,793	17,076,498.40	641,363	117.23
Quarterhorses						
Delta	42	106,854	10,946,854	236,708.77	260,639	92.86
Delta (Mixed)		92,017	9,777,600	278,010.00		
Totals	42	198,871	20,724,454	514,718.77	260,639	92.86
STATE TOTALS	580	3,050,173	356,000,247	17,591,217.17	613,793	116.71

State Statistics (1978)

RECAP OF PARI MUTUELS WAGERING IN MAINE (1978)

TRACKS	NUMBER OF RACING DAYS	TOTAL ATTENDANCE	TOTAL PARI MUTUELS HANDLE	TOTAL REVENUE TO STATE	DAILY AVERAGE	PER CAPITA
Harness Racing						
Scarborough	87	232,812	9,170,328	429,260.82	105,406	39.39
Lewiston	93	168,330	6,884,686	342,438.23	74,029	40.90
Bangor	41	61,500	2,554,263	121,783.41	62,299	41.53
Cumberland	32	53,280	2,231,683	110,703.56	69,740	41.89
Totals	253	515,922	20,840,960	1,004,186.02	82,375	40.40
Fairs						
Skowhegan	11		693,447	33,795.12	63,041	
Windsor	8		627,724	28,972.82	78,466	
Farmington	7		356,084	17,831.95	50,869	
Topsham	7		295,913	14,759.77	42,273	
Union	4		226,783	11,074.07	56,696	
Fryeburg	5		341,058	14,985.33	68,212	
Aroostook	9		112,169	5,003.86	12,463	
Northern Raceway	3		37,136	1,609.60	12,379	
Presque Isle	5		87,285	3,705.54	17,457	
Totals	59		2,777,599	131,738.06	47,078	
Miscellaneous Revenue				17,449.00		
STATE TOTALS	312	515,922	23,618,559	1,153,373.08	75,701	40.40

RECAP OF PARI MUTUELS WAGERING IN MARYLAND (1978)

TRACKS	NUMBER OF RACING DAYS	TOTAL ATTENDANCE	TOTAL PARI MUTUELS HANDLE	TOTAL REVENUE TO STATE	DAILY AVERAGE	PER CAPITA
Thoroughbreds						
Bowie	52	441,701	56,108,044	2,996,169.55	1,079,001	127.03
Pimlico	60	638,696	71,751,246	3,831,516.54	1,195,854	112.34
Laurel	61	527,655	62,154,339	3,319,041.70	1,018,924	117.79
Pimlico (Combined)	48	369,896	42,906,040	2,291,182.54	893,876	115.99
Bowie (Marlboro-Hagerstown)	35	251,915	30,103,260	1,607,514.08	860,093	119.50
Timonium	42	231,079	21,014,292	1,155,786.07	500,340	90.94
Fair Hill (Steeplechase)	4	49,526	901,079	72,086.32	225,270	18.19
Totals	302	2,510,468	284,938,300	15,273,296.80	943,504	113.50
Harness Racing						
Rosecroft	103	416,129	39,000,224	2,487,764.66	378,643	93.72
Laurel	86	398,256	34,629,934	2,142,305.79	402,674	86.95
Ocean Downs	67	175,110	13,311,051	617,787.49	198,672	68.22
Totals	256	989,495	86,941,209	5,247,857.94	339,614	87.86
Miscellaneous Revenue				1,756,551.13		
STATE TOTALS	558	3,499,963	371,879,509	22,277,705.87	666,451	106.25

RECAP OF PARI MUTUELS WAGERING IN MASSACHUSETTS (1978)

TRACKS	NUMBER OF RACING DAYS		TOTAL ATTENDANCE	TOTAL PARI MUTUELS HANDLE	TOTAL REVENUE TO STATE	DAILY AVERAGE	PER CAPITA
Thoroughbreds							
Suffolk Downs	198		1,228,225	133,816,850	10,563,256.47	675,843	108.95
Marshfield Fair	8		107,053	1,883,773	147,054.37	235,472	17.60
Northampton Fair	10		63,983	4,605,214	419,016.01	460,521	71.98
Great Barrington Fair	10		101,000	4,470,360	408,815.91	447,036	44.26
Berkshire Fair	10		18,900	2,437,379	190,176.11	243,738	128.96
Totals	236		1,519,161	147,213,576	11,728,318.87	623,786	96.90
Harness Racing							
New England Raceway	163		563,726	52,576,979	2,847,605.26	322,558	93.27
Foxboro Fair	10		41,385	3,563,544	120,208.70	356,354	86.11
Totals	173		605,111	56,140,523	2,967,813.96	324,512	92.78
Greyhounds							
Wonderland	196	6M	1,040,121	91,882,329	8,509,189.20	454,863	88.34
Raynham	126	27M	327,213	37,951,326	3,280,243.08	248,048	115.98
Taunton	142	62M	371,994	33,716,580	2,401,205.95	165,277	90.64
Middleboro Fair	10		38,007	3,297,838	264,700.43	329,784	86.77
Essex Fair	6		87,917	646,932	32,644.30	107,822	7.36
Rehoboth Fair	10		46,207	3,186,016	250,514.81	318,602	68.95
Brockton Fair	10		36,813	3,162,138	252,217.40	316,214	85.90
Weymouth Fair	10		28,299	2,424,316	172,769.63	242,432	85.67
Totals	510	95M	1,976,571	176,267,475	15,163,484.80	291,351	89.18
STATE TOTALS	919	95M	4,100,843	379,621,574	29,859,617.63	374,380	92.57

RECAP OF PARI MUTUELS WAGERING IN MICHIGAN (1978)

TRACKS	NUMBER OF RACING DAYS	TOTAL ATTENDANCE	TOTAL PARI MUTUELS HANDLE	TOTAL REVENUE TO STATE	DAILY AVERAGE	PER CAPITA
Thoroughbreds						
Detroit	102	541,979	72,519,697	5,528,493.00	710,977	133.81
Hazel Park	114	808,777	110,941,943	8,366,160.00	973,174	137.17
Totals	216	1,350,756	183,461,640	13,894,653.00	890,590	135.82
Quarterhorses						
Glendale	32	13,471	900,074	55,938.00	28,127	66.82
Totals	32	13,471	900,074	55,938.00	28,127	66.82
Harness Horses						
Hazel Park	83	548,592	73,304,518	4,341,498.00	883,186	133.62
Jackson-Northville	59	185,061	25,186,646	1,487,948.00	426,892	136.10
Jackson	94	159,842	13,134,597	780,043.00	139,729	82.17
Northville	82	251,240	33,418,397	1,993,244.00	407,541	133.01
Wolverine	84	515,165	69,268,806	4,091,549.00	824,628	134.46
Totals	402	1,659,900	214,312,964	12,694,282.00	533,117	129.11
Miscellaneous Revenue				444,961.84		
STATE TOTALS	650	3,024,127	398,674,678	27,089,834.84	613,346	131.83

RECAP OF PARI MUTUELS WAGERING IN MONTANA (1978)

TRACKS	NUMBER OF RACING DAYS	TOTAL ATTENDANCE	TOTAL PARI MUTUELS HANDLE	TOTAL REVENUE TO STATE	DAILY AVERAGE	PER CAPITA
Fairs						
Thoroughbred	102		8,060,842	130,673.32	79,028	
Quarterhorse						
Appaloosas						
STATE TOTALS	102		8,060,842	130,673.32	79,028	

Wanta Bet?

RECAP OF PARI MUTUELS WAGERING IN NEBRASKA (1978)

TRACKS	NUMBER OF RACING DAYS	TOTAL ATTENDANCE	TOTAL PARI MUTUELS HANDLE	TOTAL REVENUE TO STATE	DAILY AVERAGE	PER CAPITA
Thoroughbreds						
Fonner Park	40	205,546	19,149,353	938,907.05	478,734	93.16
Aksarben	60	961,058	96,052,047	4,958,009.70	1,600,867	99.94
Lincoln	30	184,429	16,055,349	781,841.80	535,178	87.05
Columbus	28	99,604	8,200,379	373,447.25	292,871	82.33
Atokad	36	94,160	8,456,238	384,196.90	234,895	89.81
Totals	194	1,544,797	147,913,366	7,436,402.70	762,440	95.75
Quarterhorses						
Custer County	13	10,845	342,255	993.00	26,327	31.56
Thayer County	21	26,742	726,222	2,608.80	34,582	27.16
Totals	34	37,587	1,068,477	3,601.80	31,426	28.43
STATE TOTALS	228	1,582,384	148,981,843	7,440,004.50	653,429	94.15

RECAP OF PARI MUTUELS WAGERING IN NEVADA (1978)

TRACKS	NUMBER OF RACING DAYS	TOTAL ATTENDANCE	TOTAL PARI MUTUELS HANDLE	TOTAL REVENUE TO STATE	DAILY AVERAGE	PER CAPITA
Jai Alai						
Reno (MGM)	186	173,300	3,861,431	77,228.62	20,760	22.28
Las Vegas (MGM)	294	332,903	10,652,693	213,053.86	36,234	32.00
Totals	480	506,203	14,514,124	290,282.48	30,238	28.67
Quarterhorses						
Elko	5		49,408			
STATE TOTALS	485	506,203	14,563,532	290,282.48	30,238	28.67

RECAP OF PARI MUTUELS WAGERING IN NEW HAMPSHIRE (1978)

TRACKS	NUMBER OF RACING DAYS		TOTAL ATTENDANCE	TOTAL PARI MUTUELS HANDLE	TOTAL REVENUE TO STATE	DAILY AVERAGE	PER CAPITA
Thoroughbreds							
Rockingham	65		575,640	52,767,554	4,818,162.60	811,808	91.67
Totals	65		575,640	52,767,554	4,818,162.60	811,808	91.67
Harness Racing							
Rockingham	112		387,552	26,343,268	1,944,932.65	235,208	67.97
Hinsdale	63		81,631	4,150,480	161,624.36	65,880	50.84
Rochester (Fair)	10		16,190	859,442	47,612.15	85,944	53.08
Totals	185		485,373	31,353,190	2,154,169.16	169,477	64.60
Greyhounds							
Seabrook	299	153M	1,062,610	95,804,781	7,615,742.94	211,957	90.16
Hinsdale	132	38M	160,894	12,602,154	504,601.34	74,130	78.33
Lakes Region	85	6M	82,860	4,270,606	97,897.95	46,930	51.54
Totals	516	197M	1,306,364	112,677,541	8,218,242.23	158,033	86.25
STATE TOTALS	766	197M	2,367,377	196,798,285	15,190,573.99	204,360	83.13

RECAP OF PARI MUTUELS WAGERING IN NEW JERSEY (1978)

TRACKS	NUMBER OF RACING DAYS	TOTAL ATTENDANCE	TOTAL PARI MUTUELS HANDLE	TOTAL REVENUE TO STATE	DAILY AVERAGE	PER CAPITA
Thoroughbreds						
Monmouth	97	1,015,663	135,935,733	8,645,538.00	1,401,399	133.84
Atlantic City	85	581,068	61,400,634	1,907,029.00	722,360	105.67
Meadowlands	100	1,620,430	192,619,100	952,815.00	1,926,191	118.87
Totals	282	3,217,161	389,955,467	11,505,382.00	1,382,821	121.21
Harness Racing						
Meadowlands	168	2,797,099	343,769,960	1,706,963.00	2,046,250	122.90
Atlantic City	124	417,465	50,199,263	2,573,806.00	404,833	120.25
Freehold	126	488,251	58,574,610	3,016,336.00	464,878	119.97
Totals	418	3,702,815	452,543,833	7,297,105.00	1,082,641	122.22
Miscellaneous Revenue				1,226,871.00		
State Totals	700	6,919,976	842,499,300	20,029,358.00	1,203,570	121.75

RECAP OF PARI MUTUELS WAGERING IN NEW MEXICO (1978)

TRACKS	NUMBER OF RACING DAYS	TOTAL ATTENDANCE	TOTAL PARI MUTUELS HANDLE	TOTAL REVENUE TO STATE	DAILY AVERAGE	PER CAPITA
Thoroughbreds						
La Mesa	59	116,156	7,316,172	314,911.42	202,842	103.03
Ruidoso	71	475,450	16,872,496	1,200,483.67	444,981	66.45
Santa Fe	62	215,788	13,882,743	571,673.85	314,985	90.50
Albuquerque	17	227,824	10,586,790	325,432.50	836,635	62.43
Sunland	86	293,916	15,541,868	510,742.02	233,692	68.38
Totals	295	1,329,134	64,200,069	1,948,828.99	330,206	73.29
Quarterhorses						
La Mesa	59		4,651,515		202,842	103.03
Ruidoso	71		14,721,171		444,981	66.45
Santa Fe	62		5,646,344		314,985	90.50
Albuquerque	17		3,636,005		836,635	62.43
Sunland	86		4,555,634		233,692	68.38
Totals	295		33,210,669	974,414.47	330,206	73.29
STATE TOTALS	295	1,329,134	97,410,738	2,923,243.46	330,206	73.29

All tracks held mixed meetings. No breakdown of attendance and revenue between thoroughbreds and quarterhorses.

RECAP OF PARI MUTUELS WAGERING IN NEW YORK (1978)

TRACKS	NUMBER OF RACING DAYS	TOTAL ATTENDANCE	TOTAL PARI MUTUELS HANDLE	TOTAL REVENUE TO STATE	DAILY AVERAGE	PER CAPITA
Thoroughbreds						
Aqueduct	163	2,919,303	432,689,590	18,689,455.17	2,654,537	148.22
Belmont Park	108	2,526,305	329,578,994	13,428,859.82	3,051,657	130.46
Saratoga	24	553,949	52,629,131	1,348,040.52	2,192,880	95.01
Finger Lakes	164	651,853	56,975,557	2,725,122.44	347,411	87.41
Totals	459	6,651,410	871,873,272	36,191,477.95	1,899,506	131.08
Harness Races						
Batavia	151	491,698	44,231,844	1,826,673.47	292,926	89.96
Buffalo	147	461,468	40,381,757	1,694,638.02	274,706	87.51
Buffalo (At Syracuse)	7	19,404	1,466,719	63,793.91	209,531	75.59
Goshen	4	10,617	396,227	15,512.07	99,057	37.32
Monticello	193	580,028	53,131,845	2,393,883.93	275,295	91.60
Roosevelt	154	1,777,965	250,750,372	20,160,787.77	1,628,249	141.03
Saratoga	148	490,243	37,071,525	1,372,851.06	250,483	75.62
Vernon	171	639,952	45,137,067	1,956,060.82	263,959	70.53
Yonkers	153	1,369,077	205,869,833	16,503,781.46	1,345,554	150.37
Saratoga (Orange Co.)	48	89,804	8,529,745	316,277.31	177,703	94.98
Totals	1176	5,930,256	686,966,934	46,304,259.82	584,156	115.84
Quarterhorses						
Tioga Park	24	38,208	1,657,578	64,535.66	69,066	43.38
Totals	24	38,208	1,657,578	64,535.66	69,066	43.38
STATE TOTALS	1659	12,619,874	1,560,497,784	82,560,273.43	940,626	123.65

RECAP OF OFF TRACK BETTING WAGERING IN NEW YORK (1978)

TRACK	NUMBER OF RACING DAYS	TOTAL ATTENDANCE	TOTAL PARI MUTUELS HANDLE	TOTAL REVENUE TO STATE	DAILY AVERAGE	PER CAPITA
Thoroughbreds						
Aqueduct	163		396,538,631		2,432,752	
Belmont	108		259,009,408		2,398,235	
Saratoga	24		64,492,007		2,687,167	
Finger Lakes	164		39,341,446		239,887	
Totals	459		759,381,492		1,654,426	
Harness Racing						
Roosevelt	154		157,195,565		1,020,750	
Yonkers	153		148,542,378		970,865	
Monticello	193		24,290,358		125,857	
Buffalo	147		21,384,396		145,472	
Batavia	151		23,188,260		153,565	
Saratoga	148		8,537,210		57,684	
Orange County	48		2,831,580		58,991	
Syracuse	7		9,588		1,370	
Totals	1001		385,979,335		385,594	
Out of State						
Calder			7,473,623			
Hialeah			21,597,175			
Keystone			15,503,350			
Gulfstream			9,143,588			
Flamingo Stakes			835,990			
Kentucky Derby			5,765,937			
Colonial Cup			200,611			
D.C. International			588,822			
Laurel Futurity			60,345	18,358,003.33 (Miscellaneous Revenue)		
Connecticut OTB				1,459,071.00		
Totals			61,169,441	26,575,629.20		
STATE TOTALS			1,206,530,268	46,392,703.53		

RECAP OF PARI MUTUELS WAGERING IN OHIO (1978)

TRACKS	NUMBER OF RACING DAYS	TOTAL ATTENDANCE	TOTAL PARI MUTUELS HANDLE	TOTAL REVENUE TO STATE	DAILY AVERAGE	PER CAPITA
Thoroughbreds						
Beaulah Park	78	366,230	43,486,890	2,920,732.11	557,524	118.74
Thistle Downs	174	909,475	110,788,341	7,419,743.41	636,715	121.82
River Downs	109	574,209	61,815,090	4,161,547.48	567,111	107.65
Totals	361	1,849,914	216,090,321	14,502,023.00	598,588	116.81
Quarterhorses						
River Downs (Midwest)	28	29,463	2,392,838	111,381.96	85,459	81.22
Totals	28	29,463	2,392,838	111,381.96	85,459	81.22
Harness Racing						
Northfield	195	738,143	84,122,449	5,335,621.79	431,397	113.96
Lebanon	135	150,380	23,175,384	1,269,633.35	171,670	154.11
Scioto Downs	112	635,778	46,021,257	2,928,262.46	410,904	72.39
Raceway Park	169	472,594	36,306,852	2,056,406.58	214,833	76.82
Totals	611	1,996,895	189,625,942	11,589,924.18	310,353	94.96
Fairs (57 Tracks)	177	367,709	3,626,580	178,156.49	20,489	9.86
Totals	177	367,709	3,626,580	178,156.49	20,489	9.86
STATE TOTALS	1177	4,243,981	411,735,681	26,381,485.63	349,818	97.02

RECAP OF PARI MUTUELS WAGERING IN OREGON (1978)

TRACKS	NUMBER OF RACING DAYS	TOTAL ATTENDANCE	TOTAL PARI MUTUELS HANDLE	TOTAL REVENUE TO STATE	DAILY AVERAGE	PER CAPITA
Thoroughbreds						
Portland	83	621,363	34,896,843	2,100,257.01	489,918	65.44
Oregon State Fair	30	101,692	5,241,434	121,186.37	189,966	56.04
Grants Pass	10	18,652	452,933	21,488.75	88,567	47.48
Crooked River	4	17,094	70,538	4,408.51	50,020	11.70
Totals	127	758,801	40,661,748	2,247,340.64	373,606	62.53
Quarterhorses						
Portland	83		5,766,365		489,918	65.44
Oregon State Fair	30		457,538		189,966	56.04
Grants Pass	10		432,734		88,567	47.48
Crooked River	4		129,541		50,020	11.70
Totals	127		6,786,178		373,606	62.53
All above tracks held mixed meetings. No breakdown of attendance and revenue between thoroughbreds and quarterhorses.						
Greyhounds						
Multnomah	85	570,957	46,355,486	2,843,133.67	545,359	81.19
Totals	85	570,957	46,355,486	2,843,133.67	545,359	81.19
Fairs						
Tilamook	3		104,074	2,512.36		
Eastern Oregon	3		42,615	1,768.59		
Harney County	2		29,706	1,216.41		
Lake County	2		43,678	1,419.68		
Klamath Basin	3		168,174	4,572.10		
Totals	13		388,247	11,489.14		
Miscellaneous Revenue				103,744.73		
STATE TOTALS	225	1,329,758	94,191,659	5,205,708.18	418,630	70.83

RECAP OF PARI MUTUELS WAGERING IN PENNSYLVANIA (1978)

TRACKS	NUMBER OF RACING DAYS	TOTAL ATTENDANCE	TOTAL PARI MUTUELS HANDLE	TOTAL REVENUE TO STATE	DAILY AVERAGE	PER CAPITA
Thoroughbreds						
Keystone (Continental)	96	763,206	91,300,856	4,913,344.86	951,050	119.63
Keystone (Eagle Downs)	98	827,977	100,527,490	5,378,501.19	1,025,791	121.41
Pocono (Shamrock)	97	328,078	33,123,987	1,746,348.99	341,484	100.96
Penn National	100	567,553	53,613,584	2,869,150.34	536,136	94.46
Penn National (Mountainview)	98	572,515	53,201,055	2,847,784.41	542,867	92.92
Commodore	90	236,268	17,447,715	938,240.12	193,864	73.85
Totals	579	3,295,597	349,214,687	18,693,369.91	603,134	105.30
Harness Racing						
Liberty Bell	100	541,615	59,230,288	3,549,204.53	592,303	109.36
William Penn	100	549,216	58,529,395	3,513,369.22	585,294	106.57
Washington	100	452,287	37,738,158	2,265,454.19	377,382	83.44
Mountain Laurel	100	333,447	28,898,518	1,745,649.48	288,985	86.67
Pocono	100	228,964	24,013,564	1,411,604.19	240,136	104.88
Totals	500	2,105,529	208,409,923	12,485,281.61	416,820	98.98
Miscellaneous Revenue				716,427.18		
STATE TOTALS	1079	5,401,126	557,624,610	31,895,078.70	516,798	103.24

RECAP OF PARI MUTUELS WAGERING IN RHODE ISLAND (1978)

TRACKS	NUMBER OF RACING DAYS	TOTAL ATTENDANCE	TOTAL PARI MUTUELS HANDLE	TOTAL REVENUE TO STATE	DAILY AVERAGE	PER CAPITA
Greyhounds Lincoln	211	502,600	49,103,296	2,800,939.69	232,717	97.70
Totals	211	502,600	49,103,296	2,800,939.69	232,717	97.70
Jai Alai Newport	199	492,376	28,434,073	1,454,665.84	142,885	57.75
Totals	199	492,376	28,434,073	1,454,665.84	142,885	57.75
STATE TOTALS	410	994,976	77,537,369	4,255,605.53	189,115	77.93

RECAP OF PARI MUTUELS WAGERING IN SOUTH DAKOTA (1978)

TRACKS	NUMBER OF RACING DAYS		TOTAL ATTENDANCE	TOTAL PARI MUTUELS HANDLE	TOTAL REVENUE TO STATE	DAILY AVERAGE	PER CAPITA
Thoroughbreds							
Fort Pierre	6		5,000	156,750	3,820.36	26,125	31.35
Aberdeen	6		8,000	214,366	6,091.91	35,728	26.80
Rapid City	13		4,330	136,337	3,067.59	10,487	31.49
Park Jefferson	37		61,120	4,148,568	124,457.04	112,123	67.88
Totals	62		78,450	4,656,021	137,436.90	75,097	59.35
Quarterhorses							
Fort Pierre	6		2,500	69,541	1,686.02	11,590	27.82
Aberdeen	6		4,000	106,246	2,956.98	17,708	26.56
Rapid City	13		8,660	234,294	5,271.61	18,023	27.05
Park Jefferson	37		6,113	314,083	9,422.49	8,489	51.38
Totals	62		21,273	724,164	19,337.10	11,680	34.04
Greyhounds							
Black Hills	120	1M	127,111	6,391,941	362,571.38	52,826	50.29
Sodrac	137	9M	333,397	25,986,633	1,773,150.31	177,991	77.95
Totals	257	10M	460,508	32,378,574	2,135,721.69	121,268	70.31
Miscellaneous Revenue					29,601.00		
STATE TOTALS	319	10M	560,231	37,758,759	2,322,096.69	114,768	67.40

RECAP OF PARI MUTUELS WAGERING IN VERMONT (1978)

TRACKS	NUMBER OF RACING DAYS		TOTAL ATTENDANCE	TOTAL PARI MUTUELS HANDLE	TOTAL REVENUE TO STATE	DAILY AVERAGE	PER CAPITA
Greyhounds							
Green Mountain	102	10M	203,336	14,610,422	876,926.31	130,450	71.85
Totals	102	10M	203,336	14,610,422	876,926.31	130,450	71.85
Fairs							
Rutland		8			11,131.84		
Miscellaneous Revenue					70,057.50		
STATE TOTALS	110	10M	203,336	14,610,422	958,115.65	130,450	71.85

RECAP OF PARI MUTUELS WAGERING IN WASHINGTON (1978)

TRACKS	NUMBER OF RACING DAYS	TOTAL ATTENDANCE	TOTAL PARI MUTUELS HANDLE	TOTAL REVENUE TO STATE	DAILY AVERAGE	PER CAPITA
Thoroughbreds						
Longacres	98	860,541	94,708,241	5,732,003.00	966,411	110.06
Yakima	51	136,224	12,624,819	742,578.70	247,545	92.68
Playfair	68	276,257	21,650,725	1,422,904.00	318,393	78.37
Totals	217	1,273,022	128,983,785	7,897,485.70	594,395	101.32
Fairs						
Sundown Limited	24	39,945	1,362,844	83,370.08	56,785	34.12
Days of Real Sport	2	1,500	89,564	915.64	44,782	59.71
Dayton Days	3	3,698	130,722	1,375.00	43,574	35.35
Southeastern Washington Fair	3	7,000	184,702	1,877.02	61,567	26.39
Wagonwheeler	1	2,012	69,948	709.48	69,948	34.77
Totals	33	54,155	1,837,780	88,247.22	55,690	33.94
STATE TOTALS	250	1,327,177	130,821,565	7,985,732.92	523,286	98.57

RECAP OF PARI MUTUELS WAGERING IN WEST VIRGINIA (1978)

TRACKS	NUMBER OF RACING DAYS		TOTAL ATTENDANCE	TOTAL PARI MUTUELS HANDLE	TOTAL REVENUE TO STATE	DAILY AVERAGE	PER CAPITA
Thoroughbreds							
Charlestown	134		533,331	44,516,530	2,543,212.53	332,213	83.47
Shenandoah	116		415,305	37,016,629	2,119,594.58	319,109	89.13
Waterford	292		779,778	85,221,596	4,858,548.87	291,855	109.29
Totals	542		1,728,414	166,754,755	9,521,355.98	307,666	96.48
Greyhounds							
Wheeling	300	87M	623,533	62,782,040	3,533,742.00	162,227	100.69
Totals	300	87M	623,533	62,782,040	3,533,742.00	162,227	100.69
Miscellaneous Revenue					97,236.52		
STATE TOTALS	842	87M	2,351,947	229,536,795	13,152,334.50	247,079	97.59

RECAP OF PARI MUTUELS WAGERING IN WYOMING (1978)

TRACKS	NUMBER OF RACING DAYS	TOTAL ATTENDANCE	TOTAL PARI MUTUELS HANDLE	TOTAL REVENUE TO STATE	DAILY AVERAGE	PER CAPITA
Quarterhorses						
Casper	8	28,692	744,191	15,000.00 (EST.)	93,024	25.94
STATE TOTALS	8	28,692	744,191	15,000.00 (EST.)	93,024	25.94

RECAP OF PARI MUTUELS WAGERING ON FAIRS (1978)

TRACKS	NUMBER OF RACING DAYS	TOTAL ATTENDANCE	TOTAL PARI MUTUELS HANDLE	TOTAL REVENUE TO STATE	DAILY AVERAGE	PER CAPITA
Arizona	49	—	3,798,990	—	77,530	—
California	122	1,002,095	120,445,380	7,703,032.00	987,257	120.19
Colorado	50	60,825	2,186,046	87,441.84	43,721	35.94
Montana	102	—	8,060,842	130,673.32	79,028	—
Maine	59	—	2,777,599	131,738.06	47,078	—
Ohio	177	367,709	3,626,580	178,156.49	20,489	—
Oregon	13	—	388,247	11,489.14	—	—
Vermont	8	—	—	11,131.84	—	—
Washington	33	54,155	1,837,780	88,247.22	55,690	33.94
Totals	613		143,121,464	8,341,909.91	233,477	—

Chapter Eight

National Statistics (Trend Percentages 1979-1980)

RECAP OF PARI MUTUELS WAGERING IN THE UNITED STATES (1978)

TRACKS	NUMBER OF RACING DAYS		TOTAL ATTENDANCE	TOTAL PARI MUTUELS HANDLE	TOTAL REVENUE TO STATE	DAILY AVERAGE	PER CAPITA
Thoroughbreds	6462		47,055,235	5,714,921,928	331,758,281.59	884,389	121.45
Quarterhorses	1247		2,759,949	254,031,637	12,964,234.90	204,495	92.02
Harness Horses	5621		25,389,914	2,763,771,194	156,308,437.05	491,687	108.85
Greyhounds	5598	1755M	20,816,821	1,876,660,951	135,308,517.20	255,224	90.15
Jai Alai	2256	691M	8,214,365	567,555,752	38,311,329.47	192,588	69.09
Off Track Betting				1,321,261,763	36,134,982.24		
Fairs	613			143,121,464	8,341,909.91		
Miscellaneous Revenue					29,889,621.67		
Totals	21159	2446M	104,236,284	12,641,324,689	749,017,314.03	473,498	107.23

M Denotes Matinees

RECAP OF PARI MUTUELS WAGERING ON THOROUGHBREDS (1978)

STATES	NUMBER OF RACING DAYS	TOTAL ATTENDANCE	TOTAL PARI MUTUELS HANDLE	TOTAL REVENUE TO STATE	DAILY AVERAGE	PER CAPITA
Arizona	193	658,925	62,214,791	2,585,694.46	332,356	94.42
Arkansas	49	1,037,037	114,431,968	7,392,487.50	2,335,346	110.35
California	400	6,820,014	1,058,411,082	83,250,634.00	2,646,028	155.19
Colorado	108	386,689	33,826,883	1,522,218.10	313,212	87.48
Delaware	50	340,209	39,681,444	678,197.00	793,629	116.64
Florida	329	2,426,943	363,037,656	16,785,492.16	1,103,458	149.59
Idaho	127	192,935	7,917,225	95,383.26	85,834	37.67
Illinois	459	3,434,729	437,230,158	36,444,188.00	952,571	127.30
Kentucky	272	1,983,144	214,210,367	10,174,992.33	787,538	108.02
Louisiana	538	2,851,302	335,275,793	17,076,498.60	641,363	117.23
Maryland	302	2,510,468	284,938,300	15,273,296.80	943,504	113.50
Massachusetts	236	1,519,161	147,213,576	11,728,318.87	623,786	96.90
Michigan	216	1,350,756	183,461,640	13,894,653.00	890,590	135.82
Nebraska	194	1,544,797	147,913,366	7,436,402.70	762,440	95.75
New Hampshire	65	575,640	52,767,554	4,818,162.60	811,808	91.67
New Jersey	282	3,217,161	389,955,467	11,505,382.00	1,382,821	121.21
New Mexico	295	664,567	64,200,069	1,948,828.99	330,206	73.29
New York	459	6,651,410	871,873,272	36,191,477.95	1,899,506	131.08
Ohio	361	1,849,914	216,090,321	14,502,023.00	598,588	116.81
Oregon	127	663,951	40,661,748	2,204,301.78	373,606	62.53
Pennsylvania	579	3,295,597	349,214,687	18,693,369.91	603,134	105.30
South Dakota	62	78,450	4,656,021	137,436.90	75,097	59.35
Washington	217	1,273,022	128,983,785	7,897,485.70	594,395	101.32
West Virginia	542	1,728,414	166,754,755	9,521,355.98	307,666	96.48
Totals	6462	47,055,235	5,714,921,928	331,758,281.59	884,389	121.45

PERCENTAGES OF INCREASE OR DECREASE PER PERFORMANCE IN ATTENDANCE, MUTUELS HANDLE AND PER CAPITA WAGERING ON: THOROUGHBREDS

Percentages of increase or decrease per performance in attendance, mutuels handle and per capita wagering on thoroughbred tracks by states. 1979 figures are in comparison to 1978, and 1980 figures are in comparison to 1979. 1978 figures were compiled from figures furnished by the individual State Racing Commission's Annual Reports. 1979 and 1980 figures are based on statistics published by the Daily Racing Form.

STATE	ATTENDANCE PER PERFORMANCE		HANDLE PER PERFORMANCE		PER CAPITA PER PERFORMANCE	
	1979	1980	1979	1980	1979	1980
Arizona	—	+ 6.0	− 3.0	+11.4	—	+ 5.0
Arkansas	+ 4.7	− 0.7	+ 5.7	+ 3.2	+ 0.1	+ 3.9
California	+10.6	+11.6	+14.5	+15.0	+ 3.5	+ 3.0
Colorado	−13.0	+ 3.7	− 1.5	+ 4.7	+13.3	+ 1.0
Delaware	−13.2	+ 6.4	−13.2	+10.9	—	+ 4.3
Florida	+24.5	− 5.8	− 1.8	+ 0.1	−21.1	+ 6.2
Idaho	—	−13.2	—	−15.4	+ 8.3	− 2.5
Illinois	+ 8.1	− 4.5	+13.2	− 0.5	+ 4.8	+ 4.2
Kentucky	− 0.8	+ 6.9	+ 4.5	+ 2.8	+ 5.2	− 3.8
Louisiana	+ 9.0	− 0.4	+11.1	+ 6.7	+ 5.2	+ 7.2
Maryland	− 7.7	+ 0.9	− 2.5	+ 3.9	+ 5.6	+ 3.0
Massachusetts	+ 8.7	− 1.1	+17.3	+11.2	+ 8.0	+12.4
Michigan	− 1.4	− 0.3	+ 0.1	− 7.2	+ 6.5	− 6.9
Nebraska	+ 0.5	− 0.5	+ 8.6	+ 3.2	+ 8.1	+ 3.6
New Hampshire	− 7.0	+ 8.8	− 1.2	+ 8.0	+ 6.2	− 0.1
New Jersey	−21.3	+ 9.8	−22.1	+ 9.8	− 1.0	—
New Mexico	—	−11.3	+ 7.6	− 1.1	+17.1	+11.5
New York	−16.0	+ 2.1	− 5.4	+11.0	+12.6	+ 8.7
Ohio	− 0.5	− 3.8	+ 6.3	− 2.6	+ 6.8	+ 1.4
Oregon	−10.0	− 5.2	+ 5.9	+ 6.6	+34.4	+12.5
Pennsylvania	− 2.7	+ 8.6	+ 0.1	+ 9.8	+ 3.5	+ 1.1
South Dakota	—	—	—	+ 2.8	—	+ 2.2
Washington	+ 7.4	− 2.8	+17.4	+ 1.1	+ 9.3	+ 4.0
West Virginia	− 5.0	+ 4.4	− 4.4	+ 8.0	+ 1.0	+ 3.4
California Fairs	+11.8	−15.6	−27.6	−14.6	−17.3	+ 1.2
TOTALS	+ 1.6	+ 1.4	+ 4.5	+ 5.7	+ 2.9	+ 4.3

THOROUGHBREDS

Emphasis is usually placed on thoroughbred racing when the subject of pari-mutuels wagering comes up. Actually this category of the industry provides very close to 50% of the volume of business throughout the nation, equal to the combined efforts of harness racing, quarterhorses, greyhounds and jai alai. The purpose of this book is not to weigh the merits of one category as opposed to the other four. However, it is probably easier to judge the pulse of the nation regarding the future of pari-mutuels wagering through this medium than any of the other individual categories. There are about twice as many states which legalize this sport than those which legalize quarterhorse, harness, or greyhound racing and more than six times as many than those legalizing jai alai. Actually in some cases, states have the legalization necessary for some of the categories that is not being used, including thoroughbreds, simply because it is not economically feasible to do so. At any rate, because of the above conditions, more people are better informed about this sport than the others, and therefore judge the entire industry by its successes and failures.

This phase of the industry, as a whole, is generally concentrated in more populous locations than the others due to the fact that it costs more to operate a thoroughbred track than any other kind.

Detailed statistics for the year 1978 are contained in the state charts. Percentages of increase in all categories were obtained from figures published in the Daily Racing Form. These figures show that the number of performances during 1978, 1979, and 1980 have remained fairly constant. Some areas have added racing days to their schedule, while others have cut back slightly as dictated by the situation in their particular area. To more accurately show the trend of growth pertaining to thoroughbred tracks only, the percentages are based on a per performance basis.

The national figures show attendance up 1.62% in 1979 over 1978, and 1.38% up in 1980 over 1979. The volume per performance was up 4.52% in 1979 over 1978, and 5.73% up in 1980 over 1979. Per capita wagering was up 2.86% in 1979 over 1978, and 4.29% in 1980 over 1979. We have provided a chart showing percentages of increase or decrease in each individual state where thoroughbred racing was held. This chart does much to reflect the economy and the effects that rising energy costs have had on different sections of the country.

Some interesting trends that stand out, is that the west coast is showing substantial gains in most cases with the exception of the California Fair Circuit. These fair figures are misleading, as most of the established fairs are doing well. The averages have fallen due to the addition of new dates in areas where the population is not so concentrated.

Tracks located in areas that require considerable travel to attend, have definitely been affected by the high fuel costs.

The economy crunch likewise has slowed the growth, and in some cases, reduced attendance and volume of wagering in locations which depend on the blue collar worker for the backbone of their business.

The most predominate factor is that nationwide, even though the industry is growing, the rise of attendance figures is not keeping pace with volume of wagering and per capita betting. Factors influencing these trends will be discussed in detail in another chapter.

RECAP OF PARI MUTUELS WAGERING ON QUARTERHORSES (1978)

STATES	NUMBER OF RACING DAYS	TOTAL ATTENDANCE	TOTAL PARI MUTUELS HANDLE	TOTAL REVENUE TO STATE	DAILY AVERAGE	PER CAPITA
California	232	1,255,720	161,248,187	10,445,494.00	695,035	128.41
Colorado	49	116,754	9,843,234	404,024.34	200,882	84.31
Florida	45	109,549	8,537,195	121,871.49	189,715	77.93
Idaho	127	96,467	2,983,740	40,878.65	85,834	37.67
Kentucky	32	54,477	3,161,250	150,000.00	98,789	58.03
Louisiana	147	198,871	20,724,454	514,719.27	260,639	92.86
Michigan	32	13,471	900,074	55,938.00	28,127	66.82
Nebraska	34	37,587	1,068,477	3,601.80	31,426	28.43
Nevada	5		49,408			
New Mexico	295	664,567	33,210,669	974,414.47	303,206	73.29
New York	24	38,208	1,657,578	64,535.66	69,066	43.38
Ohio	28	29,463	2,392,838	111,381.96	85,459	81.22
Oregon	127	94,850	6,786,178	43,038.16	373,606	62.53
South Dakota	62	21,273	724,164	19,337.10	11,680	34.04
Wyoming	8	28,692	744,191	15,000.00	93,024	25.94
TOTALS	1247	2,759,949	254,031,637	12,964,234.90	204,495	92.02

PERCENTAGES OF INCREASE OR DECREASE FOR NUMBER OF RACES RUN, PARI-MUTUELS HANDLE AND PURSES PAID ON: QUARTERHORSES

Percentages of increase or decrease at quarterhorse tracks by state. 1979 figures are in comparison to 1978. 1980 figures are in comparison to 1979. The detailed 1978 figures on quarterhorse tracks were compiled from figures furnished by the individual State Racing Commission's Annual Reports. 1979 and 1980 figures were furnished by the American Quarter Horse Association.

STATE	NUMBER OF RACES		MUTUELS HANDLE		PURSES	
	1979	1980	1979	1980	1979	1980
Arizona	− 6.0	—	+ 3.5	—	+ 1.2	—
California	− 10.3	—	+ 4.8	—	+ 6.9	—
Colorado	+ 6.1	—	+ 8.3	—	+ 22.5	—
Florida	+ 10.1	—	+18.4	—	+ 48.4	—
Idaho	+ 5.0	—	+17.0	—	+ 34.2	—
Illinois	—	—	—	—	—	—
Louisiana	+ 50.9	—	+17.0	—	+ 33.7	—
Michigan	+ 45.7	—	+31.5	—	+ 71.1	—
Montana	+ 11.6	—	+ 4.8	—	+ 17.8	—
Nebraska	− 2.5	—	− 3.7	—	+ 10.5	—
Nevada	+ 43.7	—	+84.3	—	+572.0	—
New Mexico	+ 6.1	—	+ 6.2	—	+ 8.3	—
Ohio	− 96.6	—	−97.5	—	− 76.4	—
Oregon	+ 3.6	—	− 3.8	—	+ 11.1	—
South Dakota	—	—	—	—	+ 13.6	—
Washington	+ 10.2	—	+27.5	—	+ 48.8	—
Wyoming	+ 22.0	—	+14.9	—	+ 31.9	—
Non Pari-Mutuels						
Texas	+ 16.2	—	—	—	+ 23.6	—
Oklahoma	+ 37.0	—	—	—	+ 35.5	—
Kansas	− 1.0	—	—	—	+ 9.3	—
Utah	+ 1.0	—	—	—	+ 20.8	—
Indiana	+ 12.0	—	—	—	+ 23.6	—
Illinois	+100.0	—	—	—	+ 62.1	—
TOTALS	+ 10.1	+4.9	+ 6.8	+14.3	+ 15.1	+14.6

)

QUARTER HORSES

Although quarter horses are still trying to catch up with their thoroughbred cousins in popularity in the United States, seventeen states held pari-mutuels meets in 1978, with six more very active in non pari-mutuels racing. Two states discontinued their commercial meets in 1979. Kentucky and New York. Both are very strong thoroughbred and harness racing areas. So far this situation has made it difficult for the quarter horse tracks to make substantial gains into these localities. Illinois, however, was added to the list, bringing the number back to sixteen. The other five states holding non pari-mutuels meets, Texas, Oklahoma, Kansas, Utah, and Indiana, have all shown marked increases in the number of races held and increases of over all purses both in 1979 and 1980. Legislation is pending in most of these five states for pari-mutuels laws, as well as in other states looking for added revenue. 1978 saw over 260 million dollars wagered on quarterhorses at commercial and fair tracks, with 1979 showing an increase of 6.8% over 1978 and 1980 up 14.3% over 1979. Number of races held in 1979 was up 10.1% in 1979 and 4.9% in 1980. Total purses showed the biggest gains; up 15.1% in 1979 and 14.6% in 1980, so all in all there are good reasons for optimism for those in the quarterhorse industry. It is virtually impossible to arrive at accurate figures for attendance and per capita betting, since many tracks offered mixed thoroughbred and quarterhorse meets. It is impossible to tell exactly how many fans attended these type meets strictly because of the quarter horse portion of the racing cards. The 1978 figures in the charts were accumulated from individual Racing Commission's Annual Reports while the 1979 and 1980 figures were taken from the figures furnished by the American Quarter Horse Association. Both are extremely accurate. Although some appear to differ, it is because some states use a fiscal year for statistics, while others use a calendar year. Fairs are handled differently by different states. Some include their statistics with the commercial tracks, others show them separately. From the latest available figures it would appear that over 280 million dollars were wagered on quarterhorses in 1979 and over 320 million in 1980. With these increases it appears that revenue to the states was close to 14 million in 1979 and near 16 million in 1980. As volume increases, revenue will increase much faster in comparison at quarter horse tracks, since many tracks have been given tax breaks to get their operations in the black. Once this is accomplished, a much bigger share of the handle will go to state revenue.

Nationally the number of races held in the United States grew from 11,931 in 1978 to 13,777 in 1980. Purses have grown even more rapidly, jumping from slightly over 29 million dollars in 1978 to more than 33 million in 1979 and 38½ million in 1980. It appears that the increase in the number of Futurities has contributed greatly to this growth.

American Quarter Horse Association membership is growing rapidly, as is registration of quarter horses themselves. Membership in 1978 was 98,483; 108,881 in 1979; and had grown to 119,406 by the end of 1980. Individual registrations in 1978 totaled 119,287; 121,575 in 1979; and 137,090 in 1980. Any enactment of currently proposed legislation in new states will cause even more rapid growth in the future.

Wanta Bet?

RECAP OF PARI MUTUELS WAGERING ON HARNESS HORSES (1978)

STATES	NUMBER OF RACING DAYS	TOTAL ATTENDANCE	TOTAL PARI MUTUELS HANDLE	TOTAL REVENUE TO STATE	DAILY AVERAGE	PER CAPITA
California	242	1,376,992	176,200,974	11,143,072.00	728,103	127.96
Delaware	294	993,640	79,811,709	1,707,005.94	271,468	80.32
Florida	196	666,750	54,828,674	2,355,315.42	279,738	82.23
Illinois	556	3,538,199	445,169,356	36,293,102.00	800,664	125.82
Kentucky	359	823,037	60,625,003	3,065,062.00	168,872	73.66
Maine	253	515,922	20,840,960	1,004,186.02	82,375	40.40
Maryland	256	989,495	86,941,209	5,247,857.94	339,614	87.86
Massachusetts	173	605,111	56,140,523	2,967,813.96	324,512	92.78
Michigan	402	1,659,900	214,312,964	12,694,282.00	533,117	129.11
New Hampshire	185	485,373	31,353,190	2,154,169.16	169,477	64.60
New Jersey	418	3,702,815	452,543,833	7,297,105.00	1,082,641	122.22
New York	1176	5,930,256	686,966,934	46,304,259.82	584,156	115.84
Ohio	611	1,996,895	189,625,942	11,589,924.18	310,353	94.96
Pennsylvania	500	2,105,529	208,409,923	12,485,281.61	416,820	98.98
TOTALS	5621	25,389,914	2,763,771,194	156,308,437.05	491,687	108.85

PERCENTAGES OF INCREASE OR DECREASE PER PERFORMANCE IN ATTENDANCE, MUTUELS HANDLE AND PER CAPITA WAGERING ON: HARNESS HORSES

Percentages of increase or decrease per performance in attendance, mutuels handle and per capita wagering on harness racing by states. 1979 figures are in comparison with 1978. 1978 figures were compiled from figures furnished by the individual State Racing Commission's Annual Reports. 1979 figures are based on statistics published by the U.S. Trotting Association. 1980 statistics are very nearly completed and will show very little differences from 1979.

STATE	ATTENDANCE PER PERFORMANCE		HANDLE PER PERFORMANCE		PER CAPITA PER PERFORMANCE	
	1979	1980	1979	1980	1979	1980
California	− 5.1		− 4.9		—	
Delaware	− 6.9		−12.8		− 6.2	
Florida	+10.5		+31.5		+19.0	
Illinois	+ 8.4		+11.3		+ 2.7	
Kentucky	+ 5.3		+12.4		+ 6.7	
Maine	− 6.2		− 2.3		+ 4.2	
Maryland	− 7.1		—		+ 7.4	
Massachusetts	− 8.7		−12.9		− 4.6	
Michigan	− 3.0		+ 3.6		+ 6.9	
New Hampshire	−29.1		−19.1		+14.0	
New Jersey	+ 1.7		+10.1		+ 8.2	
New York	− 2.0		− 0.1		+ 1.5	
Ohio	− 5.2		+ 2.1		+ 7.7	
Pennsylvania	− 2.9		− 0.2		+ 2.7	
TOTALS	− 1.3		+ 3.3		+ 4.7	

HARNESS RACING

At this writing, harness racing is keeping a very even pace. Overall figures for 1978, 1979, and 1980 are very much the same. The slight differences show the same trend as the thoroughbred commercial tracks. Mutuels totals up slightly, per capita wagering up a little more percentage-wise than the gross handle, and attendance even or down very little. The gross national volume is in the two billion, eight hundred million range, attendance at commercial tracks a little over twenty-five million per year, state revenue is consistently near one hundred fifty million and purses are nearing the three hundred million dollar mark per year.

USTA membership remains at about 45,000 and new foal registrations at close to 15,000 per year.

The same fourteen states have held racing through the 1978, 1979 and 1980 seasons. New legislation is being considered in many states. As of now, rumors have Georgia as having the best chance to be state number fifteen.

Fair race meetings continue to be popular. The 1980 Trotting and Pacing Guide listed racing dates for 286 U.S. fairs (reported to USTA by March, 1980) for the 1980 season. These states include Delaware (1), Illinois (40), Indiana (4), Iowa (23), Kansas (2), Kentucky (8), Maine (10), Michigan (36), Minnesota (2), Mississippi (1), Missouri (4), New Hampshire (1), New Jersey (8), New York (28), Ohio (89), Pennsylvania (22), Vermont (2), West Virginia (1), and Wisconsin (4). These statistics further substantiates the fact that with the exception of California and Florida, commercial harness racing tracks are much more popular in the midwest and east, than in the other sections of the country. Underlying reasons why this is true is discussed more fully in another chapter. One thing harness racing may have going for it, is the shift of population from the east and midwest where it is favorably accepted, to the south and southwest where it has never before flourished. At the present, it's a little better than holding its own with other sports.

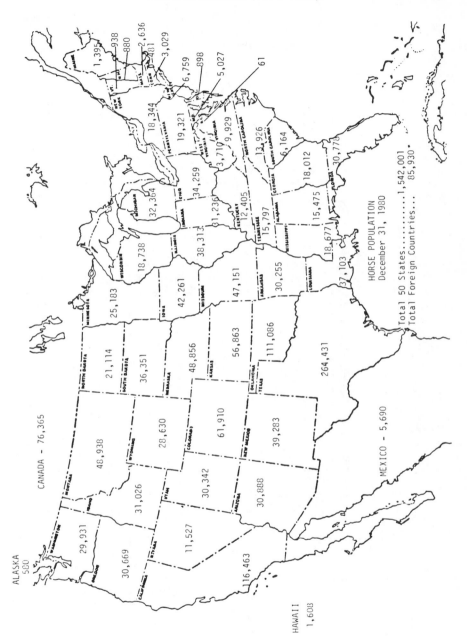

RECAP OF PARI MUTUELS WAGERING ON GREYHOUNDS (1978)

STATES	NUMBER OF RACING DAYS	TOTAL ATTENDANCE	TOTAL PARI MUTUELS HANDLE	TOTAL REVENUE TO STATE	DAILY AVERAGE	PER CAPITA
Alabama	490	154M	1,199,972	113,362,874	7,362,187.24	176,029	94.47
Arizona	497	151M	1,194,920	107,950,014	6,049,964.76	166,590	90.34
Arkansas	112	29M	1,056,755	106,046,767	6,594,105.25	752,105	100.35
Colorado	355	70M	1,245,388	121,804,108	6,090,205.40	286,598	97.80
Connecticut	284	162M	1,011,690	100,421,789	8,882,948.00	225,161	99.26
Florida	1879	790M	9,464,227	832,900,565	64,756,916.16	312,065	88.01
Massachusetts	510	95M	1,976,571	176,267,475	15,163,484.80	291,351	89.18
New Hampshire	516	197M	1,306,364	112,677,541	8,218,242.23	158,033	86.25
Oregon	85	—	570,957	46,355,486	2,843,133.67	545,359	81.19
Rhode Island	211	—	502,600	49,103,296	2,800,939.69	232,717	97.70
South Dakota	257	10M	460,508	32,378,574	2,135,721.69	121,268	70.31
Vermont	102	10M	203,336	14,610,422	876,926.31	130,450	71.85
West Virginia	300	87M	623,533	62,782,040	3,533,742.00	162,227	100.69
TOTALS	5598	1755M	20,816,821	1,876,660,951	135,308,517.20	255,224	90.15

M Denotes Matinees

PERCENTAGES OF INCREASE OR DECREASE PER PERFORMANCE IN ATTENDANCE, MUTUELS HANDLE AND PER CAPITA WAGERING ON: GREYHOUNDS

Percentage of increase or decrease per performance in attendance, mutuels handle and per capita wagering on greyhound tracks by states. 1979 figures are in comparison to 1978, except for Arizona and Florida, whose reports are on a fiscal basis. 1980 figures are in comparison to 1979. 1978 figures were compiled from figures furnished by individual State Racing Commission's Annual Reports. 1979 and 1980 figures were furnished by the offices of the American Greyhound Track Operators Association.

STATE	ATTENDANCE PER PERFORMANCE		HANDLE PER PERFORMANCE		PER CAPITA PER PERFORMANCE	
	1979	1980	1979	1980	1979	1980
Alabama	− 7.9	− 4.1	+ 4.5	+ 2.5	+13.4	+ 7.0
Arizona	—	− 5.3	—	+ 5.2	—	+11.1
Arkansas	− 7.4	+ 4.7	+ 0.3	+ 3.3	+ 8.4	− 1.3
Colorado	− 1.1	+ 4.5	+ 2.9	+ 6.3	+ 4.0	+ 1.7
Connecticut	− 5.9	−11.4	− 3.6	− 4.5	+ 2.4	+ 7.8
Florida	—	− 2.6	—	+ 6.5	—	+ 9.4
Massachusetts	−28.3	+38.9	−14.4	+39.2	+19.3	+ 0.2
New Hampshire	−15.7	−18.1	−15.1	−21.0	+ 0.7	− 3.5
Oregon	− 1.0	− 4.2	+ 4.6	+ 2.2	+ 5.5	+ 6.7
Rhode Island	+ 6.3	+12.2	+ 6.4	+40.4	+ 0.2	+25.2
South Dakota	− 5.3	− 3.5	− 3.8	+ 5.7	+ 1.7	+ 9.6
Vermont	−37.0	+33.0	−30.9	+30.6	+ 9.7	− 1.8
West Virginia	+10.3	+ 6.5	+15.6	+ 8.9	+ 4.9	+ 2.3
TOTALS	− 5.9	+ 1.0	− 1.9	+ 8.1	+ 4.2	+ 7.2

GREYHOUNDS

In the years 1978, 1979, and 1980, greyhound racing was conducted in thirteen states. Nevada joined the ranks in 1981 and proposed legislation is being considered in several others. This category of the pari-mutuels industry has shown growth the past few years, not in the addition of many new states, and very little by building new tracks in states where legislation has already been passed, but rather by increasing the number of racing days at existing tracks. Many are becoming year around operations.

Actually the increase in volume has been affected more by the trend of holding two sessions per day. For a long time, greyhound racing was almost totally a night operation. Matinees, or day racing was quite rare. Experiments in matinee racing have proven successful enough to the point where, in 1980, there were 5522 night sessions and 2234 matinees. This fact is reflected in the per centage charts. This practice has fairly well leveled off at most locations. 1980 statistics really give a more accurate picture of the industry's status at the present time. The national trend is quite comparable with other types of racing, when viewed with the above facts taken into consideration. Average increase in handles and per capita betting is slightly higher than horse racing or jai alai, while attendance is lagging at about the same degree.

Some states show drastic increases and decreases in 1979 and 1980, but there is a logical reason for this. Experiments with increased matinees proved successful in some instances, while others were forced to adjust their racing schedules back closer to their original programs. The degree of increased volume gained from added matinee racing did not prove profitable in the long run at some locations. At others, it was the answer to their financial problems.

1980 had about 400 more performances than 1978, the total nationally being almost 8000. Almost exactly the same number of people attended in 1978 as in 1980 even with the additional 400 performances (approximately 21 million). However, per capita wagering increased by over 4% in 1979 and over 7% in 1980. This fact has made it possible to raise the volume of monies wagered from about 1 billion 875 million dollars in 1978 to over 2 billion in 1980. The revenue to states of 135 million in 1978 has increased proportionately. Future growth now depends on either passing legislation in new states, building more tracks in existing states now having greyhound legislation, or adding satellite betting to their agendas. Some states are taking a close look at the latter choice. Legislation is ongoing along these lines in Colorado at this writing. Other states are watching the results in Colorado with great interest.

RECAP OF PARI MUTUELS WAGERING ON JAI ALAI (1978)

FRONTONS	NUMBER OF RACING DAYS		TOTAL ATTENDANCE	TOTAL PARI MUTUELS HANDLE	TOTAL REVENUE TO STATE	DAILY AVERAGE	PER CAPITA
Connecticut	511	178M	2,609,101	236,838,881	19,605,358.00	343,743	90.77
Florida	1066	513M	4,606,685	287,768,674	16,961,023.15	182,247	62.47
Nevada	480	—	506,203	14,514,124	290,282.48	30,238	28.67
Rhode Island	199	—	492,376	28,434,073	1,454,665.84	142,885	57.75
TOTALS	2256	691M	8,214,365	567,555,752	38,311,329.47	192,588	69.09

M Denotes Matinees

PERCENTAGES OF INCREASE OR DECREASE PER PERFORMANCE IN ATTENDANCE, MUTUELS HANDLE AND PER CAPITA WAGERING ON: JAI ALAI

Percentages of increase or decrease in attendance, mutuels handle and per capita wagering on Jai Alai frontons by states. 1979-1980 figures are in comparison to 1978. 1978 figures were compiled from figures furnished by the individual State Racing Commission's Annual Reports. 1979-1980 figures are based on statistics furnished by the National Association of Jai Alai Frontons, Inc.

STATE	ATTENDANCE PER PERFORMANCE	HANDLE PER PERFORMANCE	PER CAPITA PER PERFORMANCE
	1979-1980	1979-1980	1979-1980
Connecticut	−10.4	− 9.1	+ 1.4
Florida	− 0.1	+10.3	+10.9
Rhode Island	−37.7	−22.8	+23.7
Nevada	—	—	—
TOTALS	− 7.1	− 0.3	+ 6.6

JAI ALAI

In 1978 Jai Alai frontons were in operation in four states; Connecticut, Florida, Nevada, and Rhode Island, at sixteen different locations. Ten of these frontons were located in Florida, the first state to legalize pari-mutuels wagering on this sport in 1953. $287,768,674 was wagered by 4,606,685 paid customers during 1978. Revenue to the state of Florida was approximately 17 million dollars. The fronton at West Palm Beach was destroyed by fire since that date *and at this writing* is under construction for re-opening next season. In the past, Florida frontons operated only during the winter months to coincide with the tourist season. The Florida legislation in 1980 approved summer dates for jai alai in certain counties. The first two frontons to take advantage of this new legislation, Dania and Miami, met with very favorable results.

Connecticut had only three frontons in operation in 1978, but had 689 performances as compared to 1579 performances in Florida. Their average handle, per performance, was $343,743 as compared to $182,247 in Florida. This was largely due to exposure to more heavily populated areas and less competition from other sports than that of several of the frontons in Florida.

Rhode Island had only one fronton in operation in 1978 but averaged $148,885 per performance, a very respectable average, considering that legislation was not passed until 1976.

The two frontons operating in Nevada in 1978 are not open at this writing. Both were a part of the MGM Grand Hotel's operations, one in Las Vegas and the other in Reno. The fire at their hotel in Las Vegas forced the closing of the fronton in that city, and the one in Reno was closed because the volume of betting was not large enough to warrant keeping it open. Although the betting handle in Las Vegas is not as large as was expected, the attendance is very good. Actually, the attendance was not all that bad in Reno either, but the per capita wagering was low. Both operations appeared to be very well managed, so it seems that reasons for the volume of betting not being larger in either city were that; they were in direct competition with casino wagering; and that the customers were largely tourists. Many had never seen the game played before and were not in these cities long enough to learn the game of jai alai well enough to bet on the games to any great extent. However, the fronton in Las Vegas plans to re-open when MGM has completed its repairs, probably by the early summer of 1981.

Attendance figures in 1980 were down a little over 7% but the four states still drew approximately eight million fans, who bet close to 575 million dollars for the year. Jai Alai followed the same trend as the different categories of horse racing in per capita betting. Per capita betting was up 6.6%.

RECAP OF PARI MUTUELS WAGERING ON OTB (1978)

STATES	NUMBER OF RACING DAYS	TOTAL ATTENDANCE	TOTAL PARI MUTUELS HANDLE	TOTAL REVENUE TO STATE	DAILY AVERAGE	PER CAPITA
Connecticut			114,731,495			
New York			1,206,530,268			
TOTALS			1,321,261,763			

OTB

Off track betting is limited at the present time to Connecticut and New York except in the cases of Nevada and New Jersey where it is connected with gambling casinos. New York had a 13.7% increase in 1979 over their 1978 total of one billion two hundred six million, and another 6.6% increase in 1980 over 1979 to reach a figure of almost one billion four hundred sixty three million. These increases show up quite favorably with the handle gains at the thoroughbred and harness tracks in the same state. In 1978 the money wagered at all track sites was one billion, five hundred sixty million as opposed to OTB's one billion two hundred six million. This means that 43.6% of all monies wagered on races in New York went through OTB parlors.

Connecticut was down slightly in their 1979-1980 totals for OTB parlors, but this figure is misleading, since the Teletrack in New Haven handled fifty three and a half million dollars. It would also be misleading to say that off track betting was increased by the total handled at Teletrack, since some of that amount actually originated from OTB sites. Overall, the state showed a substantial gain in betting at locations other than the actual tracks in 1980. Combined totals from OTB and Teletrack was more than one hundred sixty six million. Another Teletrack type operation is in the plans in another part of the state and will probably be opened in the near future.

PERCENTAGE OF INCREASE OR DECREASE IN HANDLE OF OFF TRACK BETTING

Percentage of increase or decrease of Off Track Betting by states. 1979 figures are in comparison to 1978 and 1980 figures are in comparison to 1979 in the case of New York. Connecticut 1979-1980 figures are a comparison to their 1978 figures.

	1979	1979-1980
Connecticut	—	− 1.8
New York	+13.7	+ 6.6
TOTALS	+13.7	+ 5.9

Chapter Nine
The Pros and Cons of Legalizing Pari-Mutuels

The obvious questions after studying the statistics in the preceeding chapters are:

Why do some states accept and legalize pari-mutuels wagering as a means of raising revenue and others do not?

Why do the states that *have* accepted and legalized pari-mutuels wagering on one or more of the sports used for this purpose exclude the others? (Florida is the only one of the fifty states now legalizing all five sports.)

The answers are many and varied. I will list the ten answers most often offered and attempt to explain their validity or *hypocrisy*.

1. "We are a sparsely populated state, and we don't have any localities that would be able to support a pari-mutuels operation from a population standpoint." Let's use the state of Montana as an example. Dog racing has been tried there several times, and was never financially successful. Three cities have been involved; Butte, Great Falls, and Billings. Sometimes, a track is poorly planned, and badly operated. This may be the actual reason for failure. The lack of population is used as an excuse. I feel you can discount that theory in Montana. P. C. Hartwell, (who is now head of the racing department in Tijuana, Mexico and has been a racing official all of his adult life), was instrumental in one of the operations in Great Falls and it didn't go. He had a world of experience at the time, and in my estimation is extremely knowledgeable and efficient. The track probably failed because the people just weren't there to draw from. That was some time ago. Who's to say that it would fail now, considering the increase in Great Fall's population. Several states other than Montana face this problem.

2. "Our area has a history of breeding and racing a particular kind of animal." "The public would not support any of the other kinds of racing." There might be more merit to this argument than appears at first glance. Several examples exist. Arizona has fared moderately well with thoroughbred and dog racing, but when they tried harness racing in the Phoenix area, they had two disasters. The first came at Sportsman's Park, well within the city limits where numerous thoroughbred meetings had been held with moderate success, so location was not a factor. The operators had successful operations in New York, so they knew the business. The horses and drivers, as well as the officials, were of top caliber. The only logical reason left was lack of interest in that particular sport in the area. The second attempt, several years later, again had experienced promotors, good horses, and personnel, plus a very modern track. The facilities were several miles from

the downtown area, but its location could not have been a major detriment because when a thoroughbred track was built a similar distance from downtown, it's volume was higher than in its old location. Probably harness racing failed because there was no market for it. As another example, harness racing and thoroughbreds do well in New York, Ohio, and Kentucky, but when quarter horses were introduced in the same areas, support was almost nil. Promoters are still trying to interest the public in the new sport, but with little success so far. By contrast, in Louisiana and New Mexico, quarter horses hold up remarkably well. Probably the best example of all would be Denver, Colorado. I use 1976 for an example, because during that year thoroughbreds, quarter horses and harness horses were all raced at the same facility at different times of the year. Dog racing was conducted approximately ten miles away at another track. According to figures released by the Colorado Racing Commission, the average daily handle for the dogs was $557,565; thoroughbreds $301,210; quarter horses $183,524; and harness horses $107,475. The average daily attendance was 7,399 at the dogs; 3,946 at the thoroughbreds; 2,482 at the quarter horses; and 1,579 at the harness races. I can already hear cries of "foul" from the three branches of horse racing, as these figures show the greyhound industry in a very favorable light. There are several reasons the dogs might have the edge in this particular area. First of all, the greyhound dates were in the summer and at night, whereas the horses raced during the day, and their dates extended into the cold months. Undoubtedly other areas in the United States would show a different ratio. In Denver, the dogs got off to a good start from the day they first opened the gates. It's been "catch up" every since, for the horses, especially the quarter horses and harness horses who came upon the scene long after the dogs were well established.

3. "The citizens of our state have a large investment in certain areas of racing and an influx of other interests would jeopardize those investments." This point is extremely controversial. The in-fighting on this issue has done much to harm racing's image as a whole. Once one or more forms of racing has been legalized in a state, and excludes others, those excluded try to promote their interests. Those already in existence are the newcomer's strongest adversaries. It is quite understandable from a business standpoint, but the means they use to keep the others out are questionable from a moral standpoint, to say the least. Their lobbying against these newcomers vary from shading the truth to downright "dirty pool". The result can be mistrust of the entire pari-mutuels industry. The time and money spent to defeat these new efforts could be of more benefit to themselves by a constructive approach, and co-operation with the new phase of the industry. In many cases, the existing operations could convert their existing facilities and gain additional income, either by leasing them to the new business, or even adding the new form of racing to their own program. There has been a limited number of situations where this has been done, and more are in the planning

stage. It is surely worth considering by those now using the negative approach.

4. "The area is already saturated with pari-mutuels operations, and any additional ones would tend to drain the economy, regardless of the type of new racing proposed." This argument seems to have much merit in some areas, very little in others. The New England area provides proof that it is possible to over-saturate an area with too many racing dates, regardless of what kinds are involved. This problem has been magnified by the fact that several of the states are very small, and can draw business from their neighbors. Competition has become so intense that several tracks have had to either close, or convert their facilities to another form of racing in order to survive. Since each state has its own laws and rules, only voluntary co-operation can help the situation. Some of these parties, state and private concerns, do not care to compromise. I'm convinced that in the long run, this approach will be a detriment to their own interests. In larger states, some are using the New England area as an argument to further their fight against licensing additional tracks. In some cases the argument might apply, but in others it is strictly a self serving devise to avoid competition.

5. "The type of racing we now have is more honest than the ones proposed, and is easier to control." To me, any statement having to do with the degree of honesty in one branch of racing, as opposed to that of another, is nothing more than a cop-out. I might agree that some operations are easier to control than others. However, there are adequate rules and regulations governing each and every type of racing. If, in fact, some are more honest or dishonest than others, the fault lies not in the type of racing, but rather with those officials charged with seeing that the rules are followed and enforced. If an operation is dishonest, those in charge are not living up to the promise they made when racing was legalized, and when they were given a license to operate their business. It's up to the Racing Commission representatives, and the operators of the track, to co-operate with each other and maintain a constant effort to make sure the intent of the rules are followed to the letter.

6. "Our area has a low per-capita earning rate, and the people are not economically capable of supporting another business in the recreational field." Here we get into a sensitive area since it involves getting into government's role of protecting the public, as opposed to the rights of the individual of deciding for himself what he can or cannot afford. Is it fair to legalize racing in areas where the people are affluent and not in areas where they are poor? The final judgment rests with the governing body in each area.

7. "Pari-mutuel wagering of any kind would take customers away from other forms of entertainment that are already established, such as automobile racing, professional sports, etc." The question really is whether it is wise or ethical to protect the investments of one or more business groups from a new one that will undoubtedly take some profits from the former. Of

course all of the *existing* businesses did not start at one time. So at one time or another, those now operating were professing their rights to compete with others that had already been established. Where do you draw the line? This argument seems specious.

8. "Even though the public desires and would support racing, the politicians now in power are opposed to it for various reasons, and will not approve legislation to legalize it." This reasoning is what you hear least, and probably justifiably so. If the public really wants pari-mutuels wagering, they will eventually get their way. But it is becoming more and more a controversial political issue at election time.

9. "Betting would increase the crime rate, and bring an undesirable element into the community." This issue is most heatedly debated when the possibility of legalized betting is raised. I'm afraid that those who believe betting causes crime are using emotion and not facts. Opponents of pari-mutuels often use this argument, knowing full well that this might sway those who are undecided on the issue. But the question remains, does a track or fronton bring in crime? A few years ago, this issue became a major factor in an attempt to open a new track in an area that had not had racing in any form before. I sent out a questionaire to about fifty law enforcement agencies that had operating tracks in their jurisdictions. The response was great, and the results more conclusive than even I had anticipated. These law enforcement officers concluded that there was little or no increase in crime or an influx of an undesirable element in their communities. Traffic control was their greatest concern.

10. "Gambling, in any form—legal or illegal—is immoral." Obviously, you can not deal with facts when debating the pros and cons on this particular issue. I respect the rights of those who oppose gambling on these grounds, if in fact it is their true and honest belief. However, I deplore the use of this argument by those who are using it, not through conviction, but in order to further their interests in other areas. For example, in protecting *their* professional sports franchises.

These last two arguments, of course, are powerful to those who don't know much about the business of pari-mutuels. Nobody wants a business that would bring in a bad class of people, maybe even members of organized crime. And, if you believe that betting on something is morally bad, well, you just believe that. Nobody can convince you otherwise, even if someone points out that legalizing gambling gives you the means to control it. Besides, somebody in every state is always betting on something, from football to cards to whether it'll rain tomorrow. As for the charge that the pari-mutuels business brings in nothing but criminals, I'd have to deny that. Certainly there are dishonest people in the business. Name a business where there isn't, including the practice of law. But my experience convinces me that the proportion of cheaters and dishonest persons associated with this business is not greater than in other businesses. Organized crime certainly has tried to get its fingers into legitimate gambling, but its success probably has been greater with its hundreds of other legitimate enterprises from real-estate to vending machines.

All in all, it seems remiss to me not to get the revenue from pari-mutuels betting, and control it at the same time. For those who participate in the pari-mutuels, or who will in the future, it might be helpful to know just how pari-mutuel operations are set up and run.

Chapter Ten
Problems of Legislation and Regulation

In order to discuss these problems clearly it seems we must first separate the states into two categories. Those who have not legalized pari-mutuels operations in any form and those already having laws permitting wagering on one or more of the five sports involved.

For different reasons there are nineteen states which still prohibit pari-mutuels wagering.

It is especially difficult for me to rationalize the resistance of citizens to legalize pari-mutuels wagering in states that are surrounded by states that already have racing. It's a foregone conclusion that a certain percentage of their population travel to these neighboring states to attend the races. In this way, states without pari-mutuels are contributing business and revenue to a state that does. There are many areas of the country where this is now the case. A couple of good examples would be Texas and Iowa. Texas is surrounded on three sides by existing tracks. El Paso is the main contributor to Sunland Park, located a few hundred yards inside the border of New Mexico, as well as to the Juarez combination horse and dog track located in Old Mexico, but only five miles from downtown El Paso. Santa Fe Downs, Ruidoso, the New Mexico State Fair at Albuquerque and La Mesa Park, all located in New Mexico, depend largely on Texas money for their success. Louisiana Downs in Shreveport, Louisiana, and Oaklawn Park in Hot Springs, Arkansas are close enough to Dallas to draw heavily from this city, as well as the many towns between Shreveport and Dallas. The Houston and Beaumont areas are the main contributors to Delta Downs, located a few miles from the Texas border. The impact from this area is also felt at Evangeline Downs to a lesser degree, since it is 100 miles farther east, but still is great enough to influence their volume of business at different times of the year.

Iowa, although not a populous state itself, contributes considerably to three states: South Dakota, Nebraska, and Illinois. There are three tracks within ten miles of downtown Sioux City. South Dakota has a horse track and a dog track just inside the state line, and Nebraska has a horse track equally as close. Although not a large city, Sioux City provides the nucleus of customers for all three tracks. Farther to the south, tracks at Omaha and Lincoln, Nebraska are but a short drive from the Iowa line. A harness track at East Moline, Illinois is directly across the river from Davenport on the eastern side of the state.

Another factor not usually considered, is the influx of families from other areas, to work in various capacities at a new track or fronton. Assuming a state enforces the 85% local employee rule, there is still a considerable number who would not be living in this area otherwise. When you consider that the remaining portion of the 15% usually bring their families, it results in a boost in the overall economy. Rentals, supermarkets, department stores, doctors, dentists, and service stations are just a few of the businesses that are favorably affected by these additional residents.

I have never been able to understand the logic of businessmen opposing the construction of a race track in their immediate vicinity. I can understand why residents from distant counties or neighboring states would object. A small portion of their population would definitely spend some of their money in the area where the track is located, rather than in their own community.

Simply wanting a pari-mutuels operation, of course, means nothing unless the state allows betting. More and more states are considering legalizing pari-mutuels betting and other types of wagering to provide the substantial revenue lost to recent Federal budget cuts and tax cuts.

Sponsors of a racing bill usually have a certain form of operation in mind. For instance: thoroughbreds only; harness racing only; quarter horses only; greyhounds only; jai alai only; or a combination of two or more. Seldom is it a blanket bill that will permit any type of pari-mutuels wagering.

Ordinarily the attempt for new legislation reflects the need for pari-mutuels wagering as a medium to expand the interests of an already established fringe business. In states or communities where thoroughbred breeding farms and training centers are a part of the economy, a track to race these animals is needed in their immediate area in order to realize the most from their investments. The same is true of the other categories. So when legislation is proposed, these certain groups are naturally interested in their own category.

Let's assume first that the legislature has authorized wagering, and many entrepreneurs are wanting to set up their pari-mutuels operations. What's needed now is a state agency that will supervise and regulate these operations, helping to administer the many complicated details of horse and dog racing, or jai alai.

This governing body is set up within the state's executive branch, often in the Department of Commerce. In states where racing, but no jai alai, lotteries or casino betting, has been authorized, it's usually called the Racing Commission. States that permit a broad range of gambling call it by other names, for example, the Gaming Commission. By whatever name, the primary duties are the same: to oversee wagering facilities (including assigning dates for racing seasons); to audit books; to license all gaming personnel; to initiate investigations of alleged wrongdoing; to provide testing facilities for racing animals; and, to ensure that all operations are efficiently, safely and honestly run.

Permits to build racing sites and frontons must be given by the Racing Commission, Gaming Commission, or whatever body is charged with this duty by the laws of a particular state. These bodies are politically appointed, and it's they who encourage or discourage competition (meaning profit and attendance) within the state. This Commission must rule on who will be granted permits. This same Commission has the duty of deciding what dates a permittee may operate, and how many performances they can have during this period. Theoretically, this is to protect the public from being exposed to too many days of racing per year. It really protects the permittee from excessive competition, and in theory keeps the economy of the area on an even keel. Usually, the Commissioners are not to blame for what seems to be unfair allotment of dates and the issuing of racing permits. They are forced, by law, to stay within the framework of the rules passed by the legislature. There are cases, however, where permits and dates are awarded along political, rather than practical lines.

The legislators in turn, cannot be held totally responsible for seemingly unfair and impractical provisions in the pari-mutuels bill. At times it is necessary to compromise more than they would like in order to get a bill of any kind passed.

Usually the strongest opponents of the bill are not from outside interests, but from those segments of the industry being excluded or that is already legalized. A good example is the repeated failure of efforts to include greyhound racing in the pari-mutuels structure in California. Established horse interests have lobbied extensively against these proposals. Of course, in some cases, it is possible their objections were not so much against competition, as they were the way in which the bill was written, or the identity of those who would provide the competition. In cases, however, where competition is the only factor, I feel they are over reacting. If an already established business is doing a good job, they won't see a mass exodus to the new type of racing. Rather, the new form of competition will help create new business for the category already established. Certainly their objections will cast doubts on their own business, unless the nature of these objections are spelled out in a constructive and fair manner.

When original legislation passes, the Racing Commission is usually made up of members active or knowledgeable in this particular kind of sport. If later, another category is added to that particular state's program, it is only natural that the commissioners continue to favor their own sport, which they understand more fully, when it comes to granting permits and allotting dates. This can be overcome, it seems, by establishing a separate commission for each type of racing. The separate commissions still have to work in harmony to produce the best results for all. Some states are moving in this direction.

Granting new permits creates a monumental problem for a Racing Commission if there is more than one applicant for a certain location. The Commissioners are often placed in the position of weighing the advantages presented by an experienced organization with active operations in other states, or even in other communities of the same state, as opposed to an applicant new to the industry. Often, this new applicant is a resident of the community in which the new track will be built. The experienced applicant has tangible evidence of the quality of operation that he will run. Will his experience overshadow the advantages of the "newcomer", if this "newcomer" is respected in his home community? Does the "newcomer's" track record in other businesses indicate that he can adjust to the unique problems of the pari-mutuels industry? This industry has no exact counterpart. Ask Bill Veeck, the past owner of several baseball franchises, as to the differences. Or simply read his book *"Thirty Tons a Day"* which vividly describes his frustration when he switched from operating a baseball club to managing a horse track in New England. This is not to imply that previous experience is a must for an honest and successful operation. But I do believe a novice to the business must be prepared to keep an open mind, be interested in the sport (aside from its monetary gains), and be prepared to operate the business for a long period of time, not just get it started and unload it to a group that already has numerous other racing operations or jai alai frontons. It is my conviction that if the pari-mutuels industry ever rapidly declines or fails entirely, the number one cause would be the trend toward monopolies. I'm not saying a person or organization should be limited to one operation, especially in cases where permits for racing or jai alai are seasonal. It is often beneficial to everyone concerned for the same group to operate a circuit that covers practically the entire year. This may involve two or possible three different locations. This ensures year-around racing for kennel owners and racing stables and steady employment for permanent officials and employees. It often saves infighting for choice dates, and prevents overlapping dates. It makes it possible to utilize supplies and equipment on a yearly basis, a very healthy situation.

Yet competition is an incentive for better racing and operational procedures. It's already limited enough by the nature of alotting a specified number of permits at the Commission's discretion. The Commissions are not only faced with these decisions in regard to new licenses, but again when the track is sold. The Commission is responsible for the approval of the sale to a qualified person or organization. Sale situations in many cases make the decision even harder than new permits. Often the operation is for sale, because it is losing money. It may be that the only buyer available is one who has one or more successful operations elsewhere and can use these profits to upgrade the new purchase. The desire for continued operation of the facility by the local residents, plus the threat of loss of an established revenue source may encourage the Commissioners to approve a sale that they would ordinarily reject.

A lengthy court and legislative battle in Arizona illustrates the problems of Commissions, permit-seekers, and monopolies. All six greyhound tracks, plus one of the three commercial horse tracks, were owned by the same interest for many years. The legislature finally passed a bill requiring that at least two of these tracks be sold to other parties. This was finally accomplished in November, 1980. The main reason given for the bill's passage was that a monopoly was not a healthy situation for the state or for racing.

Large food and beverage concessionaires who invest in race tracks are another consideration for Commissions and those seeking permits. These investors, I believe, must be limited to a reasonable number of operations. One such company, however, is reported to have interests in tracks and frontons in twenty or more states, in addition to foreign countries. It is hard to pinpoint exactly how many actual operations they control, since they are listed under different names and subsidiary companies. Most of the inroads into these operations were made after various tracks or frontons were opened and an operation ran into financial trouble. The company often loans operating money to the tracks, secured by lengthy food and drink concession leases. Such a concession company was one of the parties involved in the Arizona legislation. The dangers can be numerous, but I will mention two: one is the threat of a pari-mutuel monopoly going hand-in-hand with immense lobbying powers that can influence the industry as a whole. The second is intangible and is a factor at tracks and frontons depending on the size and success of departments other than food and drink concessions. Specifically, where profits are higher in the concession department than in the pari-mutuels department, a good business man will give first priority to the department showing the most profit. The racing and pari-mutuels departments becomes adjunct to the food-and-drink business. I feel the Racing Commissions would be wise to concentrate more attention on this department of operations where this situation exists. Indirectly, this can do much to upgrade the racing and pari-mutuels departments.

Many potential future problems can be alleviated where tracks or frontons are able to either operate their own concessions, or lease them to a local group.

When a Racing Commissioner is appointed, his qualifications (aside from political persuasions) usually are based upon his knowledge or previous participation in the sport involved. This seems sensible. A Commissioner needs knowledge and experience to wisely supervise the pari-mutuels operations. But it also can create another problem. Often, this Commissioner is in some way financially involved in one or more aspects of this sport. Many own or have direct interests in animals that will be competing in his home state. He will inevitably be faced with making rules or decisions that will affect himself. No matter how honest or fair this person is, it is almost impossible to convince other members of his business, or the customers that he is acting impartially. I can't suggest a complete solution, but there are some things that would help. First of all, if the Commissioner is a horse or dog owner or breeder, he could limit his participation in racing to states other than the one for which he is a Commissioner. Many Commissioners might feel this is too great a sacrifice, when compared to his contributions to the sport he is trying to help. Perhaps that's true if only a short period of time is being considered, but over the long haul, he would probably end up in better shape due to the good it would do the industry as a whole. In cases where track owners or managers face the same involvement, the same would pertain. Sooner or later, commission or track employees must make decisions that will directly or indirectly benefit or hurt their employers. I'm sure it would do much to increase the public's confidence and good will if they limited their involvement to states other than their own.

Aside from the unenviable burden the Commission faces in deciding which applicants should be given licenses to operate, they must decide how many licenses should be issued in their state, how many total racing days should be allowed and what exact calendar days the allotted dates should include. Commissioners in most states find it impossible to please everyone. About the only guidelines in racing bills that make this task easier in most states are: stipulations that pari-mutuels operations must not conflict with others during the same hours within a specified distance (for instance fifty or one hundred miles); a limit on the number of racing days a permittee or particular category of racing may operate during the year; and local-option provisions where voters may include or preclude such operations. All these items help, but big problems remain. In too many states, it is nearly impossible for the Commissioners to always vote as their consciences dictate. The political pressures are great. Sometime economics force the Commissioners to make unpopular decisions. Sometimes a small track that has battled for years to get their operation in the black is suddenly faced with opposition from a new track in a much more populated area, applying for the same racing dates. In such cases, the Commission is faced with the decision of protecting the interests of the small track or favoring the larger new one that will provide much more needed revenue. Solutions to this problem takes years of compromise to keep everyone reasonably satisfied. Usually it is never solved completely. If neighboring states are in competition for the choice dates, it adds another dimension to be considered in the Commission's final decision.

Alabama, one of the last states to legalize pari-mutuels wagering, has a new approach which so far seems to be working out well. While legislation is required at the state level, it is a local option system. A separate commission is provided for each county that has approved a racing operation. Supervision is much more localized in this way. The Commissioners are much more aware of the needs and desires of their communities. The biggest difficulty is finding Commissioners with the necessary experience and background. So far, Alabama seems to have overcome this obstacle. Their plan may be followed by states that pass pari-mutuels legislation in the future.

The diversity of legislative regulations from state to state has been a barrier in co-ordinating uniform rules. Various organizations have been formed by Pari-Mutuels Operators and the Racing Commissions to provide more co-operation and uniformity. They are now all trying to solve their regulation problems. One reason behind this effort is the threat of federal intervention to control all facets of legalized gambling. The trade organizations, however, can only go so far because they must limit the degree of their co-operation in conformity with the racing bills in their home state. One positive act has been to make reciprocal agreements, whenever possible, to honor the suspensions of persons who have broken the rules of racing in states other than their own. This is doing much toward eliminating the undesirable element from the industry nationwide.

The issue of medication has similarly unified Racing Commissions for the most part. Still, this is a terribly controversial subject. There are so many different opinions as to which drugs are harmful and which are not. No one is advocating the use of stimulants or depressants that would alter the outcome of a race. But there are medications intended to ease a racing animal's pain and discomfort, and it's in this area that the agreements must be reached by all Commissions.

The three most controversial drugs in the racing industry today are phenylbutazone (bute), used to ease pain and soreness; fuorsemide (lasix) used to control bleeding; and dimethyl sulfoxide (DMSO), an analgesic pain killer and sedative. Some believe these items are harmless and necessary. Some believe that they are not only harmful and unnecessary, but that they are being used in some cases to mask illegal substances. I am certainly not qualified to say what is good and what is bad or dangerous. But I know enough to speak out strongly for the betting public's right to know what medications have been administered to each animal competing. Also, to argue that the same set of rules governing the use of medication, agreed upon by the experts, should be enforced equally in all states. So long as horses and dogs are competing in two or more states, a bettor must rely on past performances from states other than his own. If medication standards are not the same, the animal's past performances will not only not be helpful, they will be misleading. A horse used to racing with the help of "bute" for instance, and suddenly having to race without it, cannot be expected to give the same level of performance. The same is true if the circumstances are reversed. I wouldn't venture to guess the percentage of loss in handle and revenue where these conditions exist. I do know the knowledgeable bettor has a "wait and see" attitude toward the animals racing under different conditions. Those depending on purses for their success must somehow be made to realize the impact that uniform medication regulations would have on their income. The entire industry will suffer until this problem is solved. The extreme views, being espoused by each side, for and against certain medications is unnecessarily eroding the public's confidence in racing. Here once more, the all-important Racing Commissions must take a principled stand.

Chapter Eleven
Where Does the Money Go?

What exactly happens to the money that you leave with the ticket seller when you make a wager at a track or fronton? How is it divided? Who benefits from its division?

The percentage deducted from each dollar wagered varies from state to state. Each state has its own laws and the percentage withheld remains constant, unless new legislation is passed changing this percentage. Most deductions fall into the range of from 15 to 20%. New York had a trial period with a takeout of 14%, but returned to a 17% figure in 1980.

These percentages include the deductions for monies for both Track and State. Each state has laws specifying the division of this percentage between Track and State. Some states use a sliding scale. The higher the volume of business, the higher the percentage paid to the state. In some states, two take-out figures are used. For example: 17% from the win, place, and show pools; and 20% from exotic pools. The logic expounded by those using the two figures is that the exotic pools result in much higher pay-offs, and won't discourage the bettors because of low returns on their investments. Some states receive a larger portion from the greyhound tracks and jai alai. This is reconciled by the fact that greyhound purses usually don't exceed 3%, while purses for thoroughbreds is usually in the neighborhood of 6½%.

Probably the easiest way to understand the system is to picture a dollar as a pie, as shown on the following page.

We will use a 15% take-out figure for our example. Breakage, or surplus, usually amounts to approximately ½ of 1% at operations where exotic pools predominate, to a little less than 1½% where only win, place, and show wagering is offered. We will assume the breakage will average 1%. This means that 84 cents out of each dollar will be returned to the public in the form of winning tickets.

This leaves 16 cents for the Track and State to divide. Let's assume that the law stipulates that 5 of these 16 cents shall go to the State as revenue. This leaves 11 cents for the track. The biggest share of this 11 cents, at a horse track, will go for purses, usually about 6½ cents. We are now down to 4½ cents. The Totalisator Company also works on a percentage basis. They receive about ½ cent for the older equipment and 6/10 of a cent for the cash-sell systems. Mutuels employees' percentage for wages, range from 1 to 1½ per cent. Lumping the two together, they will account for about 2 more cents. The track still has 2½ cents to work with. Depending on whether the law allows the track to keep the 1% breakage, or whether the state receives the 1%, or whether it is split 50-50, the track now has only from 1½ to 2½ cents to cover the remaining expenses.

15% Commission used for:

Commissions to State
Purses (3% dogs, 6.5% horses)
Pari-mutuels payroll (1.5% - 1%)
  General payroll
  Taxes
  Insurance
  Interest on investment
  Improvements
  Maintainence
  Advertising-Publicity
  Utilities
  Supplies
  Stationery
  Totalisator equipment
  Photofinish/Video replay/Closed Circuit TV
  Armored car service
  Ambulance service
  Bankroll

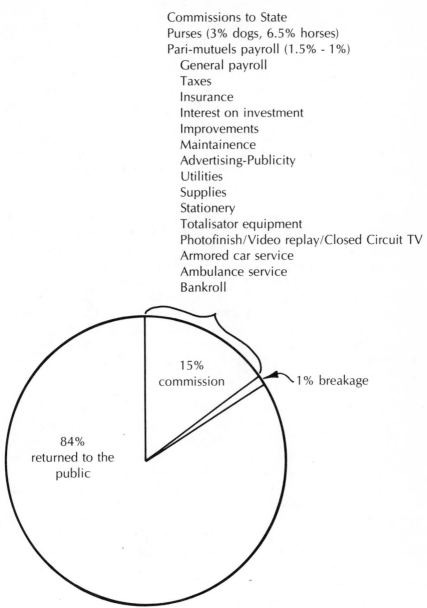

These expenses include: closed circuit TV, photo finish equipment, video replay, taxes, insurance, maintenance, utilities, advertising and publicity, improvements, interest on their investment, armored car service, ambulance service, bankroll for the mutuels department, the payroll for the racing department, legal fees, the general payroll (which includes the general manager, office personnel, parking lot attendants, admissions personnel, security, clean-up crews, doctors and first aid attendants, ushers and bartenders, cooks and waitresses, if the track also manages the concessions), equipment to condition the track, starting gates, and office equipment and supplies for the entire track. Impossible to do with even 2½ cents? You're correct! That's why the original take-out percentage often has to be increased. Assume the takeout is 17% and the track has an attitional 2 cents to work with. The problem is, that every time the take-out is increased, the volume decreases. Every state is constantly walking a tight line to reach a point where the maximum amount of revenue can be attained and still allow the track operators to show a reasonable profit for their investment and their efforts.

Fortunately, there are other sources of revenue for the track to make ends meet, even if the mutuels operation is operating at a loss. These sources include: parking fees, admissions, reserved seats, fees for feed and tack concessions, tip sheet sales, use of their facilities for things other than racing during the times of the year the track is not in operation, and souvenir shops. Some operations gain from the sale of programs, including the advertising sold that is part of the program. Others are content to make enough from the sale of programs to offset the cost of printing and distributing them. "Alpha boards" are a recent innovation for the sale of advertising between races at some tracks.

The most important source of income is the food and beverage concessions. If it weren't for this department, many tracks would have to fold. A person doesn't have to know a lot about the restaurant and bar business to figure out that if you have several thousand semi-festive people on your premises for several hours, the profits from this source has to be extensive. You have a captive audience, with no choice to shop for price or quality. Naturally, over-pricing, lack of quality, and poor service will cut into profits, but the American public expects to pay a little more for a little less, not only at tracks and frontons, but also at other entertainment and sporting events. This is not to imply that all operations are the same. Some tracks and frontons do sell good products and give good service at competitive prices, but they, unfortunately, are the exception rather than the rule. Racing is probably no better or no worse than other businesses, where captive audiences are involved. I do believe that it is an area that is not given the same degree of attention by the Racing Commission as is given to the racing and mutuels departments, even though the concessions are included in their jurisdiction.

Income from these concessions are handled in two different ways. The track or fronton may either operate this department themselves, or they may lease these concessions on a percentage basis. If the latter system is used, the lessee is either a local organization or one of several companies who specialize in food and beverage concessions on a national or international basis. Personally, I believe that, if at all possible, operating these concessions themselves or leasing to a local group will not only result in more profit to the track or fronton, but also in better relations with their customers.

So far, we have limited the concessions situation to facilities that serve the public. At most horse tracks, and some dog tracks, a "track kitchen" is maintained for employees during training hours. Horse tracks usually also have a snack bar in the jockey's quarters. Often the track will retain this portion of the concessions and lease the facilities which serve the betting public. Sometimes all concessions are leased to an outside interest.

Some tracks feel that the original cash outlay for restaurant equipment and their lack of expertise in managing this department will not justify the added income derived by keeping the concessions for themselves. Many find out very soon that they were mistaken, but by that time, it is too late. Most of the large companies insist on long term leases, and track management has no way to change directions for several years, once the leases have been signed.

The five cents going to the State in our illustration, is also distributed in many different ways, varying from state to state according to their particular laws. All states use a portion of this money to maintain the expenses involved in the operation of the Racing Commission and to pay the salaries of the Commissioners and their employees. The distribution of the balance is usually spelled out in the law legalizing pari-mutuels wagering. Some states specify in detail where this money is to go, such as a certain percentage for education, public parks, etc., while others simply specify that it be put into the General Fund of their State.

Contrary to the belief of many, the above illustrations prove that very little, if any, of the monies lost at a track by the public leaves the area in which the track is located. Most of it is actually redistributed in the form of purses, salaries, and goods and services of local businessmen. Owners of the tracks are not making huge profits, especially at horse tracks where the purses constitute a large share of the monies deducted. Some are even showing a loss in these times of inflation and rising costs. Certainly, very few recipients of these purses are showing large, if any profits. Most horse and greyhound owners are struggling to make a fair return on their investments and efforts. These owners also leave most of their purses in the local economy. Salaries of the employees are not enough to permit savings beyond their living costs. So most of the revenue and commissions going to the State and Track is returned to the general public in one form or another.

About the only money leaving the area of the track is limited to the concessionaires in the cases where this department is leased to non-local companies, the minimal profits of totalisator companies, non-local photo finish and video patrol companies, and the few ultra successful horse and dog owners. Actually, most of these owners end up being local residents, especially where long racing seasons are involved.

Many states are allotting some of their revenue for Breeders Awards. When a horse wins a race at a track in the state in which he was born, the owner of the colt at the time he was foaled, receives a part of the purse. There are also certain races where all the horses must have been born in the state where the race is being held in order to be eligible to compete. A supplement is added to the purses of these special races, so that all the horses sharing in the purse will receive more money than in races not so designated. Stipulations as to what constitutes a "local bred" may vary, to a small degree, from state to state. An example: in Louisiana, a "Louisiana Bred" is either one who was both conceived and born in Louisiana, or when it was conceived in another state but born in Louisiana. In the latter case, his mother must be bred again to a horse standing at stud in Louisiana, to be eligible. This practice is designed to improve the quality of locally bred horses and to encourage an expansion of the breeding industry in the home state. Further, in a round-about way, this serves the purpose of keeping purse money from leaving the state in which it was paid.

Accepting the fact that some portion of the take-out is leaving the area by the above groups, this figure is overshadowed by the money being brought in by tourists and customers from outlying areas of the state, which have no track of their own, or from neighboring states. Not only is this influx of money reflected in the increased revenue to the track, but also it increases the volume of business of local motel owners, service station operators, restaurants, and bars as well as many other related businesses.

PART THREE

The Pari-Mutuels System

Chapter Twelve
The Modern Pari-Mutuels System and How It Works

The betting public, and many race-track folk, probably understand the pari-mutuel system less than any other facet of the sport involved, so that, ironically, the guts of betting—how pay-offs and odds are determined—remain a mysterious portion of the sport's anatomy. A dictionary will merely tell you that pari-mutuels is "A system of betting on races or games, whereby the winners divide the net amount of monies wagered in proportion to the sums bet." Meaning, that the net amount of monies is that which is left from any individual betting pool, after the proper commissions have been deducted for distribution to the track and state, according to the laws of that particular state. But there is much more to the system than this. The tracks must make the distribution correctly, paying the right amount to the state and to the holders of winning tickets. The state must oversee and audit the track's distribution procedure, and deposit the state's share to the proper state agency in accordance with the state's legislation (or "Racing Bill").

Many bettors wonder what the track does with its share. It's used to pay for all expenses involved in the operation of the track, and for profits if any money is left. Otherwise the track acts only as an agent to distribute the monies bet. The patrons are wagering against each other and not against the track. The term "Gambler" is defined as "one who wagers on the outcome of a race, game, or a contest of any kind" one exposed to hazard or risk." Track operators do not fit this definition, but it's a term often used to describe them by persons unfamiliar with the pari-mutuels system. Their challenge is the same as any other businessman's: to generate enough business volume to meet operational costs. Race results do not reflect in their profits or losses. Only their track's attractiveness, its efficiency, and the laws governing pari-mutuel Commission (or track and state "take-outs") affect the profit. The percentages withheld vary from state to state, and some states withhold more from the Exotic Pools than from Win, Place, and Show Pools.

In any given state, incidentally, the basic take-out percentage remains constant. Any change requires a legislative act. The breakdown of the track's share and the state's share is sometimes figured on a sliding scale. When an operation reaches a certain volume, the track's share becomes less and the state's share greater. Normally, the percentages withheld are within a range of 15% to 18%.

But, how exactly does the pari-mutuels system function for bettor and track operator?

POOLS

First of all, there are several separate betting pools to deal with. Win, Place, and Show pools are used at every track in America. The other pools are "Exotic Pools" or "Gimmicks".

These include the Daily Double, Quinellas (spelled Quiniela in some states), Exactas or Perfectas, Trifectas, Big Q's, Big Perfectas or Big Exactas, and Double Doubles.

Most of these Exotic Pools, with the exception of the Daily Double, are fairly new, and came into being because sophisticated computer systems could calculate these pools rapidly and accurately. Seldom are more than two of these Exotic Pools used on any one race.

The first thing for bettors to remember is that each pool is an entity. Money bet in one pool is never transferred to another, except in very, very rare cases at small tracks, where no winning tickets have been sold on a particular entry in a particular pool. Even then, provisions are made to distribute the money to the public in accordance with the pari-mutuels rules. For example, if no winning tickets were sold on the winner in the Win Pool, the net amount of the money in the Win Pool would be distributed to the persons with Place tickets on the same entry.

WIN POOL (or The "Straight" Pool)

To share in the Win Pool, a bettor must select the entry which actually finishes first. In cases of Dead Heats (two entries tying for first place), the pool is shared by bettors on both entries. The approximate odds showing on the infield display board reflect the per cent of profit per dollar for each entry. Example: An entry showing odds of 5-1 must pay at least $12.00 for a two dollar ticket. This is determined by multiplying five times each dollar bet ($10.00 profit) plus the original cost of the ticket ($2.00).

PLACE POOL

The Place Pool is designed for second place finishers in the race. However, ticket holders of the winning entry and the entry finishing second, share equally in the profits. Finishing first or second will not change the pay-off for either entry.

SHOW POOL

The Show Pool involves the first three finishers in the race. Profits are divided equally among all three entries, and pay-offs will not change regardless of whether they finish first, second, or third.

QUINELLA or QUINIELA POOL

Winners in a Quinella Pool are required to select the first two finishers, regardless of who wins and who places second. Payoffs remain the same in either case. Example: entries finish 7-5. Holders of 5-7 tickets receive the same pay-off as if they had finished 5-7.

EXACTA or PERFECTA POOL

"Exacta" and "Perfecta" mean the same thing. Some tracks use one term, others the opposite. The requirements are the same. The first two entries to finish must be selected, as in the Quinella, but this pool requires betting on the exact order of finish. Example: If the finish is 7-5, winning tickets must read 7-5. Holders of 5-7 tickets are not winners. Only in the case of a Dead Heat, would either combination be valid, and then the pay-offs would be calculated according to the rules of a Place Pool.

TRIFECTA POOL

The Trifecta Pool is identical to the Exacta or Perfecta, except that it is required to select the first *three* finishers in the exact order of finish.

BIG "Q" POOL

The Big "Q" is in reality a parlay of two Quinellas in succession. It is a pool entirely independent of the regular Quinella Pool. Winning tickets are determined in the same manner as the regular Quinella. But instead of a bettor collecting money for selecting the first two finishers of the first Quinella race, those winning tickets must be exchanged for choices to win the second Quinella in the following race. No further money is required, but you must have a valid ticket from the first half of the Big "Q' Pool to exchange for every combination you wish to bet in the second half. If you have only one winning combination, you can only receive one ticket in return. If you have more than one winner, you can get the same number of exchange tickets. (Big "Q" tickets purchased in a race designated as the first half of a Big "Q" Pool limits the holders of winning tickets to participation in the second half of this pool (the following race.) Those who had winning tickets in the regular Quinella Pool in the race designated as the first half of a Big "Q" Pool do not have the option of participating in the Big "Q" Pool, but must cash their winning tickets for the amount of the pay-off in the regular Quinella Pool for that race.

"BIG PERFECTA" or "BIG EXACTA" POOL

The "Big Perfecta", or "Big Exacta" Pool works in the same manner as the "Big Q", the exception being that the rules of the Perfecta or Exacta, described earlier, apply in determining winning tickets. Of course, there are times when no one eligible to participate in the second half of the pool selects a winning combination. There are provisions and regulations, called

"Consolation Pools", to insure that all monies in any given pool is distributed to the public in a fair and equitable way.

DAILY DOUBLE POOL

The Daily Double Pool was the first wide-spread form of Exotic wagering. This pool usually involves the first two races of a Racing Program. It requires that you correctly select the winners of both the first and second race. Winners of this pool are not determined until after the running of the second race, but selections must be made before the start of the first race. The Double was originally used primarily to get the public to the track early, and was usually the only form of Exotic wagering offered. It has remained a popular pool in most areas, and is still used by most tracks.

DOUBLE DOUBLE POOL

The Double Double Pool is simply a system of selecting two Daily Doubles in succession on the same program, and follows the same general rules which apply to the Big "Q" and the Big Perfecta and Big Exacta. This pool usually makes for huge pay-offs for a $2.00 investment, but creates some complications since it is much harder to select winners of four successive races than it would at first appear. The Double Double has drawbacks. The pool usually ends up with the pay-offs being made in different Consolation procedures, which are fair but confusing to all but the most knowledgeable patrons. Also the monies wagered in this pool are tied up for four races before the correct pay-off can be determined. Since money volume is the chief factor in a track's income, tying up even one pool for four races reduces this volume, and so some oppose the Double Double for this reason. However, this objection must be weighed against the benefits of larger pay-offs which please the bettors and create free publicity to encourage more people to come to the track. The Big "Q", the Big Perfecta and Big Exacta Pools, it should be noted, tie up money for only two races, not four as with the Double Double.

PROFITS, PAY-OFFS, BREAKAGE, ODDS

"Profits" and "Pay-offs" are key terms in understanding how a pari-mutuels system works. Misunderstanding them causes many people to think there is dishonesty in the money distribution of the pools, especially in the Place and Show Pools. "Profits" means money available for distribution after a winner's initial investment has been paid off. "Pay-off" means both the initial investment's return and a share of the remaining profits. Let's look at these basic principles. We'll assume we are at a track where the combined commissions ("take-out") for the Track and State is 15%. When the money in any given pool has been totaled, fifteen cents is immediately deducted from each dollar wagered to cover these Commissions. This leaves eighty-five cents (less "breakage," explained soon) to pay those having winning tickets. But, the eighty-five cents is not paid off equally among the winners, as at first glance it seems it should be. First, everyone holding a winning ticket must be repaid the amount he has invested for a winning ticket. When this has been done, the monies *remaining* are "Profits." They are then divided equally. Said another way, the only profit derived from a pool is the monies bet on the losing entries, less the 15% commission, less the actual dollars used to reimburse the winning tickets, and less the "Breakage." "Breakage" and "Surplus" mean the same thing. When the profits are divided equally in the calculating process, and a pay-off figure arrived at, the amount of profits per dollar is usually figured to the nearest dime.* Since state laws require that every winning ticket must be repaid in full, plus a profit of at least five cents per dollar (in most cases, ten cents per dollar). "Breakage" enters the picture whenever the profits per dollar fall between one ten-cent level and the next ten-cent level above. Thus, if the actual "profit" is eighty-six cents per dollar the holder of the winning ticket receives eighty cents profit, and the other six cents is put into a "breakage fund." This fund goes to the State, the Track, or to both, depending on the laws of the particular state involved. Breakage will vary according to the type of pools. The more exotic the pool, the less breakage. The extremes would be from close to 1½% using only Win, Place and Show Pools, to one-half of one percent where the major portion of wagering is in the Exotic Pools. Eight-tenths of one percent is close to the average.

Once Breakage and all other "take-outs" have been calculated, it's time for the pay-off. The pay-off for holders of tickets that have been calculated to pay eighty cents profit per dollar would be $3.60 for each $2.00 ticket, the standard minimum wager—$.80 X 2 ($1.60) plus the $2.00 originally paid for the ticket. The pay-off prices announced at the track and posted on the display boards (called Odds Boards or Tote Boards), and those published in

---

*Some states have provisions whereby it may be figured to the nearest nickel, if paying to the nearest dime would result in a loss to the pool. In racetrack language, this is called a Minus Pool.

newspapers or other sources usually reflect the value of a $2.00 ticket even though one dollar is the measuring stick for the calculations, and even though tickets are available in varying amounts up to $100.00. In recent years, tickets for Pools sometimes have a minimum price of $3.00 or $5.00. In that case, the "pay-offs" are posted at *this* minimum value.

The public display boards as well as the closed circuit TV systems show the odds determining the Win Pool and Exotic Pool pay-offs. These odds change at regular intervals as the wagering progresses, and are entirely determined by the bettors. Note that it's impossible to post approximate pay-off odds in the Place and Show Pools, because those prices will vary according to the order of finish (as explained later).

Sophisticated display boards will show the amounts bet on each entry and the periodic pool totals during the pre-race betting period. A bettor who knows about profits, pay-offs, and odds can, with practice, get some idea of the pay-off he can expect. An expert can determine the minimum he will receive, by doing a rough calculation, based on his selection and the favorite finishing one-two in the Place Pool, and his selection and the two favorites finishing one-two-three in the Show Pool.

When the betting is completed for the race, and the betting windows are closed, the Final Odds, or the Final Line, are posted on the public display board. These odds are binding. Pay-offs must be at least at this rate. They may be slightly higher, but never lower.

Odds posted on the tote board *before* betting has begun, and usually printed by the entry's name on the official program, are called the "Morning Line." These are the educated guesses of a knowledgeable Oddsmaker hired by the track, and usually called the "Handicapper." Many people rely heavily on the Handicapper's odds in making their selections. But, of course, the bettors change the Morning Line. If the odds go higher as the betting proceeds, they are called "Overlays." If the odds decrease, they are called "Underlays."

In fact, some of the most heated arguments in the racing business are over the accuracy and methodology of making the morning line. Most Handicappers study a race's entries, weigh various factors, decide from top to bottom who should finish where, and make the morning line accordingly. Some are consistently accurate in their selections. Fine. They're picking winners. But perhaps those handicappers are overlooking the real purpose of the morning line, i.e. rather than trying to predict his favorites, to predict how the *bettors* will see the race. Shouldn't Handicappers try to make their line coincide as closely as possible to the final line determined by the public? The first advantage that comes to mind is that if the Morning Line accurately reflects the public's betting mood, it is possible for the bettor to wager at any time during the betting period and not have to watch the Tote Board, waiting until the last moment to get an idea of what his selection will pay should he win. Only a limited number of patrons can be served in the last moments of a betting period. The more the wagering is spread out over the entire betting time available, the less pressure on track personnel, space and equipment. At some tracks, such pressure becomes a real problem. The comfort of the patrons is also a consideration. Spread-out betting eliminates having to fight a last minute rush to the betting windows. Nothing antagonizes a customer more than, having selected a winner, to have the windows close before he has a chance to buy his tickets.

In addition, why should the morning line "winners" be regarded as definitive? The customer can get other help in handicapping a race. There are the selections at the bottom of the official program at most tracks. Various opinions by expert thoroughbred Handicappers appear in *The Daily Racing Form*. Tip Sheets are available at the entrance of most tracks, offered for sale by persons sanctioned by the track's management, which share in their proceeds. If the Tip Sheet selections are poor, the sales drop off, so it is important to be as accurate as possible, and financially advantageous to Management to give this concession to as competent a Handicapper as it can find. Lastly, accepting that the morning line accurately reflects what the finish will be harks back to before the pari-mutuels system was instituted, when the gambling aspect of racing was handled by Bookmakers. At that time, it was important, even imperative, that the odds be governed by picking winners, since pay-offs had to be made in accordance with the odds posted by the bookmaker. Obviously this is no longer true at the tracks where electronic equipment calculates the true odds. Thus, there seems to be no good reason for the morning line in conjunction with today's pari-mutuels system even though it's a safe bet that the morning line will be with bettors for a long time to come.

At any rate, these are the basic principles of profit, pay-off, and odds-making. It's more than possible, however, that a bettor still might not know exactly why he got paid what he did. What's needed now is a simple example: A single race that illustrates the track's procedures step by step (including items like the Place and Show Pools, and that bugaboo, the dead heat). Remember, the Exotic Pools are calculated in the same manner as the Win (or Straight) Pool, since only one entry is involved in calculating the Win Pool, and only one combination is involved in the Exotic Pools. Remember, too, that a dead heat in the Win or Exotic Pools is figured in exactly the same fashion as a regular Place Pool and that "Dead Heat" is the term used when two or more entries finish the race in a tie and it is impossible to separate their finish even with the aid of the photo-finish camera.

The following illustrations are to clarify procedures only, and so the same figures are used for each entry and for Pool totals. Actually, this rarely happens. The Win Pool usually is much larger than the Place Pool. Likewise, the Place Pool is usually greater than the Show Pool. Varied amounts are used on each entry to show why some winning tickets pay more than the others.

WIN POOL—WINNER #1

Horse or Dog Number	Pay-off	Dollars Wagered		Proof that pay-off is correct
1	$40.80	216	#1 $\frac{20.40}{216\overline{)4412.35}}$ = pay-off per dollar	#1 $40.80 × 216 dollars = $8812.80
2		372	$\frac{432}{923}$	÷ 2 since we have multiplied actual dollars × $2 ticket prices
3		814	$\frac{864}{5.95}$ = breakage	
4		562		
5		163		Amount to be returned to
6		412	$20.40 × 2 for $2.00 pay-off	winners $4406.40
7		602		
8		2050		15% of pool deducted for state
Total Pool		$5191.00		and track 778.65
15% Commission to track and state		−778.65		Breakage left over from winner 5.95
Net pool (85% for public)		$4412.35		$5191.00
				PRICE IS CORRECT

In case of a Dead Heat to win, the calculation is made in exactly the same manner as a Place Pool, described in the following illustration. You will see the procedure of dividing the profits, when more than one interest is involved in determining the correct pay-offs. However when there is an absence of a dead heat in the Win or any form of Exotic wagering, there remains but one pay-off in these Pools and the calculating process is simplified by needing only to divide the net Pool by the dollars bet on the winner or winning combination in the Exotic Pools.

PLACE POOL—ORDER OF FINISH 1-8

Horse or Dog Number	Pay-off	Dollars Wagered
1	$11.80	216
2		372
3		814
4		562
5		163
6		412
7		602
8	3.00	2050
Total Pool		$5191.00
15% Commission to track and state		−778.65
Net pool (85% for public)		$4412.35
Winning tickets (#1 and #8)		−2266.00
Profits to be divided equally		2146.35
Equal share of profits ÷ 2 to #1 and #8		$1073.17

#1
$$216 \overline{)1073.18} \quad 4.90 = \text{profits per dollar}$$
```
          864
          209.1
          194.4
          14.78 = breakage
```
Profits for 2 dollars = $ 9.80
Repay ticket price   2.00
                        $11.80

#8
$$2050 \overline{)1073.17} \quad .50 = \text{profits per dollar}$$
```
         1025
         48.17 = breakage
```
Profits for 2 dollars = $ 1.00
Repay ticket price   2.00
                        $ 3.00

Proof that pay-offs are correct

```
#1   $11.80 ×  216 dollars = $2548.80
#8    3.00  × 2050 dollars =  6150.00
                             $8698.80
```

÷ 2 since we have multiplied actual dollars × $2 ticket prices

Amount to be returned to winners $4349.40

15% of pool deducted for state and track   778.65

Total breakage left over from two winners   62.95

Original pool $5191.00

PRICES ARE CORRECT

This is a good spot to point out why, when your winning selection is coupled with either a favorite or a longshot, it affects your pay-off to quite a degree. We have just seen that when #1 was the winner and #8 ran second, the pay-off to place was $11.80. Using exactly the same procedure and the same pools, let's assume that the order of finish had been 1-5 instead of 1-8, and figure that combination.

Horse or Dog Number	Pay-off	Dollars Wagered
1	$20.60	216
2		372
3		814
4		562
5	$26.60	163
6		412
7		602
8		2050
Total Pool		$5191.00
15% Commission to track and state		−778.65
Net pool (85% for public)		$4412.35
Winning tickets (#1 and #5)		−379.00
Profits to be divided equally		$4033.35
Equal share of profits ÷ two to #1 and #5)		$2016.67

```
#1        9.30 = profits per dollar
     216 ) 2016.68
           1944
            72.6
            64.8
             7.88 = breakage
     Profits for 2 dollars = $18.60
     Repay ticket price       2.00
                            $20.60

#5       12.30 = profits per dollar
     163 ) 2016.67
           163
           386
           326
            60.6
            48.9
            11.77 = breakage
     Profits for 2 dollars = $24.60
     Repay ticket price       2.00
                            $26.60
```

Proof that pay-offs are correct

```
#1   $20.60 ×  216 dollars = $4449.60
#5   $26.60 ×  163 dollars =  4335.80
                            $8785.40

÷ 2 since we have multiplied
actual dollars × $2 ticket
prices

Amount to be returned to
winners                     $4392.70

15% of pool deducted for state
and track                     778.65

Total breakage left over from
two winners                    19.65

Original pool               $5191.00

        PRICES ARE CORRECT
```

In this instance the place price for #1 almost doubled as a result of #5 running second instead of #8. Without a knowledge of how the pari-mutuels system works, a relative newcomer at a track is terribly confused by the great difference in place and show prices that are posted on entries with relatively the same win odds. Even those who have been attending the tracks for years question the accuracy of the pay-offs. I hope this illustration will be reassuring to the doubtful ones.

PLACE POOL—ORDER OF FINISH 1—DEAD HEAT 2-8

Horse or Dog Number	Pay-off	Dollars Wagered
1	$10.20	216
2	4.20	372
3		814
4		562
5		163
6		412
7		602
8	2.40	2050
Total Pool		$5191.00
15% Commission to track and state		−778.65
Net pool (85% for public)		4412.35
Winning tickets (#1, #2, and #8)		−2638.00
		$1774.35
Profits to be divided		
#1		$ 887.18
#2		$ 443.59
#8		$ 443.58

#1

$$216 \overline{)887.18}$$
4.10 = profits per dollar
864
23.1
21.6
1.58 = breakage
Profits for 2 dollars = $ 8.20
Repay ticket price 2.00
$10.20

#2

$$372 \overline{)443.59}$$
1.10 = profits per dollar
372
71.5
37.2
34.39 = breakage
Profits for 2 dollars = $ 2.20
Repay ticket price 2.00
$ 4.20

#8

$$2050 \overline{)443.58}$$
.20 = profits per dollar
410.0
33.58 = breakage
Profits for 2 dollars = $ .40
Repay ticket price 2.00
$ 2.40

Proof that pay-offs are correct

#1	$10.20 × 216 dollars =	$2203.20
#2	$ 4.20 × 372 dollars =	1562.40
#8	$ 2.40 × 2050 dollars =	4920.00
		$8685.60

÷ 2 since we have multiplied actual dollars × $2 ticket prices

Amount to be returned to winners $4342.80

15% of pool deducted for track and state 778.65

Total breakage left over from three winners 69.55

Original pool $5191.00

PRICES ARE CORRECT

Note how the dead heat reduced the pay-offs for numbers 1 and 8. Number 1 still receives ½ the profits, but the profits are smaller as the result of having to repay the winning tickets for number 2 before profits are determined. Also, numbers 2 and 8 together receive the other ½ of the profits since they were in a tie for second, each receiving ¼ of the profits.

SHOW POOL—ORDER OF FINISH 1-2-8

Horse or Dog Number	Pay-off	Dollars Wagered
1	$ 7.40	216
2	5.00	372
3		814
4		562
5		163
6		412
7		602
8	2.40	2050
Total Pool		$5191.00
15% Commission to track and state		−778.65
Net pool (85% for public)		$4412.35
Winning tickets (#1, #2, and #8)		2638.00
Profits to be divided equally (#1, #2, and #8)		$1774.35
Equal share of profits ÷ 3 to #1, #2, and #8		$ 591.45

#1
```
        2.70 = profits per dollar
216 ) 591.45
      432
      159.4
      151.2
        8.25 = breakage
```
Profits for 2 dollars = $ 5.40
Repay ticket price   2.00
                          $ 7.40

#2
```
        1.50 = profits per dollar
372 ) 591.45
      372
      219.4
      186.0
       33.45 = breakage
```
Profits for 2 dollars = $ 3.00
Repay ticket price   2.00
                          $ 5.00

#8
```
         .20 = profits per dollar
2050 ) 591.45
       410.0
       181.45 = breakage
```
Profits for 2 dollars = $ .40
Repay ticket price   2.00
                          $ 2.40

Proof that pay-offs are correct

#1 $ 7.40 × 216 dollars = $1598.40
#2 $ 5.00 × 372 dollars = 1860.00
#8 $ 2.40 × 2050 dollars = 4920.00
                            $8378.40

÷ 2 since we have multiplied actual dollars × $2 ticket prices

Amount to be returned to winners $4189.20

15% of pool deducted for state and track   778.65

Total breakage left over from three winners   223.15

Original pool $5191.00

PRICES ARE CORRECT

SHOW POOL—ORDER OF FINISH 1-2 DEAD HEAT 3-8

Horse or Dog Number	Pay-off	Dollars Wagered
1	$ 4.80	216
2	3.60	372
3	2.20	814
4		562
5		163
6		412
7		602
8	2.20	2050
Total Pool		$5191.00
15% Commission to track and state		−778.65
Net pool (85% for public)		$4412.35
Winning tickets (#1, #2, #3, and #8)		3452.00
Profits to be divided (#1, #2, #3, and #8)		$ 960.35
⅓ profits to #1 and #2		$ 320.12
⅙ profits to #3 and #8		$ 160.06

```
#1        1.40 = profits per dollar
   216 ) 320.12
         216
         104.1
          86.4
          17.72 = breakage
             Profits for 2 dollars = $ 2.80
             Repay ticket price        2.00
                                     $ 4.80

#2         .80 = profits per dollar
   372 ) 320.11
         297.6
          22.51 = breakage
             Profits for 2 dollars = $ 1.60
             Repay ticket price        2.00
                                     $ 3.60

#3         .10 = profits per dollar
   814 ) 160.06
          81.4
          78.66 = breakage
             Profits for 2 dollars = $  .20
             Repay ticket price        2.00
                                     $ 2.20

#8         .10 = profits per dollar
  2050 ) 160.06
             Profits for 2 dollars = $  .20
             Repay ticket price        2.00
                                     $ 2.20

 20500
-16006
 44.94 minus breakage
```

Proof that pay-offs are correct

#1 $ 4.80 × 216 dollars =	$1036.80
#2 $ 3.60 × 372 dollars =	1339.20
#3 $ 2.20 × 814 dollars =	1790.80
#8 $ 2.20 × 2050 dollars =	4510.00
	$8676.80
÷ 2 since we have multiplied actual dollars × $2 ticket prices	
Amount to be returned to winners	$4338.40
15% of pool deducted for state and track	778.65
Total breakage left over from #1, #2, and #3 less the minus breakage from #8	73.95
Original pool	$5191.00

PRICES ARE CORRECT

We used #3 and #8 in the order of finish to illustrate how a minus pool is created. In calculating the odds of profits for #8, you will notice that the 2050 dollars wagered would not go into his share of profits of $160.06 once, but the law requires that ten cents profit be paid for each dollar of a winning ticket. Thus the minimum price of $2.20 is paid and the minus breakage is deducted from the plus breakage of the other three winners. Some states permit you to pay a five cent profit in this case. Thus the ticket price would be $2.10 and eliminate the minus breakage. Also note how the dead heat reduced the pay-offs of #1, #2 and #8. Numbers 1 and 2 still get ⅓ of the profits, but the profits are reduced as a result of having to first pay the ticket price back to those selecting #3. In the first pool this was losing money, and created a larger amount of profit to be divided. Also note that the numbers involved in the dead heat only get ⅓ of the profits between them, since they tied for third place, and thus receive only ⅙ each.

Wanta Bet?

WINNING MUTUEL TICKET RETURN

(APPROXIMATE)

ODDS	$2.00	$5.00	$10.00	$20.00	$50.00
1-2	$3.00	$7.50	$15	$30	$75
3-5	$3.20	$8.00	$16	$32	$80
4-5	$3.60	$9.00	$18	$36	$90
1-1	$4.00	$10.00	$20	$40	$100
6-5	$4.40	$11.00	$22	$44	$110
7-5	$4.80	$12.00	$24	$48	$120
3-2	$5.00	$12.50	$25	$50	$125
8-5	$5.20	$13.00	$26	$52	$130
9-5	$5.60	$14.00	$28	$56	$140
2-1	$6	$15.00	$30	$60	$150
5-2	$7	$17.50	$35	$70	$175
3-1	$8	$20.00	$40	$80	$200
7-2	$9	$22.50	$45	$90	$225
4-1	$10	$25.00	$50	$100	$250
9-2	$11	$27.50	$55	$110	$275
5-1	$12	$30	$60	$120	$300
6-1	$14	$35	$70	$140	$350
7-1	$16	$40	$80	$160	$400
8-1	$18	$45	$90	$180	$450
9-1	$20	$50	$100	$200	$500
10-1	$22	$55	$110	$220	$550
11-1	$24	$60	$120	$240	$600
12-1	$26	$65	$130	$260	$650
13-1	$28	$70	$140	$280	$700
14-1	$30	$75	$150	$300	$750
15-1	$32	$80	$160	$320	$800
16-1	$34	$85	$170	$340	$850
17-1	$36	$90	$180	$360	$900
18-1	$38	$95	$190	$380	$950
19-1	$40	$100	$200	$400	$1000
20-1	$42	$105	$210	$420	$1050
21-1	$44	$110	$220	$440	$1100
22-1	$46	$115	$230	$460	$1150
23-1	$48	$120	$240	$480	$1200
24-1	$50	$125	$250	$500	$1250
25-1	$52	$130	$260	$520	$1300
30-1	$62	$155	$310	$620	$1550
35-1	$72	$180	$360	$720	$1800
40-1	$82	$205	$410	$820	$2050
45-1	$92	$230	$460	$920	$2300
50-1	$102	$255	$510	$1020	$2550

Chapter Thirteen
Pari-Mutuels: Yesterday and Today

Calculations like those in the illustrations on the previous pages are done mostly by computers today. But computerization is a recent development in the pari-mutuels system. In fact, to fully understand today's methods, it's helpful to know something about the history of pari-mutuels wagering, right down to how it works at the track now—from who runs it to the machines that revolutionized the system.

THE OLD DAYS AND WAYS

When the pari-mutuels system was first used in the United States, pre-printed tickets were sold from a ticket rack. These vari-colored tickets were printed with the name of the track, the type of pool, and the monetary value of the ticket. The colors made the tickets identifiable for the pari-mutuels clerks and the customer. All denominations of the Win, Place and Show tickets had a coded system to designate the day of racing, the race number and the entry number. The first two numbers designated the day of the current racing meet; the third number designated the race in which the ticket was sold; and the fourth number identified the entry. At the bottom of the ticket, small numbers showed how many tickets on that particular entry had been sold. The top ticket on the rack was numbered 00, the second 01, and so on up to 99. When the rack was empty, 100 tickets had been sold. If further tickets were necessary, filler tickets were added, and the number of the filler tickets recorded so the clerks could identify winning tickets for cashing. With this system, the top ticket remaining in the rack showed how many tickets had been sold.

The illustration below will give a rough idea of how this system worked.

CHURCHILL

DOWNS

$5.00 Win

1336

09

A ticket sold at Churchill Downs. It is a $5.00 Win ticket sold on the thirteenth day of the meeting, for the third race on horse number 6. At this point, 9 tickets had been sold from this rack.

Of course, for Exotic Pools there were too many different combinations to use the simple codes for day, race, and entry. The Exotic Pools were handled this way:

CHURCHILL DOWNS
$2.00
Daily Double

5 FIVE 7 SEVEN

16432

17

Another Churchill Downs ticket, this one for the Daily Double Pool. It is a $2.00 ticket on the 5-7 combination. There was no practical way to designate the racing day, but to assure the authenticity of the ticket for any given day's races, a set of numbers were set up, e.g. 16432 would never be used for any other combination, or on any other day of that meeting. Here, 17 tickets had been sold on the 5-7 combination.

In the old days, figuring the odds took legwork. The oddsmaker would have to go to each window selling Win tickets in all denominations, and accumulate the total bets. Then he'd go back to the Calculating Room and figure the new odds from these totals. Next, he would telephone (or inter-com) the odds to the personnel across the track behind the odds board. They'd insert large printed numbers into the display board, after rechecking with the oddsmaker to insure that they had heard these numbers correctly. The board was usually made to swivel, so that personnel could hang the new odds on the back, and swing the board so that all of the new numbers would go up at once. These were called approximate odds. Altogether, it was a slow, hard, demanding process, and rarely could more than four or five odds changes be made during a betting period.

When the betting windows were closed, all the pools had to be totaled in the same manner. Pay-offs had to be figured manually, using the same calculations now done in a split second by the computers.

The last step was to call the pay-offs to the odds board where they were posted in the same way as the odds had been. It's hard for many people who work in the mutuels departments today, to comprehend the complex and demanding work involved in this system of the early days. But the system worked well, even if a little more slowly than it does now.

The first step from pre-printed tickets to the computer system as we know it today, was when an electronic totalisator was perfected. It was crude, when compared to today's systems, but was capable of totaling the bets as they were being made, and making this information available to the oddsmaker and the calculators of the various pools. It was accompanied by the electric odds-board. It was first designed to show only the approximate odds and the pay-offs in lights.

Now the system had been speeded up to a point where the oddsmaker no longer had to go to the individual selling windows to get his information. The totals were available on indicaters in the calculating room, and could be had by simply pushing a button. He still had to make the odds changes manually, but the process was much faster and more accurate. The changes on the board could be made from the calculating room, and no longer was there need for personnel to work behind the display board in the infield.

Pay-offs could be posted much more rapidly. The win, place and show calculators had the amount of money wagered on each entry and the pool totals within seconds after the betting windows closed. Calculations were still made manually, but the prices could be set up and checked in the calculating room. The moment the race was declared "Official", the prices were flashed to the odds board. Only the calculator of the exotic pools had to use the old method of compiling his pool totals and the number of winning combinations manually.

The next innovation was the odds computer, which automatically calculated odds and relieved the oddsmaker from the tedium of manually figuring the odds. Still, the oddsmaker periodically checked the accuracy of the computer and checked the final odds posted automatically on the board.

Soon afterwards, a system was developed to total the tickets on individual combinations and the pool totals for Daily Doubles, Quinielas, and Perfectas or Exactas. This enabled the calculator of the exotic pools to have the same advantages as those figuring the pay-offs for the Win, Place and Show pools. Now all the pay-offs could be posted simultaneously, without the exotic pool bettors waiting for their results—a delay that often led to suspicions that the procedures for this pool were not being carried out honestly.

Admittedly, however, there was more room for error using pre-printed ticket systems. Worse, there was greater opportunity for dishonesty on the part of a *very few* people who managed to give a bad name to the pari-mutuels business that has lasted to this day among those ignorant of how the system works. The fact is, that the few who cheated in the early days are gone, and with the advent of the electronic totalisator equipment, plus the advancement of checks and balances, it is very difficult to be dishonest in this accounting facet of racing. Unfortunately, where there are humans involved, and money is the raw material being processed, there still will undoubtedly be a few who will try to find a way to beat the system.

Their chances of success aren't good, though, which should reassure the average bettor. It's true that a couple of years ago, an ingenious scheme was discovered at one of the major greyhound tracks. A totalisator operator, and some members of the mutuels department, managed to insert some phony figures into the computer, and they were able to siphon off sizeable profits from the customers before they were caught. But they *were* caught. If something similar is tried again, it's probable that the new scheme will be discovered before much damage is done. Overall, the mutuels departments can be proud of its record over the past two decades.

At this point, I'd like to emphasize that we're dealing with the aspect of correct pay-offs and the proper handling of monies wagered. This should not be confused with dealings between the clerks and customers at the betting and cashiers windows. There remains problems in this area, and they will be discussed later in the chapter.

Many more improvements have been made in the equipment used to carry out the Pari-Mutuels system in a more sophisticated manner. I will describe some of these improvements in the following paragraphs. However, many small tracks are presently being operated with basically the same systems described up to this point. There are definite reasons why these small tracks have not taken advantage of the latest innovations that have been perfected. Their volume of business dictates how much money can be spent in this particular area of operation. Almost all of this equipment is secured on a lease basis. The Totalisator Companies must be able to lease each system for several years to be able to pay for the costs of improving and manufacturing each system. The cost of the latest in electronic equipment would be prohibitive for tracks with small Mutuels handles. Even with unlimited funds, it would be impossible to secure the sophisticated models. Drastic improvements are being perfected at a rapid pace. It is not feasible for the Totalisator Company to build too many identical systems at one time. By the time they are on the market, a better system has been perfected. There are never enough late models to go around.

The trend has been for existing tracks to race more days per year, rather than to build new facilities in States where Pari Mutuels wagering is legal. A few years ago, the same tote system was used at several different locations during a calendar year. This option is no longer possible. Every improved system has a waiting list of tracks that would like to install better equipment, when it becomes available. Naturally, the Totalisator Companies place their premium systems where the revenue will be greatest. It all boils down to a track increasing its volume to a point where it will be profitable for both the Totalisator Company and the track to install improved systems.

The public was the benefactor of the next improvement. The Display board in the infield showed the number of dollars on each entry and the totals of each pool at each cycle of the approximate win odds. This didn't decrease the work for the calculators, but it gave the public a better break, as entries being overlooked in the Place and Show Pools were reflected on the display board. By now, some calculators were using small hand calculaters to aid them in their calculations. Soon, the Totalisator Companies were offering Price Computers that could calculate the pools, one at a time, and would give a print-out of the pay-offs. A Calculator usually checked the prices manually, but the pressure had been taken from them somewhat, except when there was a breakdown in the computers. During all this time, although the totals had been furnished automatically, a breakdown of tickets had to be made manually. That is: how many tickets of each denomination had been sold to arrive at the pool and entry total. Each ticket issuing machine had a manual print-out, and these print-outs had to be consolidated for purposes of sheet writing.

The next development was total automation. The new computers sent the pay-off prices directly to the display board, as well as to monitors behind the cashiers' windows. They displayed odds on the exotic pools every few seconds, and made a complete print-out of all information needed by the mutuels department, including the "sheet writing" for the cashiers. They also kept an up-to-date record of all uncashed tickets for the entire race meeting.

As of today, the total automation system has expanded at the larger facilities to the latest electronic equipment: the "cash-sell" system. A bettor now can both buy and cash any ticket, in any denomination, in any pool, for any race, at any window. The ticket's cost appears on a read-out window like a cash register at a supermarket. When presented for cashing, the ticket is inserted into a slot in the ticket-issuing machine, and its total value appears on the read-out window.

Many who had extensive experience in pari-mutuels systems, seriously doubted that the advantages would outweigh the problems of this innovation when the idea was first proposed. Although only a few tracks have installed this equipment, both the public and management are happy with it. In time, it will probably be in use at most, if not all the tracks in the country.

Through all the above stages of advancement in the pari-mutuels system, it looked like a very simple operation to the outsider, as well as to lots of insiders, including track management and those in other departments of pari-mutuels operations. "After all", they tell you, "all you have to do is take the money in, divide it up in regulation with a basic set of rules and pass it out to the winners. It's a simple mathematical process and now you have computers to do it for you." Don't believe it. Unfortunately, in lots of cases, that's about the way it is handled. The intangible costs of this attitude are indeed great.

This attitude starts in many cases, at the very top of the pari-mutuels structure.

Some members of Racing Commissions, experts in their own field, but with little understanding of the pari-mutuels system, make unwise decisions. Progress is being made in some states by having separate commissions for different types of racing.

Track owners who have been extremely successful in other businesses, sincerely believe they can apply the same principles to racing that they used in their previous business and succeed. Some General Managers have little, or no background, in racing. Many other General Managers, who have been successful in other areas of the country, bring with them ideas that worked for them there, to a new location with different problems peculiar to this new area, and expect positive results. Frequently, this practice is counter-productive.

Many track officials in one department or another have spent most of their lives in the racing business, and do a fine job in their own area. But they have never taken the time to learn the problems of the other departments. My recommendation for all those who fit in the categories mentioned above, is to listen carefully to the words of the Gatlin Brothers song "No matter where you played before, California is a brand new game".

Of course, this doesn't apply to everyone, and I'm sure other growing industries are facing similar problems.

Since wagering is the heart of all pari-mutuels facilities and since the pari-mutuels system is the theme of this book, we will attempt to explain in detail the workings of this particular department, especially the duties and responsibilities of the Mutuels Manager. We will also touch lightly on all the other departments and the personnel involved within these departments.

THE PARI-MUTUELS DEPARTMENT

Probably the most important item in managing a Mutuels Department, aside from accuracy and honesty, is "timing". To be specific, this department must give the public enough time between events to make their selections for the coming event, without rushing themselves, yet not too much time to get bored. Correct timing keeps the money circulating from the customer to the ticket sellers, time to watch the event, ample time to cash winning tickets, have refreshments, and to repeat this routine fom the first event to the last, all in an orderly, comfortable fashion. Racing and jai alai are supposed to be entertaining. The Mutuels Department can help make it so, or it can undo the efforts of all the other departments. Another important factor is in the selection and handling of the personnel in this department. The average customer has much more contact with members of this department than with all other departments combined. The customer's assessment of the entire operation is often based on his association with the pari-mutuels clerks.

Although many references in this chapter refer to horse or greyhound racing, the general principles also apply to jai alai.

The head of the Pari-Mutuels Department is called the "Mutuels Manager". He is subject to orders of the General Manager regarding policy, and to the decisions of the Presiding Steward in cases not completely covered by the Rules of Racing. His responsibilities include: seeing that all pay-offs are correct, that the revenue is correctly divided between State and Track, the hiring and training of all personnel in his department, the conduct of personnel during working hours, job assignments (when the betting facility is unionized, his control of hiring and job assignment is limited to the union contract but he has the authority to determine whether or not a person is capable of handling a job assigned by the union representative), to determine the number and types of betting and cashing windows as dictated by volume of business, weather etc., to arbitrate and decide the outcome of disagreements between customers and clerks, to make certain that all personnel in his department are properly licensed by the State, to set post times, to see that contracts are fulfilled between Track and various contractees, (such as the Totalisator Company, the Company that furnishes Closed Circuit TV in the Mutuels area, the Pari-Mutuels Union at union tracks, and any other contractees who deal with the Pari-Mutuels Department,) to order mutuels supplies and stationery, to keep detailed records of all transactions in his Department, to determine the amount of money needed for the "bankroll", to make reports to the Racing Commission regarding any variance from normal proceeding (such as "underpays" or "overpays" resulting from equipment failure or human error,) to control the "outs tickets book", to authenticate mutilated tickets, to determine the validity of claims of patrons that they were short-changed by sellers or underpaid by cashiers, to make up the payroll for his Department, and to be the conduit between the Racing Department and the Mutuels Department, regarding order of finish, scratches, or any other situation involving the co-operation of the two Departments. Of course, one person cannot individually do all of these things, but he is responsible to see that all of these matters are handled correctly by himself, his assistant, or other members of his Department.

While computers and allied technological advances have made it possible for persons with limited experience to become Mutuels Managers, there are many areas where even the most sophisticated computer systems are no help at all. Overall knowledge and experience should still be the main criteria for selecting someone to head this department. Unfortunately at many facilities, management has opted in favor of hiring someone of limited experience for less money. It looks good on paper, but I assure you that when you reach the bottom line, it is the utmost in false economy. The intangibles which reflect profits are immeasurable. I've always maintained that written and oral tests should be required before a person can be licensed to hold the Mutuels Manager job. I believe this should apply to other personnel as well, such as Stewards, Placing Judges, Racing Secretaries, and other important department heads.

Overall, the responsibilities delegated to those in the above categories, and their pay rates are not compatible. Most are grossly underpaid. Salary increases have in no way kept pace with the inflation rates of the past decade at most pari-mutuels facilities. Especially when compared with other lines of work.

To elaborate on the importance of experience as it applies to a Mutuels Manager, let's deal with his handling of the large number of employees under him, the majority of whom will be in direct contact with the customers most of the time that they are at the track or fronton. These employees can immediately be separated into two groups. There are those, known as "racetrackers," who make their living entirely or primarily from their work at the track. Then there are "moonlighters" whose work is a supplement to their regular jobs. Naturally, both groups must be honest and efficient. But they differ in many respects. Ordinarily, a professional, a "racetracker," takes a greater interest in doing what is beneficial for the facility. His success depends on the success of his employer. Occasionally a "moonlighter" will have enough self-pride to show real interest in the operation's success, but this is not the norm. Holding two jobs takes its toll on the "moonlighter" and he will be more apt to miss work—more often—especially when social events involving his family, and holidays, coincide with the racing or jai alai schedule. Holidays are usually the big days at a race track, and they create a special problem if some "moonlighters" don't show. Here the philosophies of Mutuels Managers differ. Some insist on a hard line, treating both groups exactly the same. Others are more lenient with the "moonlighters." I've found that most professionals understand this situation and will tolerate a double standard. As for the problem of absenteeism, it's usually possible to maintain a list of standbys to fill in for the absentees. The same problem arises when a large number of students and teachers are employed and the school year and the racing dates overlap. Sometimes, too, part of the regular crew has to leave before a meet is completed in order to hold a job at another facility whose racing dates overlap. I believe in being as flexible as possible when these situations arise, if—and only if—the employee was honest about these problems when he applied for work. This approach has worked for me, but I know others who take a harder line and do a fine job.

Enforcing a dress code gets complicated at most tracks. Uniforms would seem to be the answer, but usually creates more problems than it solves. If the employee furnishes them, management is still responsible to see that they're clean and neat. What's clean and neat to one person might be sloppy to the person working next to him. The person responsible for the final decisions probably won't agree with either one. If the employer provides the uniforms, there is a problem of space to keep them while not worn, getting them cleaned regularly, and keeping a supply of the correct sizes for changing personnel. If uniforms are not used, the type of clothing that is acceptable, the length of hair and beards and mustaches become an issue. I'm convinced that the most sensible solution is to take into consideration the geographical location of the track, since different areas accept different modes of dress as acceptable. The temperature control of the working area is a factor, but probably the biggest criteria is to match the dress code with the majority of customers with whom they're dealing.

The "no betting" rule by employees at a track or fronton is probably the most difficult rule of all to enforce. Most states have this rule, but expect and demand different degrees of enforcement. It is imperative that certain officials and employees be forbidden to wager. Stewards, Placing Judges, Paddock Judges, Racing Secretaries, Starters, Assistant Starters and Blacksmiths fall into this category in horse racing. Also jockeys, drivers, owners and trainers, if they bet on any entry other than the one that they are in charge of. At dog tracks, the Placing Judges, Racing Secretary, Paddock Judge, Leadouts, and especially the Lure Operator should definitely be barred from wagering. Track maintenance personnel in both categories fall into this group, as well as Veterinarians and their assistants who are taking samples for testing for illegal medication. Judges, Matchmakers and Players are the most important figures in jai alai to be excluded. The ones listed above are the persons who can definitely change the outcome of a race or game.

Racing Commissioners, Track owners, and General Managers cannot control the results of a race or game, but could directly or indirectly influence the decisions of their employees.

While mutuels employees and other track employees are not actually able to alter the outcome of a race or game, they are in a position to watch the action of the more informed members of the betting public and may either bet or tout the selections of someone else. With the new cash sell system, this will be minimized to a great extent, since the customers making large bets may do so at any window. Before this system came into being, large bets were made at designated windows, and the action could be watched much more easily. Touting the selections of others by the clerks is another taboo, but very hard to control and harder in most cases to prove. While these employees, not in a position to alter the outcome of a contest, have a very, very little edge on the rest of the betting public, it's terribly hard to convince the majority of the public that such is the case. When meeting a stranger and they learn that you work at a track, invariably, their first words are "Oh, could you give me a winner sometime?" Little do they know that this same employee is wishing that someone could do the same for him.

Using the premise that it is virtually impossible to completely stop clerks from wagering, I find that a partial solution to the problem, is to insist that if they feel they must bet, to do so early in the betting period. In this way, no customer will be shut out by the closing of the windows when the race or game begins and their betting will not arouse the suspicions of the public that something dishonest is happening. This certainly does not mean that breaking the betting rule is being condoned, but a compromise of this sort often does wonders for over-all operation of the track and gives added confidence to the public. A lawyer once told me that a rule or law that can't be enforced often proves more harmful than no rule or law at all.

Touting (giving selections to someone in return for part of the winnings) by the mutuels clerks is another item that must be controlled. The situation is somewhat different in the case of the clerks from that of professional touts who are part of the betting public. Security guards in the betting area are constantly on the lookout for these professionals. They are ejected from the premises when they are caught. Often, they force themselves on customers and are a definite detriment to an operation. Sometimes the customer is at fault when a clerk touts. It starts with his belief that because the clerk works at the track, he has a better idea of who will win than he himself does. Sometimes this is true, but more often than not, the customer can pick more winners by himself than with the help of the clerk. Otherwise, the clerk would be outside betting rather than punching or cashing tickets. There is a certain percentage of people who are reluctant to make their own decisions, and would rather bet on someone's else's choices. This results in the customer asking the clerk who he likes, or even laying his money on the counter and saying "punch out the numbers that you like for me". Sometimes he makes his own selections, has some change left over and says, "now give me your choice". Often, the customer becomes angry if the clerk says "I can't, it's against the rules". It becomes pretty hard for the clerk to pass up a chance to make some money, with no risk involved. Especially in the cases where the customer thinks the clerk is not being co-operative if he refuses. Even under these conditions the degree of good or harm to an operation is determined by whether the clerk is giving the customer his own selections, or whether he is giving out selections that have been made by previous customers. In the latter case, it is definitely detrimental and must be stopped as much as is possible. This is not to be confused with the cases where the clerk is soliciting this type of action. At that point he is in the same boat with the touts outside. Those who follow this course are soon caught, and they are dismissed from their jobs. Another case of applying the rule of "common sense" for the good of all concerned. The manner of handling customer complaints does much to create a favorable or unfavorable opinion of a facility. The bulk of these complaints concern money. The most common are "not receiving the correct change" when buying tickets, or "not receiving the correct amount when cashing winning tickets". The new cash-sell totalisator systems will alleviate almost all of these controversies since the amount of the purchase, and the value of winning tickets, are clearly displayed where both the clerk and customer can read the totals. To dispute these figures is to argue with a highly accurate computer. However, cash-sell equipment is still not available at many tracks and frontons. In this case, someone has to act as judge and jury concerning the validity of the claim. This someone is the Mutuels Manager.

Invariably, he hears two completely different stories. Technically, it is the customer's responsibility to make certain all transactions are correct, before he leaves the seller's or cashier's window. Unfortunately, due to the rush and confusion during the betting and cashing periods, sometimes the error is not discovered until later. Clerks are responsible for their shortages and these shortages must be deducted from their wages. Many customers have the impression that if they're overpaid, it's the tracks loss. Those with this false idea, often do not feel guilty, if they believe that they're regaining some of the money they may have lost wagering. If the customers knew that the amount of extra money they were receiving would come from the pockets of the clerk, the majority of these customers would not think of keeping it.

Sometimes the clerk benefits from the mistakes. Repeated claims against any one person, usually means one thing. All of these errors are not accidents. In either case, this person must be replaced. The term used when a clerk gains money from a transaction is called a "drop" in racetrack language.

The unfortunate thing about these situations is that often they are the result of a chain reaction. The few customers who are dishonest and the few clerks who are working for "drops" can cause buying and cashing tickets to become almost as competitive as picking winners. Everyone will soon be trying to get even if it isn't stopped in time. I've often felt that some customers check their morals at the entrance of a track or fronton. They wouldn't think of keeping money overpaid them by a clerk at a store, but don't feel guilty if it happens at the track. These incidents are detrimental to management and everything possible is done to control it. This is another example where experience and finesse of a mutuels manager becomes one of the valuable intangibles mentioned earlier. Both the customers and clerks must be protected as much as possible, to benefit management as well as the actual parties involved.

A partial solution to the "drop" problem is a pay scale for the clerks large enough to make the possibility of losing their jobs a major factor, when the opportunity for taking a "drop" occurs.

The firing of clerks suspected of taking drops or deliberately touting customers becomes a more complex procedure if the clerks are members of a union. While the union certainly does not condone these practices, any more than does management, the union is bound to the concept of protecting their members, and more documented proof is needed to replace the guilty parties.

Even at non-union tracks, the mutuels manager must be certain the clerk is guilty. Suspicion alone should not be reason enough to dismiss a clerk, since if the suspicions are unjustified, it can do great harm to the clerk's integrity.

The new cash-sell system eventually will control three other age old problems; altered tickets, mutilated tickets, and the cashing of invalid tickets. These are called "pigeons". Sometimes when invalid tickets are presented for cashing intentionally, it is with the hope that the cashier will not notice that it has no value. If they do notice, which is usually the case, the customer has lost nothing but time. Once in a while, a "pigeon" slips by, and the cashier must accept the responsibility of repaying it. However, if the same customer does this repeatedly, he is usually ejected from the track by the security guards. Sometimes, however, the act is unintentional. The customer may have bought several tickets, torn up the ones he thought were losers, and saved one of the bad ones by mistake. Of course, he knows that he ordered a winner. Frustration sets in, and in many cases the customer feels he was either sold the wrong ticket or that the cashier has switched tickets on him. It is very hard to convince him that it is he who made the mistake. This is a very unfortunate situation and can cause undue ill will concerning the integrity of the employees. One way to prevent this is for the customer to not throw tickets away, until all transactions have been concluded to his satisfaction.

Mutilated tickets are most numerous when the order of finish is changed because of the disqualification of winners due to infractions of the rules during the running of a race. Technically, in most states, the track is not obligated to pay for a mutilated ticket. Programs plainly state "Not responsible for torn or mutilated tickets". Signs to this effect are often displayed in conspicuous places in the betting area. Usually the announcer will say "Please hold all tickets until the race is declared official". Novices, or those disgusted with the original order of finish, will often disregard these warnings and either throw away, or tear up their tickets as soon as the race is completed. When the change in the order of finish has been posted and the race declared official, the cashiers are swamped with tickets torn in various ways. Since time prevents the cashiers from helping reconstruct the tickets, most tracks have special windows to tape the tickets back together. Although not obligated to provide this service, most operations feel it is good public relations to do so. Parts are missing from many, and again, the mutuels manager has to make the final decision as to whether the information remaining on the ticket is enough to justify cashing the ticket. The way this situation is handled can do much to help or harm the credibility of the track. Another intangible.

This phase of the operation would not be complete without saying something about "stoopers". This is the practice of a very few people who spend their day at the track looking for valid tickets that have been thrown away by mistake. This is discouraged by all tracks and Racing Commissions. First of all, it's a profession that doesn't command much respect. It looks bad to the public, and secondly, it's a financial loss to whomever receives the value of these discarded tickets. If they are not recovered by the "stoopers", it means the tickets will never be cashed. In some states, this money is given to the State. In others, it is retained by the Track. Various states have different rules as to how long after a meet has been closed, that a customer may receive the value of these winning tickets. The longer a track is in operation, the smaller the gross amount of uncashed tickets becomes. This is due simply to a growth in the overall knowledge of the public as to how the pari-mutuels system works. I've noticed that at most tracks which have been in operation for ten or more years, this figure represents less than $1/10$th of 1% of the volume.

The act of altering tickets is rare, since it is forgery and punishable by law. Alterations are usually caught at the cashier's window, and the person presenting them is picked up by Security for prosecution whenever possible. Occasionally the alteration is professional enough to pass at this level. It is eventually found when more tickets are presented for cashing than were sold. When this occurs, it must be determined who is responsible for the loss. Again, in this case, the mutuels manager must finally decide whether the alteration was crude enough so that the cashier should have noticed it when it was presented, and therefore be responsible for the loss; whether or not it was partially the fault of the tote company because the printing was not clear to begin with; or whether the job of altering was done so well, that no one in particular can be blamed. In this case, the track usually pays for the loss. The same problem exists in rare cases where the printing on the ticket has not been actually altered, but when the printing is not completely legible. A similar situation is faced in cases of counterfeit money. Disposition of these problems, in a fair and proper manner (many of which involve large sums of money), can be made only by someone experienced in all phases of a pari-mutuels operation. Still another intangible.

When a mutuels manager, as well as other department heads, makes a decision relative or similar to the illustration above, he must know that he has the backing of the General Manager, and to understand his general philosophy on different issues. A General Manager's job is not only important, but it is also very complex. He must carry out the wishes of the owners of the track, and at the same time keep the confidence and respect of all the department heads and employees of the track. I would compare his position with that of a Second Lieutenant in the military. He gets flak from both those above and those below him on sensitive issues. Further, he must act upon his decisions in a way that will not alienate the customers.

The number of employees in the mutuels department varies greatly from track to track. Factors are: the volume of business; the physical lay-out of the facilities; the number of betting lines; and the type of totalisator equipment used. Regardless of all the above factors, management tries to keep the payroll of this department under 1½% of the total money handled and as close to 1% as possible. The larger the handle, the easier it is to keep this percentage down. Certain key personnel is a must for all size operations, so the increase in employees for a larger handle is in the lower pay scale areas such as additional cashiers and sellers. Night racing also helps to determine this percentage, since it makes it easier to utilize "moonlighters" who have daytime jobs. Whether or not the employees are members of a union also affects this figure. Standard pay scales in other businesses in an area where the track is located, also plays a role.

I am convinced that regardless of all the above factors, the most simple and effective solution to pay rates, is for management to arrive at a percentage that they can live with in their budget, and set aside a definite amount for this purpose. This is already being done at most locations to determine the size of their purses. It seems that since the mutuels department's payroll is second only to purses in the volume of expenditures, this procedure would do much to ease the never ending controversy over pay scales. Personally, I favor a lower base pay—use the percentage concept and provide incentive measures to distribute the balance of monies to those employees who are doing the most to help make a better operation.

Some tracks are very much opposed to the mutuels department being unionized. I maintain that a lot depends on whether or not the majority of the customers are union members in other businesses in the area in which the track is located. Philosophy and attitudes of different unions differ greatly, as does the attitudes of different management. For instance, I feel it is easier for owners to deal with this added dimension, who are involved with unions in other businesses which they control. Conversely it is harder for owners whose other businesses are non-union. There are many pros and cons regarding the advantages or disadvantages, that a union presents. Not only to management, but to the employees, as well. Some of the disciplinary problems confronting management, are reduced at a union track. This advantage is offset by a reduction in control of placing employees in positions where management feels they would be more productive. It is a proven fact that a mutuels operation is less flexible at a union track. The pay scale is usually the item given priority when considering a union. There is often other factors that will be more important in the long run. While the union may provide greater job security, it will also limit initiative and advancement to some of the more deserving employees. Fringe benefits, gained by union negotiations, are often overshadowed by a poorer relationship between management and employees. A track with a high percentage of "moonlighters" runs into more complications when a union is involved than does one which is staffed by predominately professional racetrack personnel. My personal opinion is that unions cause the greatest problems when a track is chiefly a weekend operation and is open four or less days per week. Tracks in this category usually have a much greater number of part-time employees. I would suggest that because of the diverse situations described above, a union might be helpful at some locations and a definte detriment to both management, and employees at others.

Many states require that a certain percentage of the personnel on the payroll of a track, must be bonafide residents of the state where the track is located. 85% is a figure commonly used. Ordinarily, the longer a track is in operation, the larger the percentage of local employees becomes. Some of the experienced personnel who come to a new area to help open a track end up staying in this community and become permanent residents. Other experienced personnel do move on after awhile, but are usually replaced by local people who have had time to learn from the experienced persons, who are leaving.

The ratio of local employees has been increasing rapidly during the past few years because of more racing days being allotted to each individual track. Many areas now have year around operations; whereas in the past, most tracks were limited to a few months or even a few weeks of racing. This trend has also increased the percentage of professional racetrack personnel, and decreased the percentage of "moonlighters". Many who started as "moonlighters" quit their other jobs when racing dates were increased, and moved into the professional bracket. This trend has also changed the image and the lifestyle of those, who for a long time have been professionals, or "racetrackers" as they are called by their peers. In the earlier years, it was not uncommon for these "racetrackers" to work at seven or eight different tracks in any given year. Many moves involved long trips, since track dates coincided with the climate. Most of the tracks in the North closed down on Labor Day or shortly thereafter. The winter tracks in the South would usually co-ordinate their dates with their tourist season, and close in the spring when the tourists left. There weren't many spring and fall dates in the early days, so these periods of the year always were a rough time for the "racetrackers" to make ends meet. There were more summer tracks than winter tracks, so it meant that many of these professionals had to settle for less important and lower paying positions in the winter than they had held during the summer.

Following the circuit in those days was quite an experience. Competition for the better paying jobs was keen. A person had to be knowledgeable about more than one facet of the operation, and he had to learn his job well in order to keep it. This was especially true in spring, winter, and fall. Workers with families were especially hard pressed. It either meant several moves per year for the entire family, or maintaining a year around base for the wife and children, and the added expense for the head of the family on the road. Families who moved from place to place with children of school age had added problems. It meant changing schools several times each year. This would seem to be very harmful to these children's future, and to some it was. But many seemed to gain from the experiences acquired by living in different parts of the country and learning the different cultures and philosophies prevelant in these different areas. Whenever this subject comes up, I'm reminded of a humorous conversation that I overheard several years ago. One of the local employees asked a "racetracker" if moving around so much didn't adversely affect his children's schooling. His reply was "Hell no, the smartest kids in the world are circus kids, and they move every week." I do know that many of the children who complained the loudest about moving around are now grown and working at racetracks or frontons.

Housing was always a serious problem, especially after World War II, when the housing shortage was at it's peak. It was hard enough for a permanent resident to find a rental, let alone someone with a family who would be staying only a few weeks or months. The fact that the tourist season was also the racing season, magnified this problem to a great degree.

Despite the competition for the better paying jobs, the "racetrackers" of the eras before the 1970s, were a close knit group. Today the professionals are scattered. Now that the trend of longer seasons prevail in each area, most of the professionals can maintain a base where few, if any, moves are necessary. Even if each individual track doesn't operate year around, one in the approximate area does. A couple of good illustrations would be the St. Petersburg, Tampa, Sarasota circuit in Florida. The racing dates are allotted so that there is no overlap, and the same employees can work all three and still be within reasonable driving distances from their homes at all times of the year. California has two circuits, one in the northern part of the state, centering in the San Francisco area, and the other in the Los Angeles area. The allotment of dates permits the employees to work year around without having to move. Many of the states have similar circuits.

There were several reasons why the "racetrackers" were so close knit in the early days. One, of course, was their common interest in a growing business. It was necessary to keep in touch with each other, when not working at the same track, to keep up on job possibilities and racing dates in different sections of the country. At that time, there were few trade magazines as such, so personal contact was the only means to keep each other informed. Simple economics probably played the biggest role in keeping them together. Accidents, illnesses in the family, tracks that were forced to shut down, unexpectedly because of financial losses, and many other factors, might leave a family almost destitute in an area where they weren't well known. Banks and other lending institutions seldom would loan money to someone moving constantly and with no definite job commitments for any lengthy period of time. It was even hard to finance an automobile, a "must" for a racetracker. Their alternative was to look out for each other. There was no organization to go through, so it was always a one-on-one situation. A person's reputation was his credit card. The group was small enough so that if one racetracker didn't know another one personally, he knew someone who did. You are probably wondering by now, why people would face all of these adversities to stay in the racing business. It was interesting work and the pay scale was excellent at that time in comparison with other lines of work. Unfortunately, the scale did not grow in proportion to other businesses. Good salaries are no longer the case in most areas of the country. This fact applies to officials in all departments of racing, not just those in the mutuels department.

The four categories of racing and jai alai combined, attracts more spectators than any other sport in the United States. Yet this is accomplished at only about 275 locations. Since one person, or a group of persons, often control several of these facilities, the owners move their key personnel from one location to another during the year. This means that there is probably less than two-hundred experienced Mutuels Managers and less than one-thousand key racing Officials, such as Stewards and Racing Secretaries. A large percentage of this small number are more than fifty years of age. It is becoming increasingly difficult to find competent replacements for key personnel. Pay incentives, fringe benefits, and job security is not great enough to attract young people with exceptional ability. Computers have reduced the number of key personnel in the mutuels department to the extent that there are very few in a position where they can learn the necessary procedures to become a competent Mutuels Manager. This dilemma is further complicated by the fact that the individuals who make up this group of less than fifteen-hundred racing officials, are locked into these positions after a few years. Their skills in this area have few, if any, counterparts in other businesses. Their experience is of little use, if they choose to change their line of work.

Few, if any retirement benefits are available to this group. Group health insurance is available to some, but is not the norm. They fall into a category of being semi-self employed, without the benefits of either the self employed or the benefits usually provided to the employees of most large companies. A continuous record of efficiency and integrity provides their only chance of job security.

TRACK OWNERS

BOARD MEMBERS

GENERAL MANAGER

RACING DEPT.

Dir. of Racing
Stewards
Placing Judges
Racing Sec'y
Asst. Racing Sec'y
Paddock Judge
Patrol Judges
Identifier
Clerk of Scales
Starter
Track Supt.
Veterinarian
Announcer
Stall Supt.
Jockey Room
  Custodian
Horsemen's Bkpr.
Clockers
Entry Clerks
Valets

Asst. Starters
Outriders
Ambulance Drivers
Security (Barn)
Physician
Nurses
Bugler
Maintenance Crew
  (Barn)

MUTUELS DEPT.

Mutuels Mgr.
Asst. Mutuels Mgr.
Calculators
Sheetwriters
Money Room Mgr.
  & Counters
Ticket Room Mgr.
  & Counters
Payroll Clerk
Head Supervisor
Line Supervisors
Sellers
Cashiers
Messengers

**MISC. RACING DEPT.
CONTRACTEES AND
PERSONNEL**

Horse Owners
Authorized Agts.
Trainers
Grooms
Pony Riders

Jockeys
Exercise Boys
Jockey's Agts.
Blacksmiths
Feed Concess.
Tack Shop Concess.

Photo Finish
  Contractee
  & Operator
Film Patrol
  Contractee &
  Technicians
Closed Circuit TV
  Contractee &
  Technicians
Racing Form
  Contractee
Form Chart
  Contractee
Chart Caller
Chart Taker
Printing Contractee

**MISC. MUTUELS
DEPT. CONTRACTEES
AND PERSONNEL**

Totalisator
  Contractee,
  Operator &
  Technicians
Closed Circuit TV
  Contractee &
  Technicians
Intercommunication
  Contractee &
  Technicians
Armored Car
  Contractee

OPERATIONS DEPT.

Comptroller
Operations Mgr.
Secretaries
Office & Payroll Clerks
PBX Operators
Publicity
Publicity Dir.
Dir. Special Events
Souvenir Shop Mgr. & Clerks
Admissions
Admissions Mgr.
Reservationist
Clubhouse Mgr.
Reserved Seat Sales Personnel
Admission Sales Clerks
Ushers & Elevator Operators
Parking
Valet Parking Mgr. & Attdnts.
Parking+Sales Personnel
Official Programs & Tipsheets
Tipsheet Contractees & Sales
  Personnel
Program Sales Personnel
Form Chart Sales Personnel
Track Maintenance
Maintenance Chief
Track Electrician
Handymen, Clean-up Crew &
  Restroom Attdnts.
Security
Security Chief or Contractee
Guards & Nightwatchmen
Safety
Track Physician
First Aid Attdnts.

CONCESSIONS DEPT.

Concessions Mgr.
  or Contractee
Maitre d'
Chefs
Bartenders
Waiters
Waitresses
Concession Booth
  Operators
Bus Boys
Dishwashers
Track Kitchen Mgr.
  or Contractee
Jockey Room Snack Bar
  Mgr. or Contractee

Chapter Fourteen
Personnel Needed to Operate a Pari-Mutuels Facility

Let's assume a permit has been given to a group to operate a pari-mutuels operation at a dog or horse track or a jai alai fronton. Certain requirements are spelled out in the permit concerning the alloted number of racing days and the physical requirements for the facility. The Racing Commission must inspect and approve these facilities before the organization can open for business. Next, the organization must submit to the Commission a list of names who will be in key positions, for the Commission's approval. These include the General Manager, Stewards and various other Department Heads as required by a particular Commission. The Commission also appoints personnel to act in their behalf to assure that the operation is carried out so as to conform with the provisions in the permit and to follow the Commission rules as pertains to the track's actual operation. A general outline of the structure of personnel necessary for a complete operation both from the standpoint of track management and the Racing Commission is described on the following pages for each category of racing as well as for jai alai.

RACING DEPARTMENT

GENERAL MANAGER

The General Manager is the conduit between Track Owners and all other employees, Department heads, the Racing Commission and various contractees connected with the operation of the Track. His duties are numerous and varied. He carries out the policies of the owners, and must have an all around knowledge of racing and the Pari-Mutuels System. He is the Track's representative at Commission meetings and signs contracts with various concessionaires. His policies, and his selection of efficient Officials and Department heads often make the difference between a successful operation and an unsuccessful one. His decisions are final, except during racing hours, when it is possible for these decisions to be overridden by the Presiding Steward.

Racing Officials, in fact the entire Racing Department is identical for Thoroughbreds and Quarterhorses. At some of the smaller operations, it is possible to double up on many of the jobs listed in this department. This is necessary in some cases, to make it economically feasible to operate. The Racing Commission will usually grant the request to double up, if they feel the need is justified.

DIRECTOR OF RACING

Under the direction of the General Manager, the Director of Racing sets the policies of the Racing Department and oversees this branch of the operation.

STEWARDS

There are usually three Stewards, two representing the track, but approved by the Racing Commission, and one representing the State. They must see that all rules governing racing in that particular state, are carried out to the letter. They have the power to change the order of finish, if in their judgment, this finish was influenced by any infraction of rules during the running of the race. They may order money refunded on any entry whose start was impeded by mechanical failure of the starting gate. They have the power to suspend the license of any employee, or anyone else who is licensed in any capacity, for rules infractions, or conduct detrimental to the conduct of racing. They set the specific time for a formal hearing of those suspended. They have the authority to levy fines, suspensions, or probations as they see fit. The party punished does have the right to appeal the verdict to the Racing Commission, and the final dispensation is made by the Commission's governing body. But during racing hours, the Steward designated as the Presiding Judge (usually the state-appointed Steward) has the authority to overrule any decision made by any employee or department head licensed at this particular track. He also has the authority to take action against any unlicensed person whose conduct conflicts with the rules of racing. The Stewards may also order any horse to be scratched before the start of a race, if, in their judgment, the horse is not physically fit. Most often, this is done upon the advice of the Track Veterinarians. The Stewards are also responsible for pushing the button to close the betting windows at the start of the race, and to declare the race "Official" when everything is in order to their satisfaction. Written reports of any actions taken by the Stewards must be reported to the Racing Commission daily.

PLACING JUDGES

The Placing Judges determine the order of finish of every race, and report these results to the Mutuels Department immediately for calculation of the pay-off prices. They sometimes need the aid of the pictures from the Photo Finish camera, and co-ordinate their duties with the Photo Finish Operator. However, the decision of the Placing Judges regarding the order of finish is final. They must also send, in writing, the results of each race to various departments, including the Racing Commission, and the Horsemen's Bookkeeper. Another of their duties is to watch the infield board for electrical malfunctions or discrepancies.

RACING SECRETARY

The Racing Secretary screens applications for stall space from owners and trainers, and determines which horses are acceptable for competition at the track. After acceptance, he must make sure the Registration Papers for these horses are accurate and up to date. He writes what is known as a "Condition Book." This book describes contemplated future races for each day of the racing meet. This description includes: what age the horses must be; the distance of the race; the basic weight to be carried; the race classification (claiming, allowance, etc.); the claiming price if a claiming race; and all other conditions that must be met before a horse is elegible to enter and to receive weight allowances. The Condition Book is issued well in advance of the actual race date, so the Racing Secretary must know the past records of all the horses available, and thus ensure that there are enough entries to make each race competitive. Conditions are set for all types of races to give all entries as equal a chance as is possible. A good Condition Book will use all the horses available, giving trainers a chance to enter all the horses in his care.

There are several categories of races. The most common is the "Claiming Race". This means that in any given claiming race, you are willing to sell this horse for the amount specified in the condition book via the claiming procedure. Any licensed owner, or authorized agent of an owner, has the option of claiming any horse from any race, so designated, by depositing the amount specified, along with the horse's name, prior to the race, in accordance with the claiming rules. If more than one claim is properly filed for the same horse, the new owner is determined by a drawing. If the claimed horse earns any portion of the purse in the race in which he is claimed, the money goes to the original owner. If anything happens to the horse during the running of the race, even if he should die, the loss and expenses are the obligation of the new owner. Once the horse sets foot on the track for the race, the deal is binding. Of course the horse must meet all other conditions outlined in the condition book for the race in which he is entered. A horse that has been claimed cannot be entered in another race within a thirty-day period after claiming for less than a 25%-higher claiming price. For example, a horse claimed for $2000 would have to be entered in at least a $2500 claiming race within thirty days after he'd been claimed. Usually, a horse must remain under the same ownership for thirty days after claiming, unless reclaimed during that period.

"Maiden Races" are for horses that have never won a race. Horses begin racing when they are two years old, so there are lots of Maiden Races written for two-year-olds. The winners become ineligible for further Maiden Races, and therefore give those left a chance to also graduate from the Maiden class. There are races written for Maiden three-year-olds only, and races that include a mixture of three- and four-year-olds. Some races written for Maidens include a claiming price.

"Allowance Races" are made with similar conditions to Claiming Races, as to age, distance, weight, etc. But an owner or trainer cannot lose his horse in these races by the claiming procedure.

"Handicap Races" are usually those which draw the best class of horses at the track, with the exception of a few Stakes Races and Futurities. There are no set conditions as to which horses can or cannot be entered for Handicaps, but this causes few problems, since it would be foolish to enter a horse with limited speed against the best at the track. The races are called Handicaps because the weight each horse must carry is determined by the Racing Secretary in such a way as to give each horse in the race as much of a chance as is possible.

"Stakes Races" require an entry fee from the owner or trainer, and the track adds a specified amount to the purse. There are various kinds of Stakes Races. Allowance Stakes have weights determined by Allowance conditions. In Handicap Stakes, the weights are assigned by the Racing Secretary. Derby Stakes are limited to three year olds. The supplemental entry fees vary according to which kind of Stakes Race is involved. In most races, certain time limits are set for each supplemental fee. After each such date, it is no longer possible to keep the entrant eligible by making the supplemental payment.

"Futurities" Stakes are limited to two-year-olds. The first entry payment must be paid while the horse is still a yearling. Supplemental rules apply after the horses reach two years of age, as governed by the rules applying to that particular Futurity.

All two-year-old fillies are assigned three less pounds of weight than the colts and geldings. (For racing purposes, all horses become one year older on January 1st, regardless of their actual date of birth.) Fillies and mares three years old and older receive a five pound weight allowance until September 1st, after which the allowance is reduced to three pounds.

Lastly, the Racing Secretary is responsible for submitting complete, accurate information on the entries for each day's racing to the printer of the Official Program, after the entries have been closed and post positions drawn.

ASSISTANT RACING SECRETARY

The Assistant Racing Secretary helps the Racing Secretary, and is usually very active during the time entries are being taken in the racing office.

PADDOCK JUDGE

The Paddock Judge is in charge of the saddling area. He makes certain the trainers in the barn area are notified by public address system when it is time to bring their horses to the paddock. He must make sure that all the horses are in the paddock at a designated time, that they are properly identified, and that they are saddled correctly. He reports to the Track Veterinarian any horse's questionable physical condition and reports any trainer who gets his horse to the paddock late. He tells the jockeys when it is time to mount, and makes sure the horses enter the track at the proper time for the Parade to Post. Twelve minutes is the normal time alloted for the Post Parade. The Paddock Judge must also keep a written record of all equipment on each horse saddled, and report any changes of this equipment to the Stewards. He must also inspect the bandages on each horse. If the weather is extremely bad, the Judge keeps the horses in the paddock until just before the race. It is announced to the public that this is being done. The bulk of betting occurs after the horses start their Post Parade because many customers like to look at the horses before they make their wager. The Paddock Judge is also responsible for the conduct of the owners, trainers, grooms, valets and jockeys while they are in the paddock area.

PATROL JUDGES

Patrol Judges have been practically eliminated at some smaller tracks who rely on the "film patrol" to detect infractions. Still, some states require that at least four be placed in towers at advantageous locations to observe the running of the race. They are equipped with intercom head-sets, as is one of the Stewards. If there is a question of a foul at any point, the Patrol Judge reports this suspected infraction, so that the Stewards can more carefully study the film furnished by the film patrol at that particular point in the race, and determine if the outcome of the race was affected in any way. A written report is submitted after each race by the Patrol Judges.

IDENTIFIER

In the paddock, the identifier must check the number tattooed inside the upper lip of each entry, and compare it with the number from the horse's registration papers to make sure the correct horse is being raced. His immediate superior is the Paddock Judge.

CLERK OF SCALES

The Clerk of Scales must weigh the jockeys before the race, record any overweights on the "change board," and notify the Track Announcer of these overweight changes so that they can be announced to the public as the horses enter the track for the Post Parade. Overweights occur when the jockey and his tack weighs more than the assigned weight printed on the Official Programs. He must weigh the Jockey in again after the race. The jockey must finish the race not weighing less than his assigned weight. Otherwise his mount will be disqualified from his position of finish in the race.

STARTER

The Starter has charge of the horses from the time they leave the paddock until the actual start of the race. The Starter directs the Assistant Starters who help load the horses in the starting gate. He submits a program to the Stewards at the end of the day, showing the name of each Assistant Starter who handled each individual horse. He is responsible to see that all horses are securely in place, and therefore get a fair start when he unlocks the gate to start the race. He must see that all horses are in the correct gate according to the post position listed on the Official Program. He must submit a list of unruly horses who are to be schooled in the starting gate during training hours. He is also charged with immediately notifying the Stewards of any gate malfunctions that cause an uneven race start. He may also recommend fines or suspensions of personnel not following his orders during the start of a race.

TRACK SUPERINTENDENT

The Track Superintendant is responsible for the condition of the racing strip and the equipment necessary for its maintenance, such as tractors, harrows, drags, water trucks, etc.

TRACK VETERINARIANS

Veterinarians practicing at any track must be licensed by the Commission to treat any horse racing, whether the horse is treated on or off the track grounds. The official Track Veterinarian may not treat any horses registered to run at the track at which he works, but he is responsible to check the horses in the paddock, and at the starting gate, prior to the running of each race, to make sure all are physically able to compete.

TRACK ANNOUNCER

The Track Announcer's main purpose is to describe the running of the race, during its progress. Before the first race, he receives the scratches, jockey changes, and overweights for the entire racing program from the Clerk of Scales. These changes are announced to the public, and are repeated before each race, along with any additional changes as the races progress. He relays messages from all other departments to the public by means of a public address system, and gives a rundown of the horses and jockeys' names as they enter the track for the Post Parade. He also announces the results when each race becomes "official."

STALL SUPERINTENDANT

The Stall Superintendant receives the number of stalls assigned to each individual trainer from the Racing Secretary. He then locates them in particular barns and stalls. He must keep a record of all stalls being used, and by whom. He also keeps a list of vacant stalls for incoming horses, which he assigns at the newcomers arrival.

JOCKEY ROOM CUSTODIAN

The Jockey Room Custodian assists the Clerk of Scales in any way this Official requests, seeing that order, decorum and cleanliness are kept in the jockey and scales room, overseeing the care and storage of all racing colors (jockey's uniforms), supervising the jockeys' valets, and arranging their rotation among jockeys in the manner of weighing out. He must report any irregularities to the Stewards, and see that all jockeys and valets are neat in appearance and attire when they leave the room for the running of the race. He must also keep all unauthorized persons outside these areas.

HORSEMEN'S BOOKKEEPER

Each Racing Association (the organization that is licensed to hold the race meeting) is required to provide an office in order to keep a separate bank account, known as the Horsemen's Account. At all times this account must contain sufficient funds to cover all monies due horsemen: purses, jockey fees, stakes, rewards, claims and deposits. The account is subject to audit by the Commission at all times. The track provides a person, known as the Horsemen's Bookkeeper, to handle this office. He keeps a separate ledger on each owner, or owner's authorized agent, and credits cash deposits and shares of purses after he receives word that the urinalysis of the winning animals proved that no illegal drugs were used on the horse. The Bookkeeper is also required to see that jockey fees are collected from each individual owner and credited to the appropriate jockey. He compiles a weekly report of each jockey's earnings and the total taken from the Horsemen's Account for the jockey's payroll. Cash withdrawals may be made against their account by the owners during the race meeting and any balance remaining at the close of operations is paid to them to close all accounts.

CLOCKERS

Clockers are required to be at the track during training hours to time the horses in their workouts. They keep records of these workouts, turn in copies to the Racing Office, and also to the person at the track who represents the Form Chart.

ENTRY CLERKS

The Entry Clerks are on duty at the Racing Office in the mornings when entries are being taken. The entry slips are checked for corrections, processed and turned over to the Assistant Racing Secretary for further checking.

VALETS

The Valets are under the supervision of the Jockey Room Custodian, and are paid by the track at the rate of so much per horse saddled. Sometimes, they are given extra money by the jockeys that they service in the form of a tip. They keep the jockey's tack (boots, saddles, whips, etc.) clean and in place, see that the jockey's equipment, plus his own weight, is in conformity with the assigned weight. A valet returns the tack to the jockey room from the unsaddling area after the completion of each race.

ASSISTANT STARTERS

The Assistant Starters are often called "Gate Men." They work under the Starter at the starting gate, and follow his orders in loading the horses in the starting gate and keeping them in position for an equal start.

OUTRIDERS

Outriders lead the entries from the paddock area to the starting gate during the Post Parade. They also give any assistance needed to the pony riders during this period. (Pony riders are people used by the trainers to help the jockeys with their horses during the Parade to the Post.) Outriders also are assigned to catch runaway horses during the Post Parade, and any who break free from the starting gate during the process of loading.

AMBULANCE DRIVERS

Ambulance Drivers are stationed so that they can reach any Assistant Starter or jockey injured during the Parade to the Post, at the starting gate, or during the running of the race. Two ambulances must be available, so that there will always be one on hand in case the other is enroute to or from the hospital with an injured person.

SECURITY PERSONNEL

The security personnel in the barn area are part of the overall security force, but they have the added responsibility of patrolling the barn area—not only for misconduct such as vandalism or drugging, but to guard against fires. They must also keep all unauthorized persons out of this area. The entire barn area *must* be securely fenced. All entrances must be manned by security guards to see that only properly licensed persons are permitted in this area.

TRACK PHYSICIAN

A Track Physician must be on hand during racing hours to care for customers, employees, or other personnel who are part of the operation. A physician is on call during training hours.

TRACK NURSES

Nurses are present at the First Aid station during training and racing hours to minister to patrons as well as the employees. Normally, the nurses' station is in the betting and spectator area, readily accessible to patrons.

BUGLER

Some tracks still employ a bugler to play the Call to Post, the traditional summons for the horses to come onto the track for the next race. But most tracks now use a recording, broadcast over the public address system.

BARN MAINTENANCE CREW

The maintenance crew of a barn area at a horse track usually answers to the Track Superintendant and other department heads with responsibilities for the barn area. Their work consists mainly in keeping the barn area clean and in repair. This includes the disposal of the manure, unless a contractee takes care of this responsibility.

All of the above personnel are paid a salary by the Track. In the categories below, most are self-employed, or are paid by those who themselves are self-employed. A few are contractees, or are paid by these contractees. However, they are all subject to being licensed by the Racing Commission, and must abide by the rules of racing at the particular track where they are presently working.

HORSE OWNERS

Horse Owners sometimes train their own horses, but more often employ a Licensed Trainer to carry out the duties of training and racing them. Any person's name appearing on the horse's Certification Papers must be licensed as an owner, even if the horse is jointly owned and each is subject to the rules and regulations of the State and Track. The Owner may assign another person, called an Authorized Agent, often his Trainer, the Power of Attorney to handle financial transactions and conduct business as pertains to the horses he owns. These Authorized Agents must be approved by the Commission. If he wishes to race his horses at a certain Track, he must apply for stalls and submit the Certification Papers for each horse to the Racing

Secretary for approval. These papers must be up to date and correct. The Racing Secretary examines these applications and grants him a certain number of stalls. In turn, the Stall Superintendant assigns the approved horses to a certain barn, and to certain stalls within this barn. He may replace these horses with others under his ownership which have been approved during a current race Meeting. Next, he must set up an account with the Horsemens Bookkeeper, to take care of jockey mounts etc. When he is properly licensed, he is issued identification allowing him in the barn area and the Paddock during the saddling periods, when his horses are involved. During the time he is licensed as an owner, he may not be in the employ of the Track in any other capacity, in most, if not all states. He is responsible for picking up any identification used for access to the Barn area or Paddock of any discharged employees. He must file in writing, the termination of any agreement with his Authorized Agents. When applying for his license, he must also submit satisfactory evidence of his financial stability, and ability to care for, and maintain any horses he may own. He must also have a satisfactory moral background. Further, he must report any changes of personnel to the Stewards within twenty four hours of the change.

AUTHORIZED AGENTS

An authorized agent may be an agent for more than one party, but must obtain a license for each person that he represents. He is permitted to appoint a sub-agent, but only when authorized to do so by the document under which he was licensed.

TRAINERS

A trainer must demonstrate enough previous track experience with a racing stable (usually for a period of at least two years) to satisfy the Stewards that he is capable of carrying out the duties necessary to train a horse for racing. Usually, he must be recommended in a written statement by two persons known by the Stewards, attesting that he is a person of good reputation and has adequate knowledge of training procedures. A trainer usually must take a written test proving his competance. Once approved, he is held responsible for the condition of all horses under his care, and must be in the paddock to supervise the saddling of these horses or receive permission from the Stewards for an assistant trainer or another licensed trainer to perform these duties. A trainer is usually required to keep an up-to-date list of his employees on file with the Commission. Obviously, all of these employees must be properly licensed. Like owners, trainers must pick up identifications from discharged employees. The same general rules apply to assistant trainers.

GROOMS

Grooms are hired by the trainers. They feed and groom the horses, take them to the paddock, and return them to the barns after the race to cool them out.

PONY RIDERS

In addition to helping the jockeys with their horses during the Post Parade from the paddock to the starting gate, the riders help regulate horses during training periods.

JOCKEYS

There are many requirements that must be met before a person can become a jockey. Upon recommendations from trainers, starters, or others knowledgeable in racing (and having worked for a racing stable in some capacity for at least one year), the Stewards may permit a person to ride in two races on a probationary basis. At the Stewards request, he must also furnish a medical affidavit, stating that he is physically and mentally capable of riding in a race without jeopardizing the safety of the other jockeys. Anyone under the state's legal age must have written consent from their parent or guardian to apply for a license; all candidates must be at least sixteen years old. If the probationary rides are satisfactory to the Stewards, and all other license requirements are met, this person can become an apprentice jockey. Rules differ in some states, but in a typical situation, an apprentice jockey will start riding with a five pound weight allowance (i.e. may ride five pounds lighter than the assigned weight). He will continue to get this allowance for one year from the date of his fifth winner, after which, if he has not ridden forty winners in the year following the date of his fifth winner, this allowance will continue for a period not to exceed three years from the date of his first winner, or until he has ridden forty winners, whichever occurs first. Often an apprentice jockey will have a contract with an owner or trainer. If this is the case, after the above provisions have been completed, he may still receive a three-pound allowance for an additional year when riding for the party holding his contract.

Contracts are for different lengths of time, but most contain provisions for fair remuneration, adequate medical care, and an option for either party to cancel the contract after two years from the date of execution. Jockeys *not* under contract are paid by the owners of the horse, or by their authorized agent, through the Horsemen's Bookkeeper. The Horsemen's Bookkeeper withholds the amounts earned by the jockeys from the owner's accounts. He then transfers this amount of money to the department making up the jockeys' payroll. Pay standards (called "jock mounts") differ according to the size of the purses. An example: a guaranteed thirty-five dollars per ride, with the winning horse's jockey receiving 10% of the net proceeds received by the owner.

All jockeys are subject to the rules of racing, and are accountable to the Stewards for actions both on and off the track. The Stewards may levy fines or order suspensions for infractions of these rules. Jockeys have certain responsibilities. A list of these requirements is posted by the Jockey Room Custodian in the jockey room. For example, a jockey may be required to view films of races in which he has ridden. He is required to watch these films, so that the Stewards may point out riding infractions, or careless riding. Most jockeys belong to the Jockeys' Guild, an organization which represents them in their contracts with the Commissions, the tracks, and owners and trainers (see section on the Guild).

An explanation of the terms "weight allowances," "weighing in," "weighing out" and "overweights" is probably in order here.

When a weight has been assigned for a horse to carry during a race, either by the Racing Secretary's Condition Book or by his assignments of weights for a handicap race, the jockey and certain items of his equipment may not weigh *less* than this amount. Failure to carry this assigned weight results in the disqualification of the horse. When the total weight of the jockey and his "tack" does not equal this figure, lead weights are inserted in the saddle blanket to make up the difference. (Items excluded in the weight total include: the whip, bridle, blinkers, head number, bit, reins, safety helmet and the number cloth.) Many times, the jockey that the trainer has named to ride his horse cannot meet this weight. This results in an "overweight" that must be posted and announced to the public when the horses enter the track for the Post Parade. "Weighing in" means just that: the jockey's and tack's weight before the race. "Weighing out" is the weight check *after* the race.

A claim of "foul" during the running of a race must be filed with the Stewards immediately upon completion of a race. A direct phone line is installed from the Winner's Circle to the Stewards office on the roof for this purpose. Only the owner, trainer or the jockey of the horse allegedly fouled can make the claim. When a foul is alleged, the Stewards must carefully study the films of the race to make a determination of the claim's merits, before they can declare the race "official."

If the claim is upheld and a horse is disqualified, he may be placed either directly behind the horse impeded, or he may be placed last. The fouled horse moves up in the order of finish accordingly, but may never be placed ahead of a horse that has beaten him and was not involved in the rules infraction. For example, if the horse finishing first fouls the horse finishing fourth, the horse originally finishing second becomes the winner of the race. The horse finishing third is then moved up to second place, the fouled horse who finished fourth is moved to third place, and the winner who committed the foul is placed fourth.

On the other hand, a meritless foul claim may be classified as a "frivolous claim." The party making such a claim may then be reprimanded or even fined by the Stewards.

If a disqualified horse is part of an entry (an entry is two or more horses racing for the same interest, and coupled as one for betting purposes), the other parts of the entry are also disqualified, even though they were not involved in the rules infraction. This, of course, is to prevent one horse and jockey of an entry from helping another part of the entry improve his position in the race.

JOCKEY AGENTS

Most jockeys have a person—called a jockey's agent—who acts in his behalf to obtain riding assignments for him from the owners and trainers. (A jockey may also act in his own behalf.) Before being licensed to act in this capacity, the jockey's agent must prove to the Stewards, through a written and oral examination, that he is qualified to handle the duties of this job. He must also provide an authorizing signature from the jockey he is to represent. Jockey's agents are limited to the number of jockeys they can represent at any one time, usually three. If an agent's agreement with any jockey is terminated, the agent must immediately make this known to the Stewards, along with any unfulfilled engagements he has made for this rider. No agent is permitted within the saddling enclosure, the jockeys' room, or the winner's circle during racing hours without the permission of the Stewards. Neither he (nor his immediate family) may own any part of a horse racing in that particular state. Agents are subject to all rules of racing, and are paid by the jockeys they represent, usually at the rate of 25% of the jockey's gross earnings.

EXERCISE PERSONNEL

Persons may be licensed to exercise horses during training hours, but they do not ride in official races. Sometimes a regular or apprentice jockey fulfills these duties (but they are not required to do so).

BLACKSMITHS

The blacksmith (or "plater") is licensed to shoe horses at the owner's or trainer's request. At least one blacksmith who works for the track only, must be present in the paddock area during racing hours to inspect shoes. He must report any discrepancies pertaining to shoeing to the Stewards, and also makes necessary repairs.

FEED CONCESSIONAIRE

The feed concessionaire, located in the barn area, sells hay, grain and bedding to the owners and trainers. Like all backstretch people, the feed concessionaire must be licensed and display the proper identification in order to be present in the barn area.

TACK ROOM CONCESSIONAIRE

Many times, the tack room concession is granted in conjunction with the feed concession. If it is a separate operation, the same requirements must be met as those of the feed concessionaire. This concession stocks all necessary tack, such as halters, bridles, saddles, lead straps, jockeys' boots, whips, etc.

COMMUNICATION AND ALLIED SERVICES

PHOTO FINISH

The Photo Finish is designed to aid the Placing Judges in making an accurate and impartial determination of the order of finish. The developed photos are then displayed in conspicuous locations for the public's inspection.

FILM PATROL

The Film Patrol crew and cameras furnish a complete film or video-tape recording of all races run. This film is used by various groups.

The Stewards review these films immediately after the running of each race to aid them in determining whether or not the race was run free from infractions.

The public is furnished replays on the closed circuit TV monitors within minutes after the race has been declared "official." These viewings enable the fans to see what happened to the entry they backed, and are used as an aid in handicapping in the future.

The track specifies certain times during training hours when replays of the previous day's races will be shown to horsemen and jockeys. This makes it possible for the owners and trainers to determine the extent of effort put out by their horse and jockey, and to look for signs of any physical problems their horse might have.

The jockeys may be required to view these films in company with the Stewards, so that their errors of the previous day can be pointed out. Many jockeys voluntarily view these films, to pick up pointers on how to improve their performances in the future.

CLOSED CIRCUIT TV

The closed circuit TV systems serve two purposes. They aid the public by keeping them up to date on odds, pay-offs, and results. Secondly, this TV system helps employees and department heads coordinate their efforts, by informing them visually of what is happening in areas other than the one in which they have jurisdiction.

INTERCOMMUNICATION AND PUBLIC ADDRESS SYSTEMS

The intercommunication system provides immediate contact of all departments with one another, concerning information not pertinent to the public.

The public address system gives the bettors important information, not possible to display on the Totalisator Board, or on the closed circuit TV system. The PA system also broadcasts the Track Announcer's description of the race while it is being run.

DAILY RACING FORM

The Daily Racing Form has representatives at the track, including a supervisor, a chart caller, and a chart taker. They compile information at most thoroughbred tracks, and send the data to their headquarters for processing. The end result is an accurate account of the past performances of all entries, selections on each individual race by experienced handicappers, latest results from other tracks, the racing dates of all thoroughbred tracks, and general information and news of interest to the racing public. The *Form* is on sale at the entrance to most tracks.

PRINTING CONCESSIONAIRE FOR THE OFFICIAL PROGRAM

This concessionaire and his employees usually do their printing at a facility away from the track, but their work must conform to the Commission's standards.

OPERATIONS DEPARTMENT

OPERATIONS MANAGER

The Operations Manager, appointed by and answerable to the General Manager, oversees the different Department Heads described below, and is directly in charge of the personnel who run the General Office, including the secretaries, pay roll clerks, office clerks and PBX operators. He often carries the title of Asistant General Manager, and frequently also acts as the Comptroller.

COMPTROLLER

The Comptroller audits the deposits from the various departments, including those from the pari-mutuels operation, admission tickets, parking fees, tip sheets and program sales, and the various concessions. He makes checks payable to the State for its share of the revenue. He must also approve purchase orders for materials and supplies, and keep records on the entire operation subject to audit by the Commission.

PUBLICITY DIRECTOR

The Publicity Director works within a budget to promote the facilities' business in various ways. Most common are; advertising by way of billboards, television, radio, newspapers, etc, and to sell advertising spots in the official program. He must call in entries and results and write articles to and for the various news medias, and should be present at the Track during business hours to promote good will among the customers. Ordinarily he has an assistant to set up special events, and to arrange for transportation for groups needing bus transportation. The Publicity Director also hosts visiting dignitaries and participates in presentations of trophies and other awards. At tracks that have curio shops, he is in charge of the material and personnel needed to operate this shop.

ADMISSIONS MANAGER

The Manager of the Admissions Department hires the numerous employees needed to sell and collect admission tickets. Each day he sets up money boxes with the proper change for each person collecting admissions at their particular booths, periodically checks to see that their change is adequate during their selling periods, and counts their money for overages or shortages when the booths are closed. He puts together receipts of all the combined booths, and totals them for deposit. He also keeps records of the total number of admissions sold and the amount of money collected.

RESERVATIONIST

The Reservationist has a seating plan with all available seats listed in the different sections. This person works during pre-race hours and takes phone reservations, as well as reservations from those appearing in person. Tickets are set aside for these seats or tables, and the seating plan marked with the name of the parties making these early reservations. When the Reservation Sales clerks arrive for work during business hours, the partially completed seating plan for their particular section, plus the tickets and money collected is turned over to these clerks for completion. The clerks check in at the end of the day, with the Admissions Manager, turning over the unsold tickets and money collected, for him to audit. The General Admission Ticket sellers need not have a seating plan, but simply sell tokens, in most cases, for use in turnstiles. The Admissions Manager checks the turnstile figures against the sellers money and tokens to balance this group of sellers.

CLUBHOUSE MANAGER

The Clubhouse Manager supervises the Reserved Seat clerks and ushers in his area, and takes care of any misunderstandings in regards to seating that can't be resolved by the ushers. Often patrons have to be removed from seats or areas that they have not paid for. If he has problems in this area that he can't control, he may call upon the Security Guards as a last resort. He is also available to answer questions from the patrons and look after their overall comfort and safety, such as keeping aisles and entrances clear.

USHERS

The ushers simply guide the customers to their correct seats and keep unauthorized patrons from using these accomodations.

ELEVATOR OPERATORS

Elevator operators take the patrons to the correct floor level, after checking their credentials to see that they are entitled to be in this particular section of the track.

VALET PARKING

The Valet Parking Manager is in charge of the employees actually parking the cars for the patrons and those collecting money for this added service. He must set up a system of parking that is fast and efficient. He must also start those employees collecting money with adequate change, check this situation periodically, count the number of cars parked, and justify this number with the amount of money collected. He must turn in a report at days end, of the number of cars parked and deposit the correct amount of money.

MANAGER OF GENERAL PARKING

The Manager of General Parking is in charge of those collecting money at the entrance to the general parking lot, and those directing the flow of traffic. He must give those collecting money the proper change, and periodically check this situation. He also must check the money collected at the end of the day and make a proper deposit. His employees see that parked cars are properly guarded, and report any cars that are locked with the motor running, or with the lights on. He must also direct an orderly flow of traffic to the exits after the day's racing is completed. (Employees are assigned to a certain area for parking, and it's the Parking Lot Manager's responsibility to report employees parked in other areas.)

TIP SHEET

Most tracks contract with one or more handicappers to make up a daily tip sheet for sale, as an aid to the patrons in helping them make their selections. Usually, the handicapper gives a percentage of his sales to the track for this privilege. The handicappers must be licensed, and so, too, must be the persons who sell these sheets at the entrances to the track. Most states require that each sheet contain the name of its owner and handicapper.

OFFICIAL PROGRAMS AND RACING FORMS

At most tracks, the same person is in charge of sales for both the programs and *Racing Forms* (sometimes forms and programs are split into two operations). He (or they) is responsible for furnishing the booths with the programs and *Forms* and the change to start selling, replenishing each when necessary. He must also balance the money of each seller, save the unsold programs and forms for counting, make the appropriate reports regarding sales, and make the deposits for these departments. He's also responsible for delivering the publications for sale at off-track sites, such as news stands and pharmacies. He picks up the unsold items, and collects the money for those that were sold.

Note: Most quarter horse tracks are not serviced by *The Daily Racing Form,* but incorporate past performances in the Official Program. This information is obtained from the American Quarter Horse Association by Telex. The quarter horse track hires the personnel to chart the races at the track site. These employees have the same duties as those from *The Daily Racing Form* at thoroughbred tracks.

MAINTENANCE CHIEF

The Maintenance Chief is in charge of keeping the premises clean and in repair. Under his supervision are: the track electrician; carpenters; handymen; and, clean-up crews who clean the parking lot, the grandstand, the Clubhouse areas, the paddock, jockeys' quarters, mutuels department, and offices, including those of the racing officials and the press. Sometimes the kitchens are included, if the concession department isn't assigned to take care of its own cleaning. The Maintenance Chief ensures that the rest rooms are clean and supplied, and that personnel are stationed in the rest rooms during business hours. He's also responsible for the tools, supplies, and equipment necessary for use in general maintenance.

SECURITY

Security is handled in three ways. Some facilities set up their own security system. Others contract for the service with an outside agency. Frequently, a combination of both provide security, working together with separate jurisdictions. The largest, and best known of the outside agencies is the TRPB (Thoroughbred Racing Protective Bureau), described earlier. Whatever the arrangement, this department is responsible for maintaining order and enforcing the Rules of Racing pertaining to the particular track and state. In addition, the security people provide twenty-four-hour surveillance in all areas of the track grounds. The Chief of Security works closely with the local, state and national law-enforcement agencies.

FOOD AND BEVERAGE CONCESSIONS

The food and beverage concessions may also be handled in three ways. The facility may retain sole control of all concessions; it may lease all concessions to a person or company; or it might lease some areas, and operate other areas in its own interest.

This department furnishes four different kinds of service. There are areas where full meals are served at tables, complete with maitre d's, chefs, waiters, waitresses, and bus boys. There are snack bars in the General Admission sections, selling liquor, beer, sandwiches, soft drinks and pop corn. There is the track kitchen in the barn area, serving only track personnel like horse owners, trainers, jockeys, grooms, exercise personnel, etc. And there is the snack bar in the jockey's quarters, serving the jockeys and jockey room personnel during racing hours.

The Concessions Manager is in charge of the full-service areas, operating them as would a private restauranteur. He supervises the maitre d', the chefs, bartenders, waiters, waitresses, cashiers, bus boys, dishwashers, etc. He may also be in charge of the snack bars and back-stretch services. If these are operated by a different interest, a department head would be required to purchase supplies, keep records of this particular phase of the concession department, set up and check cash registers of each booth, and hire the necessary personnel to operate the booths, the track kitchen, and the jockey room snack bar.

PARI-MUTUELS MANAGER

Duties of the Pari-Mutuels Manager has been described in detail earlier in the book.

ASSISTANT MUTUELS MANAGER

The Assistant Mutuels Manager aids the Mutuels Manager with all of his responsibilities.

CALCULATORS

The Calculators figure the pay-offs (as described earlier.)

SHEET WRITERS

Sheet Writers make a breakdown of tickets by pool and denomination, and keep a continuous record of how many and which tickets have been cashed, and how much money each cashier has paid out during the day. They determine whether the cashier's accounts balance, or are short or over. In a very small operation, calculators often double up as sheet writers.

ODDS MAN

Most tracks have electronic odds computers incorporated in their totalisator systems. For small operations that do not, the win odds are calculated manually. An odds man figures periodic odds changes based on information the system is furnishing, and calculates the final odds.

TICKET ROOM MANAGER

A room is set aside to check winning tickets that have been cashed and turned in by the cashiers for both the accuracy of the count, and the validity of each ticket. Each ticket has been stamped with the number of the window at which it was cashed, and is actually a receipt for the money paid the customer by the cashier. The Ticket Room Manager directs the personnel doing the actual counting and checking, and is responsible for the storage of these tickets for future reference or for auditing by the Racing Commission.

TICKET CHECKERS

The Ticket Checkers are responsible to the Ticket Room Manager, and carry out the duties described above.

MONEY ROOM MANAGER

The Money Room at a track acts in much the same manner as a bank, opening each racing day with a specified amount of money called the "bankroll". The Money Room Manager is in charge of the personnel counting the money, and is also responsible for keeping records of all transactions with sellers and cashiers. At day's end he must balance with the mutuels manager as to the amount of gross sales (the "handle") and the gross gains from the day's business. He deposits these gains daily, and keeps the bankroll at its specified level in the correct denominations for the next day's business. The gains from the daily operation consists of commissions withheld for State and Track, the breakage, and the winning tickets that will be cashed at a later date ("outs tickets").

MONEY COUNTERS

The Money Counters are responsible to the Money Room Manager, and are required to verify the money returned in each race by the sellers, as well as the money returned at the end of the day by each cashier.

HEAD SUPERVISOR

The Head Supervisor is in charge of all the ticket sellers and their immediate line supervisors. He must keep an accurate inventory of the ticket paper on hand, and is in charge of distributing codes for each race to the line supervisors.

LINE SUPERVISORS

A Line Supervisor is in charge of each ticket selling line throughout the facility. He must check test tickets issued by each machine on his line before selling begins each race, to verify its correctness as to pool, denomination and code being used for that race, and to keep these test tickets for future reference and audit. He must keep each machine supplied with the correct ticket paper, and assist the personnel representing the Totalisator company in keeping each ticket issuing machine in proper working order. He must notify the tote operator when his line is ready to start selling tickets on the current race. He must be sure that the correct window sign is displayed above each ticket machine for the customer's benefit. He is also in charge of the personnel operating each ticket issuing machine.

TICKET SELLERS

The ticket sellers are directly responsible to their line supervisor. They simply sell tickets from their machine as they are ordered, and make correct change. They keep a record of their sales for each race, and send this information, along with the money collected to the Money Room for verification.

CHANGE RUNNERS (MESSENGERS)

Most tracks use change runners for their selling lines. Since each seller turns over all his money from the previous race to the Money Room, he starts selling the following race with no money for making change. The change runner is issued a specified amount of money at the beginning of each day. He exchanges the large bills from the customers for smaller ones so that transactions between the customer and the ticket seller can be made easily. The Change Runner then takes the large bills to the Money Room and exchanges them for the denominations necessary to make further change. At day's end, he returns the original amount he was issued to the Money Room.

INFORMATION AND CHANGE

The information and change window is usually assigned to a person with extensive experience in the Pari-Mutuels Department, and who has a good all-around knowledge of the entire track operation. He answers questions from the patrons and changes money for customers in the denominations they request. He writes up claims from customers who feel they did not receive the correct change from sellers, or did not receive the proper pay from the cashiers. (Claims against the sellers can be determined immediately, since their money is balanced after each race. In cases of claims against the cashiers, it is necessary to wait until their entire day's work has been audited at the end of the day.) If these claims prove valid, because of the cashier being over the amount claimed, the customer can receive this money at a later date from the information window, or have the correct amount mailed to him, if he so desires.

At some tracks, the information window also provides a check cashing service for the customers.

PREVIOUS DAY'S TICKETS

Special windows cash valid tickets from previous days of a race meeting. Records of outstanding tickets are kept in an "Outs Book." This window is closed several races before the final race of the day at most tracks, to allow time for the ticket room to check the validity of the tickets and to balance the cashier performing this service.

CASHIERS

The cashiers learn the pay offs from the calculating room as soon as the race has been declared "official." These pay-offs are provided by different methods, the most common by closed circuit TV monitors installed on the wall behind the cashier's windows.

The cashiers determine the validity of the tickets presented to them by the patrons, and pay the customer accordingly. Corners are torn from the valid tickets, and stamped on the back with the window number to assure proper credit for the monies paid out.

Lists of the tickets cashed are made in duplicate. One slip is sent with the tickets to the ticket checkers to be verified, and the other to the sheet writers, who are keeping a record of the tickets cashed and their value, for each cashier, in order to balance their work at the end of the day. When sheetwriting is done by computer, this second copy is sent to the key punch operator for credit to the appropriate cashier.

Current race tickets are sent in every race. Previous race tickets (called "stragglers") are sent periodically, or at the end of each day, whichever system is preferred by the Mutuels Manager. Stragglers are processed and credited in the same manner as current race tickets.

CASHIERS' RUNNERS (MESSENGERS)

Cashiers' runners deliver the cashed tickets to the ticket room, and take the second copy of the ticket-list to the appropriate person handling the sheet writing.

They also take requisitions for additional money needed by the cashiers to the Money Room, and deliver this money to the appropriate cashier, after the amount on the requisition slip has been verified.

TOTALISATOR COMPANIES

The Totalisator companies provide the calculating systems used in pari-mutuels operations on a lease basis, and furnish a crew of highly trained technicians to install, operate, maintain, and service this equipment.

Day-to-day operations call for at least two persons, the operator and his assistant, to be present in the Totalisator room, where most of the central equipment is located. Usually one technician (machine mechanic) is provided for each selling line (unless two lines are small and close to each other so that one technician is able to service both).

Like the track's employees, these personnel must be licensed. They are subject to the state's rules of racing. Contracts provide that the Totalisator operator defer to the Mutuels Manager in regard to procedure policies as much as possible, and to instruct the other personnel under his supervision to do the same.

ARMORED CAR SERVICE

Normally, an armored car service delivers the Mutuels Department's bankroll each day from the banking facility used by the track.

The money is delivered at a time designated by the Mutuels Manager; the day's receipts is picked up at a specified time when the racing day is over.

The service must provide a satisfactory security force to be present when loading and unloading the money. Usually the track provides its own security people after the money is delivered to the Money Room and until the armored car arrives later to take the money back to the bank.

* * * *

Most thoroughbred and quarterhorse tracks operate as I've described it here, with the equally important but separate functions of the different departments, combining to make the track run smoothly and efficiently. Obviously, there will be variations from track to track, as management changes personnel and duties to fit their particular needs. Harness racing, greyhound racing, and jai alai operations, while quite similar to the thoroughbreds and quarter horses, do things a little differently. We will attempt to explain briefly these minor differences in the following pages.

HARNESS RACING

STEWARDS

Harness Track Stewards have the added responsibility of determining whether or not a horse going off-stride during a race should be disqualified. Their criterion is whether or not the horse gained position in a race, while traveling at a gait other than the gait designated for that particular race. A harness track Steward also rules on "lapped on breaks" at the finish line, meaning deciding if a horse broke stride at the finish line while one or more horse's noses were opposite the breaking horse's hindquarters. If this is the case, the Steward disqualifies the horse even though he did not gain ground during the break.

The other duties of the Stewards at harness tracks are nearly identical with those of Stewards at thoroughbred and quarter horse tracks

RACING SECRETARY

Although the Racing Secretary at a harness meeting has the same duties as he does with thoroughbreds and quarter horses, some categories of races are named differently. All three groups have claiming races, and all called by the same name. The allowance races, described earlier, are called "Conditioned Races" at harness tracks. Harness tracks also have races known as early or late closing events. These require nominations a specified period before the event. They almost always require one or more entry fees, often added to the purse before race time. Stakes and Futurities are the same in all three kinds of horse racing. "Handicap's" counterpart in harness racing is called an "Open Race", or sometimes a "Free for All". These events draw the best horses available. The difference is that there is no way the Secretary can even the entries chances by assigning weights, as he does with thoroughbreds and quarter horses.

A few tracks use "classified" racing, whereby the Racing Secretary places horses in letter classification groups (similar, as described later, to the greyhound system).

PADDOCK JUDGE

The duties of the Paddock Judge in harness racing have one glaring difference from thoroughbred and quarter horse procedures. Only one race is handled at a time in thoroughbred and quarter horse paddocks. But harness horses must usually be in the paddock two hours before post time, so horses from several different races are in the paddock at the same time.

PATROL JUDGES

Patrol Judges have the same responsibilities at harness tracks, but are positioned a little differently during the race due to the use of the mobile gate in harness racing. The Patrol Judges sometimes ride with the starter and watches the entire race closely, since the starting gate continues to move beside the horses near the outside rail, with its barriers folded parallel to the vehicle, while the horses are racing.

CLERK OF SCALES

No Clerk of Scales is needed for harness racing, since the weight of the drivers doesn't matter.

STARTER

The Starter of harness races has the same general responsibility as the Starter of thoroughbreds and quarter horses, but the starting method is different.

The Starter works from a mobile gate (a high-powered vehicle with hinged wings attached to the rear of the vehicle). The back-seat section is open, in the manner of a pick-up truck, with a chair attached, facing the rear. The Starter sits in his chair, with an excellent view of the field of horses, as they approach the starting gate. He uses a microphone to give instructions to the drivers of the horses and the driver of the vehicle, to insure an even smooth start. Both the horses and the vehicle gradually increase their speeds to the starting point of the race, at which time, the wings fold forward against the side of the vehicle. At this point, the driver accelerates the vehicle, moving ahead and to the outside portion of the track to leave clear passage for the horses. The gate continues around the outside of the track during the race, so that the Patrol Judge may observe any infractions of the rules. At some tracks, the Patrol Judge watches the progress of the race from his office on the roof of the grandstand.

ASSISTANT STARTERS AND PONY RIDERS

There is no need for assistant starters or pony riders in harness racing. The driver of the harness horse can control his horse without help.

JOCKEY ROOM CUSTODIAN

The Paddock Judge fulfills the duties of the jockey room custodian in harness racing.

DRIVERS

Regulations for drivers are basically the same as for jockeys.

A driver must be at least 16 years of age to get a license to drive at county fairs, and at least 18 years of age to participate at tracks with a pari-mutuels license. Whereas apprentice jockeys get weight allowances, apprentice drivers are simply designated on Official Programs by a (P) beside their names instead of the (*) beside a jockey's weight. An apprentice driver carries this status for one year or until he has had 25 starts at a pari-mutuels track, whichever occurs last. The same general qualifications are required for both drivers and jockeys to receive their apprentice license.

DAILY RACING FORM

The Daily Racing Form's services are used almost exclusively for thoroughbred operations. Past performances for harness races are usually compiled by employees of the track who follow the same procedures used by *The Daily Racing Form.* This information is incorporated in the Official Program. (Greyhound tracks and most quarter horse tracks use similar systems.)

GREYHOUND RACING

As with harness racing, the personnel requirements for a greyhound racing operation vary from those of a thoroughbred or quarter horse operation. Again, most of the differences are in the Racing Department.

STEWARDS

Greyhound operations do not require both Stewards and Placing Judges. Ordinarily, a Presiding Judge and two Associate Judges (one of whom is appointed by the state) can handle the duties of the Stewards and Placing Judges described in the thoroughbred operation. For one reason, there are no disqualifications in dog racing because one dog interferes with another. If, however, the Judges decide the interference was intentional, the dog is given a "strike." Before racing again in an official race, this dog must run in a schooling race under racing conditions and perform to the satisfaction of the Judges. If he continues to interfere, he is no longer allowed to compete.

RACING SECRETARY

A Racing Secretary at greyhound tracks has about the same duties as a Racing Secretary at horse tracks. The biggest difference is in the procedure of making up races. Whereas trainers of horses enter their horses in a race of their choice, a greyhound trainer simply puts the names of his dogs that are available to compete in the hands of the Racing Secretary. These dogs are then put in a certain grade to compete with other dogs in this same grade. Although different tracks use different letter or number combinations, their grading systems work basically the same. Some might use AA for their top grade and regress through A, BB, B, etc. Others might use A, B, C, D, E. Still others might designate the grade by numbers; 1 usually being the top grade, 2 for the next best and so on down to the "Maidens" (dogs that never have won an official race). Each track's grading system is followed by the Racing Secretary. To make up fair and competitive races, a dog is moved up one grade when he wins, and lowered one grade after a certain number of losses. The names of dogs in a particular grade are drawn by lot by the Racing Secretary. The post positions are decided in the same way as in horse racing.

Most grading system allow the Secretary to "make up" a certain number of special races per week. Some are limited to the top dogs racing at the track (in race track terms, the "Hot Box"). Others to certain distances different from the most common race distance of $5/16$ of a mile. Post positions are determined in the same manner as the ordinary graded races.

The Secretary also checks the correctness of the information provided on the Official Program, including the dog's past performance (usually his last six races). He is responsible for the dog racing in his correct grade and that he is meeting all requirements of the grading system used at this particular track.

PADDOCK JUDGE

Whereas thoroughbred and quarter horses are brought to the paddock by the trainer or his authorized representative *immediately* before each race, all the dogs that are going to compete in the current day's program must be delivered to the Paddock Judge (sometimes called a Kennelmaster) a certain number of hours before the first race. They remain under his supervision until each dog enters the track for his particular race. No one, other than the Track or State Veterinarian, the Paddock Judge and his assistants are permitted in the paddock area during this time (except if the dog becomes ill or is injured).

Upon delivery to the paddock, the Paddock Judge must weigh the dogs to be sure they are within the weight limits outlined in the Rules of Racing and to be sure the proper racing muzzle is provided. He must be sure that the dog is the same one listed on the official program. This is determined by a tattoo number on the inside of the dog's ear and by a bertillion card which details the dog's physical description (color, sex, scars, etc.).

When it's time for each dog to be prepared for his particular race, he is taken from his cage (these cages are called the "ginny pit") by the Paddock Judge's assistants. He is again weighed by the Paddock Judge, and his identification rechecked. The Judge then checks to be sure the dog has the proper racing blanket, that the blanket is secure and fitted properly, so that it will not impede his running. The muzzle is also checked.

Other Paddock Judge duties include supervising his aids, assigning each dog to the person who will take the dog from the paddock to the starting box (these persons are called "leadouts"), and keeping unauthorized persons out of the paddock area. The nature of greyhound racing makes it possible for the Paddock Judge to handle the duties usually assigned to the Clerk of Scales, Identifier and Jockey Room Custodian in horse racing.

PATROL JUDGE

The Patrol Judge in greyhound racing has limited but important duties. He is responsible for the welfare of the dogs and the conduct and performance of the leadout personnel from the time the dogs leave the paddock until they reach the starting box. He rechecks the blankets and racing muzzles when the entries are introduced to the public, makes sure the dogs are handled properly by the leadout personnel and helps the starter in the proper loading of the dogs into the starting box.

STARTER

The Starter at greyhound tracks sometimes assumes the added duties of the Track Superintendant. Besides keeping the racing strip in good condition, he must constantly check the working condition of the starting boxes as well as to supervise the loading of the greyhounds and making sure the starting box opens efficiently and at the right time. The Patrol Judge and the leadouts act as assistant starters in dog racing.

VETERINARIANS

The veterinarians at greyhound tracks have the same duties as those in horse racing. They must be present at weigh-in time (when the dogs are turned over to the Paddock Judge). They must then inspect the dogs to certify the dogs are in proper condition to compete. They must be available to inspect dogs becoming ill or hurt while in the paddock area and during the post-parade. They follow basically the same procedure in obtaining specimens for chemical testing of dogs for possible drug abuse, as do veterinarians in horse racing, and they also police the kennel area for cleanliness and conformance to the rules of racing.

ANNOUNCER

An announcer for greyhound racing has identical duties to those of a horse-track announcer, except that the greyhound announcer describes the running of a race by numbers, not names.

LURE OPERATOR

The lure operator has no counterpart in horse racing. A lure operator sees that the electric lure and the rail on which it rides is kept in repair. He operates the lure from a room on the roof of the grandstand. His most important duty is to keep the lure at a proper and consistent distance in front of the lead dog at all times during a race.

CHART WRITER

Past performances of the greyhounds are incorporated in the official program. A track employee usually called the Chart Writer charts the races in the same manner as the representatives of *The Daily Racing Form* do in thoroughbred operations. An assistant types the charts after each race and delivers them to the company printing the official programs.

All other aspects of a greyhound track operation are nearly identical with those of the different kinds of horse racing.

JAI ALAI

Jai alai obviously differs significantly from horse and dog racing.

Accordingly, this least understood pari-mutuel sport, has several operating requirements that differ from horse and dog tracks. For one thing, jai alai facilities require fewer personnel. The players regulate their own training. They need no special care or supervision by the fronton. Results of games can be determined without the aid of photo-finish cameras. There are no dead heats, because ties are broken simply by the players playing for additional playoff points. Maintenance is reduced to a minimum since the sports area is a small, enclosed building. Weather is no factor.

So the duties of officials regulating the games differ from the other sports. I'll merely list and describe the functions of the officials most necessary in conducting a jai alai operation, rather than make comparisons with horse and dog racing.

PLAYERS' MANAGER (DIRECTOR OF PERSONNEL)

The Players' Manager negotiates each individual player's base salary, working within a budget set up by the fronton's management. He also acts as a "Matchmaker," making up games with players who have basically the same abilities, so as to make the games as competitive as possible.

The Players' Manager establishes the rules for the players both on and off the confines of the fronton, in much the same manner as does a baseball manager or football coach. He sees that these rules are obeyed.

ASSISTANT TO THE PLAYERS' MANAGER

The Assistant to the Players' Manager, along with aiding his superior, usually is in charge of the game operations during business hours.

JUDGES

Ordinarily, there are three Judges whose duties are similar to those of a judge at tennis matches. One is responsible for the back court, one for the front court and the third for the middle section of the court. They rule on whether or not the ball (pelota) is in or out of bounds when the play is close, and determine if one player has interfered with the play of another. The Judge in the front court has the most dangerous job, since the balls are traveling at a much higher rate of speed in this area.

TRAINER (MASSEUSE)

A trainer at a jai alai fronton is like a trainer for baseball, football, or basketball. The condition of the legs, the right hand, and the right arm and shoulder of a jai alai player require most of the trainer's attention. NOTE: All jai alai players *must* play right-handed. If a person is naturally left-handed, he must make the switch when he begins his training period.

NURSE

A nurse is ordinarily required to be present during training periods, and must be on the premises during actual competition. A doctor is required to be present during the games, but only needs to be on-call during training hours.

BALL (PELOTA) MAKER

Ball makers—a person in charge and one or two assistants—work full time to keep the balls in repair. Most new balls are made in Spain, although a small percentage now come from the Phillipines.

Besides keeping these balls in repair, the ball makers rotate the balls for use, and keep them stored in proper atmospheric conditions to get maximum performance. After a day's use, the balls are "rested"; stored for as long as possible before being used again, to get a better and more uniform performance from them.

The ball-makers keep the balls marked indicating their "grades". Tightly wrapped balls, for instance, are more lively. Balls of the highest quality are usually reserved for the more experienced players.

CESTA MAKERS

The cesta maker and his assistants keep the cestas in repair and order new cestas when necessary. The player pays for his own cestas, but the fronton management provides specialized personnel to maintain and store the cestas.

STATE REPRESENTATIVE

The State Representative from the regulatory commission simply oversees all facets of jai alai operations to ensure compliance with that state's laws and rules.

We have covered all those personnel who are hired and paid by the Track Operators. I must again remind the reader that each operation has it's own system and some categories listed above are consolidated with one person having jurisdiction in two or more categories, while others may designate more than one person to handle one duty listed above. They may use different titles to describe a person's responsibility.

RACING COMMISSION STAFF

RACING COMMISSION

FIELD PERSONNEL	MUTUELS DEPARTMENT	OPERATIONS DEPARTMENT
OFFICE PERSONNEL	Pari-Mutuels Auditors	Admissions Auditor
RACING DEPARTMENT	LICENSING DEPARTMENT	Executive Secretary
State Steward	License Clerk	Legal Counsel
State Veterinarian	Fingerprint Clerk	Auditor
Test Barn Personnel	Photographer	State Chemist
Secretaries		Clerks
		Secretaries

Commissions vary widely, of course, from state to state. But a proto-typical commission for a state allowing only horse or dog racing would have the following general shape. First, the Commissioners themselves. The legis-lative act legalizing betting specifies the number of Commissioners, usually appointed by the State's Governor. The personnel under the supervision of these Commissioners are usually divided into two groups (executive and field personnel).

The executive branch ordinarily includes the Executive Secretary of the Commission, in charge of executing the rules set forth by the Commission and conducting the business necessary to run this agency. His personnel usually include the Legal Counsel, the State Auditor for pari-mutuels opera-tions (responsible to assure the accuracy of the revenues paid from the Track to the State), and the State Chemist (who oversees the testing of blood, urine, and saliva samples taken at the track from winning horses and dogs). The Executive Secretary ensures that the pertinent records and statistics are kept for use in annual reports to the Governor, Legislature and public. He co-ordinates this information with that of other states having pari-mutuels wa-gering, and with the National Association of Racing Commissioners (if his Commission is a member of this association). The Secretary is responsible for hiring and supervising the office force necessary to carry out the above duties, including the Field Personnel assigned to the various betting opera-tions under the Commissions' jurisdiction.

This field personnel consists of State Stewards, usually one for each track, to work in harmony with the Track Stewards, the duties of which were explained previously; a State Veterinarian whose main duty is to supervise the taking of samples from winning animals and others at random and to forward these samples to the State Chemist for analysis. He must also ob-serve the conduct and efficiency of the track appointed veterinarians; make inspections of the barn area for cleanliness; and insure that living and work-ing conditions are compatible with the standards set by the Commission for the horses or dogs, and the personnel in the racing department. Also in-cluded in this department are the secretaries and office clerks to assist the State Steward and the personnel to assist the Veterinarian in his collection of samples.

Chapter Fifteen
Totalisator Companies

Contrary to popular belief, the totalisator equipment used to process the betting at a track or fronton, is usually not owned by management, but is almost always leased from a totalisator company specializing in manufacturing and operating this equipment. Statistics in early 1980 showed that almost 95% of this equipment was supplied by two major companies.

The largest, American Totalisator Company (Amtote), recently became a division of General Instruments with headquarters in Towson, Maryland. It has concentrated mostly on the United States market. This company has serviced most of the larger United States track installations, the off-track betting facilities, and several state lotteries, processing in recent years, more than ten-billion dollars in wagers per year. It is also expanding to the new satellite betting market, as well as to some foreign tracks. The Sha Tin track, located in Hong Kong and San Isidro in Buenos Aires are two examples of this expansion.

The other major company, Automatic Totalisators, Ltd., has been active almost world-wide. Based in Sydney, Australia, their chief markets were in Australia, New Zealand, Great Britian, Asia, and Canada, with a few spots in Europe and South America, as well as the United States. For the most part, "Autotote's" early inroads into the United States market were confined to comparatively small operations. But by 1980 they were active in thirteen states with approximately 20% of the United States totalisator business. The U.S. division is based at Newark, Delaware, and was acquired in 1979 by a U.S. holding company. Autotote now has the right to service the North, Central, and South American countries, while Automatic Totalisators, Ltd. retains exclusive rights to Australia and Asia.

Both of these companies have provided excellent systems and service in the past. Over one-thousand employees are involved in the manufacture and service of their equipment being used in our country.

Many smaller companies have attempted to compete with these two organizations, with little success in the past.

But today's technological revolution suggests smaller companies may now be able to compete successfully in the totalisator business. New companies can concentrate on new systems, without the problems of phasing out the old ones. This alone gives them a chance to compete.

Another trend favoring new companies is the year-round operation of race tracks and jai alai frontons, or at least the operation of greatly expanded seasons.

The giant companies have for several decades been able to provide enough equipment and manpower to service operations with short racing seasons. Many times the same tote equipment was used at several locations each year. This permitted the major companies to provide equipment and service for the small betting operations at a competitive price with the larger ones. It also gave the two large companies a chance, during the slower periods of the year, to return their surplus equipment to their home base for maintenance and give their temporarily idle employees a chance to receive updated training on new systems. Smaller companies, in most cases, were unable to find locations to keep their equipment and employees busy for enough days per year to compete with the large companies' lease prices.

Since this equipment and service is almost always furnished on a lease basis, it takes several years to make a profit on the original investment of manufacturing and installing this equipment. A large amount of capital is involved. In recent years, and especially at the present, the computer age has dictated the demand for more sophisticated systems at a rapid pace. In order to meet these needs in many case, it has meant replacing old systems with new ones before the old systems had generated a profit for themselves. Further, even with their expansive facilities, building the vast number of new systems, as well as training their employees to operate and maintain the more sophisticated equipment, has become a challenge for the major companies.

These changed situations will undoubtedly enable some of the emerging new companies to survive and gain a small portion of the industry's business. I don't see that Amtote and Autotote will be adversely affected drastically by this trend. In fact, the new competition will probably be beneficial to them. They both have established excellent reputations to date, and the new competition should be an added incentive to continue and improve their performance, and stimulate the growth of new outlets for business.

There are many new companies surfacing. As in other businesses, a certain percentage will undoubtedly fail. Three companies come to mind which seem to have a good chance to survive and prosper. They are Southern Technology, based in San Antonio, Texas; United Totalisator with offices in Shepherd, Montana, and San Diego, California; and Dynatote, Inc., located in Pennsylvania.

Whatever success these companies have with their equipment, the bettors can be sure that the electronic revolution will continue, and that parimutuels service will continue to improve.

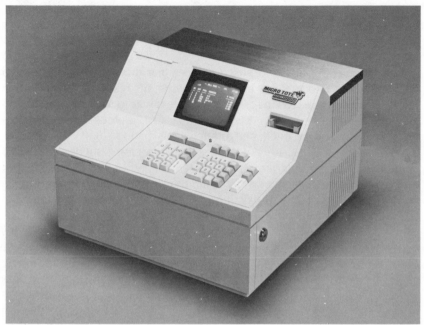

Cash-Sell Terminal (Courtesy of United Totalisator Co.)

Central Computer System—Cash-Sell (Courtesy of United Totalisator Co.)

Chapter Sixteen
Photo Finish

Most people would be surprised to hear that the conventional motion picture camera is actually a result of experiments made to record racing horses in action. The reason for this experiment was to study their form and therefore be able to improve their speed. At first, a group of still cameras were located along the track; and arrangements made to snap the shutters in rapid sequence. From a study of these still pictures, the motions of the horse could be visualized. Further improved methods led to the development of the motion picture camera in which a rapid succession of exposures is made through a single lens on a strip of film whose forward motion is intermittent.

Some kind of an aid to determine the winners of races where close finishes occured became extremely important as pari-mutuels betting grew. It's necessity became more apparent after photo finish cameras were perfected. Over and over it is proven that the naked eye is incapable of accurately calling the correct order of finish, of a race. Anyone doubting this, need only to work in the calculating room at a racetrack for a period of time. An original call is made by the Placing Judges before they have studied the film so as to speed up the calculation process.

Many, many times a change must be made after the films are examined. Most of these Judges are experienced and skilled individuals and have the advantage of the best spot at the track to observe the finish. When it is proven that often times their collective opinions of the order of finish is incorrect before viewing the film, it is no wonder that some times you hear disgruntled fans thinking they were cheated on the final results. We're now absolutely sure that such was the case in the old days. But not usually for the reason most people think. It is probable that a tiny few in number made calls to benefit themselves or their friends, but in most cases it was simply a matter of not being physically capable of judging finishes correctly 100% of the time. Judges in those days had a thankless job to say the least and at times it became downright dangerous. No so any more. Modern technology has taken the guesswork and mistakes out of this portion of the industry in the same manner that the sophisticated tote equipment has affected the calculation process. Like the tote equipment, the photo finish process was improved in stages until it reached its rapid accurate performance of today.

The forerunner of today's equipment was first used at Santa Anita, California on Christmas Day of 1934. It took about three minutes to produce pictures that would help the Judges make their decisions. It is not possible to document the improvements as they happened to any degree, since many companies made contributions at different times. However, for the benefit of the skeptical fans who still think their judgement, based on observations by the naked eye is more accurate than the photo finish camera, we will try to explain how the modern photo finish system works.

The judges determine places at the finish wire in the following manner. The nose is the deciding factor for all positions. The photo finish cameras are activated as the leading animal, or animals, approach the finish line. (The technical operations of this process, along with illustrations and examples will immediately follow this general information.)

The animal's nose must reach or pass the finish line in advance of all the others in the race. However, it is possible for "dead heats" to occur for either first, second, or third positions. For this reason, each race is recorded on film by a photo finish camera. High speed development immediately separates the noses of the animals at the finish line and thereby determines the winner of the race.

The photo finish camera is located in the Judges' stand above the track. It is fixed directly on the finish line where it is both stationary and immovable; and it's accuracy, in relation to the finish line, is periodically checked by a licensed surveyor.

A small vertical slot of approximately one ten-thousandths of an inch is made to coincide with the finish line and the film in the camera travels past this opening at the same speed of the horses or greyhounds. It records objects moving in one direction only—from left to right (in the United States).

No horse or greyhound, whether finishing on the *inside* or the extreme *outside* of the track can be photographed until they reach this band width of vision.

By virtue of the properly synchronized moving film, only objects in motion will photograph. Stationary objects such as hoof prints and dirt irregularities are recorded only as continual horizontal lines, an inherent feature of the camera in providing a substantially uniform background.

Each horse or greyhound is recorded as it's nose penetrates the finish line and this recording continues until all of it's body has passed the slot. This process is automatically repeated until the last horse or greyhound has finished the race. Thus, when a picture shows the results of a race, the animals behind the winner are also shown in exactly the order that they crossed the finish line. In racing, it is generally accepted that the time required for a horse to travel one length, (distance from the horse's nose to the end of his body) is one-fifth of a second. Greyhounds are estimated at .07 of a second per length.

To identify the race in the photo finish picture a spinner box is located on the inside rail exactly at the finish line. A drum inside the box containing the name of the track, the date, and the race number rotates at the same speed as the film in the photo finish camera. This information is photographed along with the finish of the race to assure authenticity of the picture.

The system for photo finish uses, for insuring accurate alignment, an engraved data bearing cylinder which rotates in synchronization with the moving film and records on the extreme edges of the film, alternately spaced vertical lines and numerical guides.

Every photo finish picture shows the finish line bisecting the exact numerical guide at the top of the print and the exact same guide at the bottom of the print—thus preventing any deviation from a right angle of the perpendicular finish wire.

The following is a detailed explanation and illustration of the above:

By referring to the following illustration the camera lens (figure 4) focuses the image of the horses through the vertical aperture (figure 6) onto the moving film.

The aperture consists of two rectangular plates (figures 6A and 6B) designed to facilitate an extremely narrow opening between the surface of the stationary edge (figure 6A) which determines at what point the cameras actually begin recording and, the adjusting edge (figure 6B) that controls the time factor the images are exposed to the film.

The width dimension of the aperture measures approximately ten one-thousands of an inch. This opening creates a narrow band of approximately four inches in width across the race track precisely paralleling the surveyed finish line (figure 2).

Referring to the illustration of the hypothetical race finish it can be seen that the tip of horse #1 has reached the finish line. At this point in time, only his nose has been photographed. A fraction of a second of time remains before horse #2 arrives at the finish line and begins his recording process, along with the completion of the image formation of horse #1. After horse #1 and #2 pass the finish line and are photographed in their precise positions respective to each other, the film continues to advance until horse #3 and #4 have been recorded. The camera continues this process until every contestant in a race has been photographed at the exact moment they individually arrived at the finish line.

As stated previously, it is generally accepted that the time required to travel one length is one-fifth of a second.

By using this formula one can determine that horse #3 is approximately two lengths or two-fifths of a second behind horse #1 at the moment horse #1 begins recording. Horse #3 cannot be photographed until two-fifths of a second have elapsed and he has moved into the cameras vertical aperture field of view. The subjective result is a continuous photograph of the finish, indicating the exact position of each horse as he crossed the finish line.

Occasionally there is a race finish wherein the Judges require a Win and Show photo finish picture. When these are displayed for public viewing the question arises—these seem to be the exact same photographs—with only the labeling changed to indicate Win or Show positions.

It is essential to remember—the camera does not photograph a conventional "still picture"—(a still picture would show the field of horses in their respective positions when the winning horse reached the finish line) therefore, a thorough analysis of the preceding paragraphs relative to the "elapsed time phase" will clarify this misunderstanding.

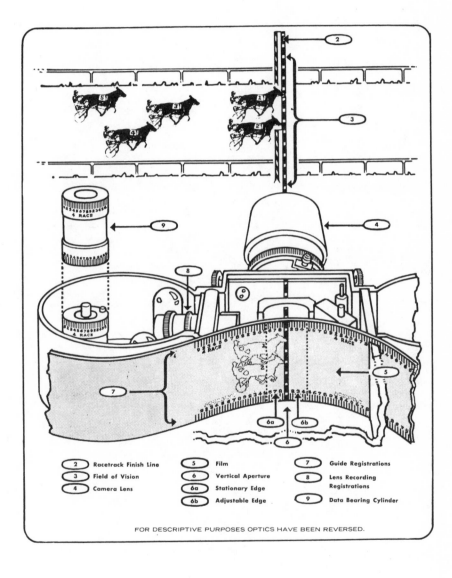

2	Racetrack Finish Line	**5**	Film	**7**	Guide Registrations
3	Field of Vision	**6**	Vertical Aperture	**8**	Lens Recording
4	Camera Lens	**6a**	Stationary Edge		Registrations
		6b	Adjustable Edge	**9**	Data Bearing Cylinder

FOR DESCRIPTIVE PURPOSES OPTICS HAVE BEEN REVERSED.

PART FOUR

Handicapping

Chapter Seventeen
Racing and Jai Alai Fans—Who Are They?

Nobody bets to lose, but simple mathematics tell us that there must be losers in order to keep this huge pari-mutuels industry alive.

Customers at tracks and frontons fall into three categories. First, the dyed-in-the-wool fan. A few of these fans actually enjoy the sport involved, but most are more interested in trying to make a living by betting, or at least in making some extra money. They go to the track or fronton almost every day of the meeting. They work hard at handicapping and have a very broad knowledge of everything that goes on. They often are very critical of operational procedures. Management might be well advised to listen more often to these regulars. Their complaints or suggestions could help their operation. These true fans are the ones with whom the clerks like to deal. They order their tickets correctly, have their money ready when the transaction is completed, know how much they have coming at the cashier's window and in most all cases will return money overpaid them voluntarily. A large percentage of this group are professional or semi-professional gamblers. I can't overemphasize how often the term "gambler" is used to describe people who are not gamblers at all.

Track owners are not gamblers because they own a track. It's possible that a track owner can also be a gambler, but the two are separate entities. Track owners are businessmen. The fact that a person owns a football franchise does not make that individual a football player. The principle is the same. A tout is not a gambler—he is a tout. A person who tries to fix races is not a gambler. In rare cases, gamblers have tried to fix races. But when this happens, he no longer fits the definition of a gambler. He becomes simply a race-fixer.

A bookie isn't a gambler either. A gambler bets with bookies. I should note that it's possible for a bookie to lose money in the bookmaking business, but he is still not gambling. If his bankroll is large enough, he must eventually come out on top. He is getting the same edge in percentages as the combined take-out figure for Track and State, because he is paying track prices. Plus he imposes betting limits and fixes the maximum odds he will pay, even though the track odds were higher. A true gambler is betting against the odds either at a track or with a bookie. If the take-out figure at a track is 17%, the gambler *must* have knowledge and handicapping capabilities consistently in excess of 17% over the rest of the participants in the pool in which he is wagering. Money, or his "bankroll" as a gambler calls it, is the same thing to him as carpenter tools are to a carpenter. It is necessary for him to maintain a large enough bankroll to get through his losing streaks, which are bound to happen periodically. When a gambler hits a long losing streak, his bankroll may be completely wiped out. Because this is inevitable at times, he must have proven to his peers, during his winning periods, that he is honest and trustworthy and capable of bouncing back. He must turn to them to re-plenish his bankroll, since it's obvious that he can't go to the bank and use comtemplated future winnings as collateral for a loan. A real gambler is usually willing to help another gambler during his lean periods.

All in all, gambling, as they say, is "a hard way to make an easy living". So, why would a person want to become a professional gambler? Not long ago, I overheard a conversation between a young lady who was a novice to racing and a gambler who had just cashed a large bet. She asked him, seriously, "What does it take to become a successful gambler?" His answer pretty well summed it up: "Well, first of all you have to have a bankroll; then you have to work hard at it; you must have confidence in yourself; you have to be patient; you definitely have to have your share of luck, but most of all, you just have to be loaded with plain old guts!" I would add to this profile that a gambler must be basically honest, that he must enjoy being indepen-dent, be of a competitive nature, be able to handle adversity in all its forms, and keep a sense of humor. Further, he must treat his winnings not as "easy come, easy go", but rather in the same manner as a steel-worker does his paycheck. This may be the most important item that separates a successful gambler from those who fail. A gambler who spends his winnings foolishly, and who devotes less time to his handicapping when he's winning, won't last long. It's easy to fall into this trap, since when on a winning streak, a gambler may think it will last forever. But luck will change, so he has to make the most of the good luck that he's experiencing at the time. In his way, he's worked just as hard as has the steel-worker.

The second category of customers consider racing as a combination of gambling and entertainment. A fan in this category is not at the track every day. Often he will go to a ballgame, go fishing, or use some other form of recreation during his free time. But he does come often enough to under-stand the basics of a track operation, and the gambling aspect is part of the reason why he is there. He may be a regular weekend and holiday customer if his job conflicts with the hours the track is open.

Category-three patrons attend pari-mutuels events almost exclusively for recreation. They usually bet lightly and aren't greatly upset if they lose. If they are lucky enough to win enough to pay their expenses, they consider the trip to the track a success. You will usually find them in the clubhouse at a table, having a few drinks and a dinner. They attend infrequently, some-times once or twice a season, or maybe only when they have guests from out of town, who they feel might enjoy going to the track or fronton.

A facility must cater to all three groups, if it is to get the maximum returns from their operations. If handled correctly, a percentage of category-two will eventually graduate into category-one, and some of the customers in category-three will soon be in category-two. New customers must be courted constantly to replace customers who drop out entirely from the racing scene for one reason or another.

I've found too, that most fans in all three categories prefer one kind of racing to others, or stick strictly with jai alai. This is true for the most part even with thoroughbred or quarter horse followers, even though these two sports are more nearly alike than any of the others. For these reasons, I sincerely believe that owners of any one kind of pari-mutuels operations over-react when they face the possibility of competition from another kind. Especially if they operate at different times of the day or year. They won't lose many customers to the new competition unless they aren't doing a good job of satisfying their customers to begin with. If this is the case, the competition is a blessing. They'll have to do what should have been done already—improve their operation.

Customers interested primarily in the betting aspect are constantly in search of systems or methods of handicapping, so that they can show a profit at the track. There is always a percentage of people who find it hard to make decisions on their own. This group will seldom attempt to make selections themselves but will depend on information from those whom they feel are better qualified. There are various sources where they can find this help. Most programs have selections at the bottom of each page, made by employees of the track, who are theoretically better informed than the average fan. It is possible to buy tip sheets, the selections of professional handicappers at the entrance to the track. *The Daily Racing Form* also contains selections from three more handicappers.

Some will look for someone to tout them. Friends, trainers, owners or as mentioned previously, a person at the mutuels window.

But most people want to do their own handicapping and make their own selections. There are literally hundreds of books in the country that have been written on the subject of handicapping. No two are exactly alike. Nor do most apply to more than one type of racing. Some of these books will advocate systems that will take hours for a bettor to prepare for just one day's races. A book like this may be helpful to those who have lots of spare time and are interested in regularly attending races to make money. This group, as I've said, is a small percentage of racing fans. For those who have other priorities and who limit their handicapping to the time they are actually at the track, books with complicated systems will be of little value. Of course, some books claim to be able to simplify the methods of handicapping, stressing a limited number of factors that can be evaluated rapidly. Following one of these systems, it's possible to have some winning days, or at least reduce your losses, so these quick-study guides are an asset to the industry.

The following chapter is devoted to my personel assessment of factors that should be considered by those who enjoy doing their own handicapping.

Certain principles apply to all five sports, but there are others which are very important to one sport, yet of little value to the others.

Therefore, I will treat each sport separately.

Chapter Eighteen
Handicapping Hints

Thoroughbreds are still number-one in attendance and volume of wagering. I'll start with this sport with the belief that a person looking for a real challenge in handicapping will find it at the thoroughbred track.

First of all, the distance of races is more varied in this sport, than in the others. Thoroughbreds compete at every distance from 2 furlongs to more than 2 miles. Two-year olds making their first few starts will sometimes go 2 furlongs. Most however, begin their careers at 4 furlongs (½ mile) or 4½ furlongs. Races at most tracks will also include distances of 5 furlongs, 5½ furlongs, 6 furlongs (¾ mile), 6½ furlongs, 7 furlongs, 7½ furlongs, one mile, one mile and 40 yards, one mile and 70 yards, 1¹/₁₆ miles, 1⅛ miles, 1³/₁₆ miles, 1¼ miles, 1½ miles, 1⅝ miles, 1¾ miles and 2 miles. Six furlongs (¾ mile) is probably the most common distance, followed by 5½ and 5 furlongs. Most stakes races are held at more than one mile for 3-year-olds and up, while 2-year-olds seldom compete at more than a mile and usually less, especially during their first six months of competition. The famous Triple Crown for 3-year-olds consists of the "Kentucky Derby (1¼ miles), the "Preakness" (1³/₁₆ miles), and the "Belmont Stakes" (1½ miles). Track size is a big factor in determining which distances are used. In earlier days there were many half-mile tracks, but most have been lengthened to one mile. There are a few ⅝ mile tracks left, fewer ¾ milers and even fewer measuring ⅞ of a mile.

Races are more formful when the horses have a longer distance to run before they get to the first turn. For example, it's unwise to have races at six furlongs when they are being held on a ¾ mile track. This would mean starting at the finish line, which is quite close to the first turn. So tracks of this size usually feature races of 5½ furlongs or 6½ furlongs. Also, some tracks of the same distance differ in shape. Some have much sharper turns than others. Chutes leading to the oval itself also differ in length. Distances from the last turn to the finish line also differ.

It seems that it would be wise to have all tracks built one mile in circumference, but there are logical reasons why this is not true. The two most important reasons are: availability of space, especially in instances where a particular track was built many years ago at a distance of less than a mile. By the time it was economically feasible to lengthen the course, the space needed had already been used to enlarge barn, parking, and grandstand facilities. The other factor usually prevalent and often overlooked, is that the customers get a much better view of the races at smaller tracks that conduct their business at night under the lights. Not to mention the added expense of installation of lights and the higher cost of utilities at larger sized tracks.

Obviously, these considerations affect the handicapping process. The shorter the run to the first turn, the more important the post position becomes. Horses on the inside, with any degree of early speed, will ordinarily travel a shorter distance from start to finish than those on the outside. The longer the run to the first turn, the less advantage to the inside post position. Some handicappers feel that a long run to the first turn actually favors the outside. Many times the inside horses find less running room unless they are blessed with early speed characteristics.

Track size also affects a horse's performance to varying degrees because of his conformation and individual style of running. Some horses are able to negotiate turns much better than others. A match race between two horses on a ⅝ mile oval, and then on a mile track, will often produce different results. Some horses have big, long strides—fast on the straightaways but who find it difficult to negotiate the turns as fast as their slower competitors with more maneuverability. Usually these long-striding horses require more distance to resume their maximum speed if they are forced, for any reason, to break stride during the race. Wider turns and longer straightaways are a decided advantage to the long-striding horse.

The composition and condition of a track are big items in handicapping thoroughbreds. No two tracks are exactly the same. Some have more sand and less dirt than others. Drainage varies from track to track. Assuming that weather conditions are ideal and that tracks are in the best condition possible, some horses will fare better on different tracks. When you hear a jockey or trainer explaining his horse's poor performance, he'll often say "He just couldn't seem to get a hold of the track". Sometimes this is due to improper shoeing, but usually it is the size and shape of the hoof. Moisture in the track's texture accentuates the problem. Officials post the present condition of the track, starting with "sloppy" after a big rain. The drying out process changes the track condition. After "sloppy" comes "muddy", then "heavy", "slow", "good", and finally "fast". Running times on a truly "sloppy" track will *not* vary greatly from those on a fast one. A real "sloppy" track will usually help a front-runner, since he and the jockey are not getting mud thrown in their faces. This factor is bound to influence the performance of trailing horses and jockeys. The "in-between" conditions—"muddy," "heavy," "slow," and "good"—usually present the biggest problem for a professional handicapper unless his research and memory are good enough to evaluate all or most of the entries from their past performances on a similar surface. Ordinarily, these "off track" conditions make for a higher percentage of winning "long shots", and some bad performances by favorites. "Class", as explained later, becomes less important when tracks are in a drying out process. The expression "this horse likes the mud" or "this horse doesn't like the mud", is misleading. I can't picture any horse stupid enough to like mud thrown in his face. The amount of dirt being thrown by the front runners makes it not just unpleasant, but also a little painful to both horses and jockeys coming from behind. The reasons that a particular horse may fare better under these conditions are: first, the confirmation of his hooves might make it possible for him to "get hold of the track" better than most of his competitors; and second, he might have soreness in his legs that is diminished by a softer surface, rather than the discomfort produced by running on a dry, hard track.

Different handicappers place varying degrees of emphasis on the weight a horse is required to carry during a race. Weight is supposed to be an equalizer to make races more competitive, and without a doubt this concept has merit. I would suggest that it's importance becomes greater as the distance of the race increases. However, this factor should not be emphasized without considering the past record of each horse. Weight does not seem to affect speed to any great degree, but rather the stamina of the horse in question.

Wind is an item seldom considered, but I'm not sure that it shouldn't be. The stronger the head wind, the bigger the disadvantage to a front runner. A horse coming from behind has had the wind broken for him for a large portion of the race, and this fact will definitely increase his stamina in the final stages.

There is no question that the jockey makes a big difference in a horse's performance. I have noticed that it doesn't seem to be as a great a factor at the major tracks as it is at the smaller ones. I believe it can be compared with major and minor leagues in baseball, or with college and professional football. In order to get mounts at a major track, a jockey must be extremely competent. Many of the riders at the smaller tracks are phased out quickly because of weight problems or because they are just plain not good enough to make a decent living at their trade. The smaller tracks also have a certain number of jockeys who have been to the "big time" and are on their way out, because of age, injuries, or various other reasons. Usually a large percentage of races are won by a relatively few jockeys at the smaller tracks. This group usually consists of good apprentice riders who will end up at the major tracks and are getting more experience faster than they could at the big tracks. There are also those who are marginal in ability. Not quite good enough for the big tracks but standouts at the smaller ones. This is sometimes due to their weight. Many riders have trouble in keeping their weight below 115 to 118 pounds, and still keep the strength necessary for top competition. Trainers at the smaller tracks usually are willing to sacrifice a few pounds to get a jockey with experience and ability. Trainers at the major tracks have a larger pool of excellent riders who can ride effectively at lighter weights to draw from. Thus the difference between the best and worst jockeys at major tracks is much less. At all tracks, jockeys usually end up in two categories. Those who excel at getting extra effort from front running horses and those whose chief asset is being able to improve the efforts of the "finishers". The ideal rider can do both, but they are few and far between. Often this does not reflect differences in their abilities, so much as it does their physical strength. Some horses need a great amount of forceful urging. Others will run pretty close to their potential on their own. In most cases a horse who runs better near the front needs a jockey with a good sense of pace, and who excels at getting a horse out of the gate quickly.

Maybe the most important item to look for when handicapping, as pertains to jockeys, is when a different jockey is riding a horse than has ridden him previously. If the change is to one of the leading jockeys at the track, besides the advantage of a better rider, it probably means that the trainer thinks that his horse is at the stage of training, where he is ready to give his best effort. The jockey or his agent, or both, also believe this particular horse has a good chance of winning. The pay for riding a winning horse is much greater than for riding a loser. Most leading riders have offers to ride several horses in the same race and will accept the mount on the one which he feels has the best chance. Even if the jockey hasn't selected the best horse, he at least feels that he has. I am convinced that this intangible factor means a lot.

Time elapsed since a horse's last previous start is another big factor, and a tough one to consider. Some need an actual race or two before they give a good effort. A few run well "fresh". Unless you are familiar with the horse's record under similar conditions in the past, about all you can do is watch the odds board to see if his odds indicate that others believe he will be a factor. The same is true if it is the horse's first official start ever.

I hesitate to discuss the factor of "time". I am in the minority in my assessment of it's importance. I don't believe that knowing the actual running time for a thoroughbred or a greyhound helps much in the handicapping process. In fact, in many cases I believe this knowledge to be counterproductive. This may not be entirely true in regards to standardbreds or quarter horses, which I'll discuss later in the chapter. It is my contention that the combination of three other factors determine the running time of a thoroughbred race: track conditions, pace, and class. First we'll consider track conditions. It is next to impossible for a track's condition to be identical on different days. Weather alone makes this a positive fact. A thoroughbred rarely starts more than once a week and usually much more time has elapsed between starts. Even though tracks are watered and conditioned during a racing card, the track will be faster for some races than for others. A windy day will not only dry out a track faster, but it will help determine pace. Drainage after rains often leaves the inside or outside of the track faster for a time no matter how expert and conscientious a maintenance crew may be. Crowding at the break, or close quarters during the race will change the final time to some degree. I will agree time is helpful in two ways. First the fractions (time of the first ¼ mile, ½ mile, etc.) helps dictate the ultimate final time of the race. But this reflects pace. A horse leaving the gate in front by himself creates an entirely different situation than if he has another horse along side. This not only dictates the strategy of the front runners, but the finishers as well. Often, on the same day, a $3000 claiming race will be run as fast as a $10,000 claiming race. I think most knowledgeable handicappers will agree that several lengths would separate these two winners should they race against each other. This can only be logically explained by the impossible to define word—"class". The other instance where time can help, is to compare the winning times of the first few races with the same horses' time the last time they ran. It will give a clue as to the actual condition of the track at the present time.

I have said that class is impossible to define. I say this because it is more or less a composite factor of all variances being considered. Since each handicapper puts emphasis on different factors, one's definition of class will not exactly fit the definition of another. Perhaps one definition that will not offend the majority is "a horse that has a history of competing with horses of greater ability than the ones in the current race in which he is entered". If we accept this premise, we have to know the background of all the horses entered in a particular race. A professional handicapper has the edge in this aspect. A few clues for a novice to consider in recognizing class are: Have they been racing at tracks having a larger volume of business than where they are now racing? (Volume of betting determines the size of the purses and better horses compete for higher purses.) Were they able to give respectable competition to these better horses? What type of races have they been competing in? Handicaps, allowances, claiming races where the claiming price was higher or lower than the claiming price of the current race? What odds was the horse when he competed with better horses? If all of these factors are too complicated, an easy way to find class in many, but not all cases, is to divide the horse's purse earnings by the number of times he has raced in the past two years. This information is available in the Racing Form.

A change of trainers is responsible for better or worse performances of horses in varying degrees. About the only way a novice can know about a trainer change is when the claim of a horse is shown on the Racing Form. It is important to determine if the horse has fared better or worse since he was claimed.

Age and sex must be considered in many cases. Fillies ordinarily mature slower as a two and three-year-old. This factor becomes less important from late summer to the end of the year. Many races are limited to horses three and four years old. Other factors being equal, the four-year-old usually is more mature and has had more experience. The time of the year applies in this case also. The nearer to the end of the calendar year, the less important this difference becomes in most cases.

Speed ratings are posted in the Daily Racing Form. Some handicappers use this information sparingly, others rely heavily upon it's importance.

Since horses compete at many different distances, most will eventually find a distance most suited to his particular style of racing and physical qualities.

His chances with horses of relative equal qualifications increase when he is racing at his favorite distance.

All of the above is designed for picking winners. Applying this knowledge is of little importance if a bettor doesn't handle his money wisely. Since this factor applies to all types of racing and jai alai, we'll discuss this in a general way after we compare handicapping procedures of quarter horses, harness horses, greyhounds, and jai alai contests, with those above as applies to thoroughbreds.

QUARTER HORSES

Many of the factors to consider in handicapping quarter horses are identical to those that apply to thoroughbreds, so rather than repeat them, we'll attempt to list those that are different.

Quarter horses also have many different distances at which they compete, but almost always race on a straightaway without having to go around a turn. Distances vary from 200 to 600 yards, with 440 yards (¼ mile) the distance most prevalent. Some states permit races of 870 yards, and allow entries of both thoroughbreds and quarter horses. In these rare cases, they must start on the backside and thus have to race around the upper turn.

Those not familiar with quarter horse racing, at once notice that many races are decided by inches or feet rather than lengths, and that often almost the entire field can literally be covered with a blanket at the finish line. Immediately, most decide that picking a winner in such close finishes is strictly luck, and that handicapping is a waste of time. This can readily be disproved by the fact that the percentage of winning favorites is usually greater at quarter horse tracks than at any other medium used for pari-mutuels wagering. This doesn't prove that quarter horse racing is more honest or dishonest than other sports but is primarily because no turns are involved. Pace and strategy are minimal. Post position loses much of it's importance, since all entries will run exactly the same distance. The extreme inside or outside post position might give a little edge, since it reduces the chance of crowding at the break, but that's about the extent of this advantage. A few quarter horses have a tendency to want to run near the inner rail and might cause the jockeys some problems in keeping them in a straight line from outside post positions. Rains, drainage, or poor track maintenance will occasionally result in either the inside or outside portion of the track being slightly better at times. When this situation occurs, it will affect a quarter horse race more than a thoroughbred race, since usually a quarter horse will be forced to stay in the same area of the track for the entire race, whereas a jockey on a thoroughbred can often guide his horse to the best footing on the track during the longer distance of the race.

It appears that if all these factors are relatively unimportant, handicapping quarter horses is simple. Not so! The length of the race, quality of the jockey, track conditions, reputation of the trainer, weight carried, age of the horse, and class are some of the variables to be assessed in the same general way as applies to thoroughbreds. In my estimation, time is a valid factor in quarter horse handicapping. The amount of ground covered at any given distance is more consistent, with no turns to negotiate, and the absence of pace to any degree.

Finally, in general, quarter horses are more sturdy, requires fewer training procedures and are less vulnerable to injuries than thoroughbreds, which will make his time more consistent.

HARNESS HORSES

Of all the different types of racing, harness racing is the sport where time appears to be the greatest factor in the handicapping process. At least, it is usually the first consideration and all the other variants are weighed against it. This is easily explained, since training procedures are much different. Pacers and trotters are worked several miles per day, even on the days they actually compete. They become almost like a machine and their maximum capabilities can be pretty well documented. So a handicapper will pretty well know who is actually the fastest horse in the race, all other factors being equal. Arriving at an eventual choice is another matter. In many cases the driver is also the trainer, or at least the same driver is used more often for the same horse, than in the case of jockeys in thoroughbred and quarter horse races. Most handicappers feel that the weight of the driver makes little, if any, difference. Track conditions does not seem to make as much difference in this type of racing, although it merits consideration to a smaller degree. Age and sex does not seem to make as much difference in harness racing. As with thoroughbreds, pace, post position, and class seem to be the most important variants to be considered. Pace can be used often to offset the advantage of class. Post position is important since it can be used as an advantage for actual position in the early stages of a race. Early position in a harness race has increased importance, since more distance is lost in passing other horses because of the width of the sulky. Pace is easier to control for the same reason. In order to change the pace that the leader is establishing, it means passing the lead horse and involves the loss of more ground, again because of the sulky's width.

The different distances used in harness racing are few. A very large percentage of races are contested at a flat 1 mile distance. Occasionally a track will offer a few races at slightly less, or slightly more distance, than the conventional mile, but these instances are rare.

The size of the track is a very important factor. Many harness tracks are ½ mile or ⅝ mile in circumference. Since most races are at a 1 mile distance, several turns are involved in a race at the smaller tracks. Horses coming from behind often have to pass on these turns and, of course, travels much farther than those racing on the inside. A horse, two or three sulky widths wide for very long, has to be much faster in order to win.

When a reasonably normal pace is being set, most drivers prefer to be in second or third position. The leader is breaking the wind for him, yet he needs only to pass one or two horses when making his bid to win the race. Strategy is a big item, since the advantage of being second or third in the early stages of the race is often negated by horses coming from the rear, blocking him on the rail. Racing room is accentuated in harness races, because a horse in a trotting or pacing gait needs more distance to regain his top speed, should he be blocked temporarily, than is the case of the thoroughbred or quarter horse.

A trotter or pacer showing rapid improvement may be attributable to several reasons and should be carefully considered when handicapping a race. This situation could be due to a change of drivers, a change of trainers, or changes in the equipment used on the horse, or a combination of any of the three. These factors may apply conversely, when recent performances are less favorable than his overall past record indicates. Changes in shoes, harness, or other racing aids—such as hopples, shadow rolls, etc., can make drastic changes in a horse's performance. The number of possible changes in the combinations of equipment is almost incalculable.

GREYHOUNDS

Different procedures used in handicapping greyhounds are due largely to the lesser degree of human involvement. Once a greyhound is placed in the starting box, he is on his own. There is one exception rarely noticed except by professional handicappers. The lure operator. He plays a much greater part in the performance of these greyhounds than most people are willing to acknowledge. Some lure operators keep the lure close to the lead dog ("short rabbit"). Others maintain greater distance between the lead dog and the lure ("long rabbit"). Some handicappers prefer a "short rabbit" while others prefer a longer one. But in either case, it must be consistent and at an even distance in front of the lead dog throughout the entire race if formful racing is to be accomplished. Failure to do so, whether dictated by dishonesty or incompetence, can make a "front runner" quit or a "closer" finish better, or vice versa. A "short rabbit" usually benefits an early speed dog. It should be closely watched by the racing officials and in no case, should a lure operator be permitted to wager on races while working in this capacity.

Texture of the racing strip: "sloppy," "muddy," or "drying-out," tracks; uniformity of footing on the inside, middle, and outside of the track; should be given about the same priority with greyhounds as when handicapping thoroughbreds. Sloppy tracks might receive slightly more attention, since there is no jockey to urge a greyhound to greater efforts while having mud thrown in his face. Experience of the dog's trainer or a change in trainers would seem to merit about the same amount of consideration as is given in horse racing.

I feel time of the race to be of even lesser importance than in thoroughbred racing, although many handicappers feel more comfortable by using it as a major factor. If some way of accurately timing the run from the starting box to the first turn could be accomplished, it would seem to be a great help in evaluating early speed and determining a dog's position in the race when entering the backstretch. Being able to determine in advance the approximate order in which the dogs will be running at this particular stage of the race, is probably the one most important factor in the handicapping of greyhounds.

Since dogs have no driver or jockey, the ever important factor of pace is determined by the dog himself. Most dogs will develop a pattern of racing after a few official starts that will remain virtually unchanged during their entire career. They will prefer to run on a particular section of the track. Different handicappers will use different terms to describe each section. I prefer the practice of dividing the track into five sections: rail, off-rail, some-wide, wide, and very-wide. Most dogs will work their way to their favorite section as soon as possible after leaving the starting box. Thus, post position becomes more important in dog racing than in horse racing. For example: a rail runner will benefit from drawing an inside post position and a wide runner will ordinarily do better when starting from an outside box.

Almost all dog tracks in the United States offer eight entries in each race. A few have increased the number to nine at various times, but this practice is rare. Most dogs also can be classified as "breakers" or "closers" after a few starts. The "breakers" leave the starting box quickly and must be in contention early in the race in order to have a chance of winning. The "closers" break more slowly and give their best efforts near the finish of the race. Although the "closers" appear to be running faster at the end of the race, they really aren't. It looks that way because the "breakers" are slowing down from their early efforts more rapidly the the "closers" who maintain a more even pace for the entire race. Most handicappers divide the "breakers", or early speed dogs, into two distinct groups. The first usually leaves the box very rapidly but sometimes will be outrun to the turn by the second group in the early speed classification. This second group may not leave the box exteremely fast but will accelerate more rapidly than the closers before they reach the first turn and usually are in contention by the time they start down the backstretch. Many refer to this group as having "run-up-speed". Seldom does either group of early speed dogs improve their position to any great degree from the start of the backstretch to the finish line, and many will not try too hard from that point on, unless they are very close to the leader. A logical explanation is that dogs with these particular characteristics need to be able to see the lure clearly at all times, while the "closers" keep extending themselves until they have passed enough dogs to also be able to see the rabbit.

Most dog tracks in the United States are ¼ mile in circumference. A few measure 495 yards and are known as "Futurity" tracks. The ¼ mile tracks are oblong in shape while the futurity tracks are more oval. Turns are much wider and gradual on the futurity tracks. Standard distances for races at both kinds of tracks are usually limited to $5/16$ of a mile (550 yards) and $3/8$ of a mile (660 yards). These distances might very slightly at some tracks but not by much. Some tracks include a few marathon races, usually a $7/16$ of a mile. A few occasionally feature even longer races. Once in a while a dash race of approximately $3/16$ of a mile is used. Since such a large percentage of races are either approximately $5/16$ or $3/8$ of a mile in length, we will limit handicapping techniques to these two distances. It is obvious that since the distance of races are compatible at ¼ mile and futurity tracks, the starting points must be located differently. This means that the racing characteristics of dogs will affect their performance in varying degrees at ¼ mile tracks as opposed to the futurity tracks. The two factors affecting this difference is the distance traveled from the starting box to the first turn (much longer for $5/16$ mile races on a ¼ mile track) and a dog's ability to race well on the turns. While a larger portion of a race is run on turns at the futurity track, the turns are more gradual than on a ¼ mile track. Less crowding is usually the norm on the turns of a futurity track. Each size track has its advantages and disadvantages, and each has its advocates among the professional handicappers. Most of the details listed above are directed primarily for races $5/16$ of a mile in length. I would estimate that approximately two-thirds of all greyhound races in the United States are run at that distance. The second most popular distance ($3/8$ of a mile) presents a few different circumstances to be considered by the handicapper. The distance from the starting box to the first turn is much shorter for the $3/8$ mile races. Therefore, the first group of early speed dogs are favored at this distance, provided that they have the stamina to remain competitive for the extra 110 yards. This is the group that consistently leave the box rapidly but sometimes are beaten to the turn by the run-up speed type. Since the distance from the starting box to the turn is much shorter, often the first group reach the turn before the second group has caught up with them. Thus the advantages of the second group's run-up speed are diminished since acceleration is more difficult in the turns. The field is usually more bunched in the first turn in the $3/8$ races, causing more crowding and favors the lead dogs who are running free and clear. Conversely, some of the "closers" will be much closer to the pace at this distance since the early speed dogs can't increase their lead to any degree in the first turn. Some dogs will break faster from the $3/8$ box than from the $5/16$ box, and vice versa. The explanation for this is really very simple when you analyze the situation. While the dogs are in the starting box the lure is moving around the track to the point in front of the starting box where the box is opened. At the ¼ mile tracks, the starting box for ⁵/₁₆ mile races is located in a chute at the head of the stretch. Therefore the lure is in front of the starting box at all times, and the dogs break primarily by sight. The ⅜ starting point is relatively close to the middle of the backstretch. Therefore, the lure passes the starting box just before it is opened. The dogs can hear the lure approaching and passing the box very clearly and many dogs time their break primarily by sound, rather than sight. The only way to know which dogs will fall into this category, is to study very carefully their past performances.

Size of the dog does not seem to be a major factor. The big difference in weight is due to the sex of the animal. Males will average about 68-70 pounds, while females average approximately 58-60 pounds, or about a 10 pound spread. The heavier dogs can withstand crowding a little better, but this is offset by the maneuverability of the smaller ones. Females and smaller males do as well, or possibly better, at the longer distances. The dog's weight change from race to race is important. Rules to prevent drastic changes are in effect at all licensed tracks, but the changes within these limits are watched closely by some handicappers, while others treat this factor lightly. Some dogs lose considerable weight due to nervousness from the time they are brought to the track until the time the race is run. A chronic weight loser will sometimes give a better effort if he runs in the early races. This is due simply to the fact that he has less time to fret and worry while in the paddock.

Class is easier to determine in greyhounds, due to grading systems used at all tracks. Grading systems may vary slightly from track to track, but all are based upon dogs being raised or lowered in grade according to each dog's performance. For example, dogs are raised a grade after winning, and lowered a grade after finishing out of the money in a specified number of consecutive starts.

Age of the greyhound is definitely worth considering in some instances. A young dog showing improvement is more likely to compete successfully in a higher grade than one who is in the twilight of his racing career. Most dogs rach their peak when they are about 2 years old. With few exceptions they will not surpass their best efforts at this age in later years.

Many newcomers to greyhound racing will become discouraged by the frequent bumping and jamming that occurs during the course of a race. They will feel that luck, rather than handicapping determines most of the winners. Luck does play it's part in dog racing the same as in horse racing and other sports. But the fact remains that many of the jams, lack of racing room, and other impediments can be foreseen by a good handicapper. This is true because of the reasons described earlier in the chapter. An example would be that if #1 forced #5 wide on the first turn, it might not be luck, but rather that the handicapper knows that #1 wants to run on the outside of the track, and that #5 wants to get to the rail on the turn. If they have shown about the same speed to the turn in past races, it would be luck if they *didn't* collide at that point, or that one or the other is not running to his usual form. It is hard for those who are not well acquainted with greyhound racing to understand that once a dog has established a definite pattern of running, he will seldom deviate from this pattern during his entire career.

JAI ALAI

I an not qualified to elaborate on the details that are necessary to success-fully handicap jai alai games, although I'm sure that regular followers of the sport could do so. Common logic tells me that it is probably likely that the same procedures and variables would be used for jai alai that are considered when predicting the winner of a baseball, football, or basketball game. I've noticed that league leaders in these sports have teams far down in the standings that give them more trouble than their nearest rivals. This is un-doubtedly due to the type of play of each particular team. A mediocre hitter often has a better average against certain pitchers than does the batting champion of the league. A good defensive guard in basketball often has less success with an opponent averaging 10 points per game than with one who averages 20 points per game. Probably tennis would be an even better example, since it is more similar to jai alai. It all boils down to the match-ups that sportscasters are always calling to our attention on TV. One other factor that would appear important is the measurements of the frontons. They are not all exactly the same size as is the case in professional baseball. A long fly ball resulting in an easy out in one park would be a home run in another. It seems regular attendance, in order to learn each player's weak points and strong points, and one player's success over another over an extended period would be necessary to intelligently handicap jai alai games. Beyond that, I have no idea which other variables are really important and which are not.

APPLICATION OF HANDICAPPING HINTS

Up to this point we have tried to point out the information necessary to pick winners. I've known many handicappers who pick lots of winners, but don't make money. I've known others who pick a much smaller number of winners who do make money. Self-descipline, a good understanding of percentages and the ability to handle money accounts for this fact. A person would be stupid to deny that luck is a necessary ingrediant but luck will pretty well average out over the long haul and in many cases what seems to be luck is really something else. Lack of work could account for some of the failures. Impatience often plays a big part. Mental toughness to stick to the

basic handicapping procedures during a losing streak is a must to be successful. You will hear professional gamblers say that they have lost their
rhythm. They may be betting $2 on winners, and $20 on losers. I heard a
true story about four gamblers who visited a track for the first time. Realizing
that they were totally unprepared to handicap dogs with which they were
unfamiliar, but still wanting to make a few wagers, they went to a mutual
friend who was working at the track. He marked each of their four programs
with his selections in exactly the same way. When the races were over, one
had lost considerably, one had broken even, one had made a little money,
and the fourth had a good night financially. This is not an unusual case.
Intelligent handling of money is the equalizer for those who don't handicap
so well. I will try to list and explain a few ways that will improve the
handling of money as well as factors which are important and almost identical for each of the sports used for pari-mutuels wagering.

The first thing every handicapper must realize is that it is impossible for a
jai alai player or a racing animal to give a peak performance every time he is
in a contest. This is true in all sports, in fact in all walks of life. Some days we
feel good and our mental attitude is good, so we have a productive day.
Racing animals fall into the same category. Physical condition of contestants
in highly competetive sports seem to go in complete cycles. When they have
reached their peak and start on the downward swing, they usually have to
make the complete cycle before they reach the top again. Some athletes are
able to stay at their peak for a longer period of time than others. They are
usually the ones who become super stars. Racing animals follow the same
pattern. Trainers should be given more credit, when they are able to keep
their charges near their peak for extended periods. Handicappers need to
recognize the clues, sometimes very minor, when these changes start to
occur. Further they should be able to evaluate the limits of a horse or a dog's
ability at it's peak and adjust accordingly during the cycle.

Still another important factor for a handicapper is, after deciding which
horse or dog he favors, to decide in his mind what odds he should receive if
his decision is correct. If he feels his selection is outstanding, he can afford to
take lesser odds and wager more heavily. If he feels his chances are marginal, he must get greater odds. If at race time the odds are not as high as he
feels they should be, he should pass the race, or in some cases, bet on his
second or third choice if their odds are higher than he feels they should be. It
takes courage to pass the race or bet against his first choice, but he must do
this in order to be successful over a period of time. Next, he should study the
race after it is run. Especially if he loses. He must see if he was wrong
because of luck, or was it because he overlooked one or more factors that
were important. Even when he wins it pays to review his bet. Was he right or
was he lucky? The race can't be run over, but it will help him prepare for
better handicapping in the future. He must also be flexible in his thinking. If
the track conditions change during the day because of the weather, is it wise

to change his selections that were made before he came to the track, or adjust as he goes along? If a stable or kennel has been doing badly and an entry from the same kennel or stable shows improvement in an early race, should he reconsider entries from the same source in later races? Or vice versa.

I have yet to find a person who likes to lose. It is human nature to increase the amounts he had planned to bet when he is losing, in order to avoid a losing day. Or if he has won several bets in a row, he may feel the law of average has to catch up pretty soon and will reduce the size of his bet. A good handicapper will do the opposite. He'll double up on his bets when he's hot and cut down when he's cold. After all, there's another day, and maybe the rhythm will improve.

Another good idea is to watch the changing of odds as much as possible. If the odds on your selection is much higher than you expected, recheck your calculations. If you still think you're right, bet more than you had planned. Most people will bet less. You don't have to win as often if you follow this procedure. Even more important, if you see an entry that has much lower odds than you expected, recheck and if there still seems to be no logical reason for this trend, consider this entry for use in an exotic pool. It's entirely possible this entry is being bet by someone with information not available to you.

Exotic pools (daily doubles, quinielas, exactas, trifectas, big Q's, big P's, etc.) are drawing a bigger percentage of the handle each year in all the sports. Most handicappers and gamblers are concentrating more on these pools than the conventional win, place, and show pools. The pay-offs are larger and the practice of multiple choice betting seems to favor a professional handicapper more than the fans who attend the races and jai alai less frequently. It undoubtedly makes the factor of handling money more important. Plus it makes handicapping these pools more complex and again favors the professional. A couple of examples should explain in a small way why this is true. When I was discussing early speed and closers as pertains to horses and dogs earlier in this chapter, it was meant to help pick a winner only. Most exotic pools require that you pick combinations, either the first two finishers in quinielas and exactas, or the first three finishers in trifectas. Each race will present different possibilities. First of all, the first two finishers in any given race will more often than not, consist of one early speed entry and one that is classified as a closer. Of course there are exceptions, but not too many. You almost have to look at races as two separate contests. Which of the early speed entries will establish supremacy in the early going? The ones that don't, seldom finish close. Handicapping procedures might determine that the three best horses or dogs are all "early speed" or they may be all "finishers". The winner representing the finishers usually is the one getting the best break in finding racing room. Winning trifecta combinations are usually made up of two from one group and one from the other. A handicapper still has to decide which early speed or which closer to key in his multiple choice bet. It is often asked which is the best way to bet these exotic pools, but there is no easy answer. Different conditions are apparent in every race. If it appears that one early speed entry stands out in the mind of the handicapper, it might be wise to use him with every other entry in the race. This is called "wheeling". Or if his odds are low, he may be keyed with only a few of the "closers". Obviously if a "closer" is the handicapper's choice, the system will work in reverse by keying the "closer" with several early speed entries. Odds are often good using this premise, since the less experienced handicappers will be tying the fastest entries together regardless of whether they are "closers" or "early speed". In some cases it will appear to a handicapper that three or four entries stand out so far over the rest of the field that a race of this kind will be one of the few where two early speed or two closers will finish first and second. When this occurs the handicapper will usually tie all the possibilities of these three or four entries together so that if any two of the three or four are first to finish, a winning combination is assured. This is called "boxing".

From what we have discussed it is apparent that, of the fans who are attending these sports only periodically, and for the primary purpose of entertainment, only a few will have the time or the inclination to examine all the variables connected with handicapping. Those in this category should be able to pick out a few factors that will make a day or evening more enjoyable to him and to cash in on a winner a little more often. For those who are regular customers and who think they can show a profit from handicapping, it should help convince them that it is time consuming and hard work. It's possible for a few who have the desire and the patience to become consistent winners. I have known some. But as I said in the previous chapter, I think most will find it "a hard way to make an easy living".

PART FIVE

The Future

Chapter Nineteen
Cash-Sell—Betting by Telephone—
O.T.B.—Satellite Wagering

The racing industry and jai alai would at first glance, seem to be an area where modern technology and computers would not have a great impact. Of course it is obvious that the advanced computer capabilities would give the bettors a much greater chance to know approximately what he will receive, should he win, at the time he makes his bet. He also will know exactly what he has won or lost much more rapidly after the completion of the contest. And he will have more confidence that his money is being handled more accurately by the sophisticated systems developed in the past few years. The accuracy of the pay-offs in pari-mutuels systems has actually been well above the 99% level for several decades. Except for isolated cases, this facet of the racing industry has been accurate and honest since the advent of automatic totalisators, although the early systems were crude compared to those of today. This is not to imply that the people involved in this department of racing were more honest or more efficient than their counterparts in other departments of racing or other businesses. It was just plain mandatory that they be so, to re-establish the integrity that was lost by the abuses which were common during the period when hand tickets were sold. This department has been rigidly supervised and checked ever since, long after such close scrutiny was necessary.

But aside from the mutuels department, the heart of this unique industry depends on the performance of highly skilled athletes in the case of jai alai, and finely trained animals in the four racing categories. The performance of these animals of course depends on people with certain skills, both in their training and supervision. Racing and jai alai are quite comparable to professional sports and other entertainment fields, where a very small portion of the business can actually be carried out by computers.

The growth of entertainment and professional sports has been phenomenal in recent years. Few can deny that the most dominant factor for its growth has been television. Baseball, football, basketball, tennis, golf, hockey, boxing, soccer, automobile racing, and other lesser sports are drawing crowds in excess of the wildest dreams of the owners and administrators at the professional and college levels. But even these huge crowds attending these events are dwarfed by the number of persons watching these same contests on television. The same is true of entertainers. The popularity of a comedian, for instance, on television is not based on his success at the clubs across the country, but rather his drawing power at the clubs is based on his success on television. A large percentage of fans attending any of these functions, at their point of origin, became interested in one or more of these sports by watching it on television at home. Experienced sportscasters are actually teachers of the games they are covering. Many would never become an avid fan of a sport by attending in person, before they had learned the basic rules and strategies that make an event interesting and exciting. It's not possible for a person to be caught up in the emotions of a contest by watching it on television to the extent that he is when actually there, but he can get involved to a greater degree, by the number of contests he sees on television. Other factors of late keeps the fan at his TV set. The most important two that comes to mind are inflation and the energy crisis. Even if there were no sell-outs, the rise in the cost of admission tickets and the costs of driving to locations not easily accessible by public transportation makes regular attendance by many almost impossible.

There are some factors that make it impossible for jai alai and racing to follow exactly the same pattern that has been described above for professional sports. There are, however, some parallels and possibilities to apply the constructive benefits of television to pari-mutuels sports in a slightly different way.

First of all, racing and jai alai operations are dependent primarily on volume of monies wagered, rather than on income from admissions for their success. The length of time needed to complete a day's program is roughly four hours for jai alai and horse racing, and slightly less for most greyhound tracks. During this time, the time consumed for actual competition is less than ten minutes for quarter horses, less than fifteen minutes for greyhounds and thoroughbreds, and about twenty minutes for harness horses. The only exception is jai alai, where competition usually consumes a little over two hours per performance. The rest of the time is spent in selection procedures, betting and cashing tickets, and patronizing the food and drink concessions. This fact practically eliminates the option of showing an entire racing program on television. Jai alai might possibly be able to adjust to the point where they could televise some programs for entertainment only, but this would be difficult. Further, it would require a lengthy and expensive educational program to acquaint the public with this exciting sport, since the vast majority know little or nothing about the workings of jai alai. It might be a good promotional idea to consider, if legislation permits more widespread locations.

CASH-SELL

The latest in electronic totalisator equipment is called the cash-sell system. This enables customers to complete all their betting and cashing transactions at one window, through one machine. Some systems even have the capability of accepting slips or cards with selection information that im-

cut. Marginal tracks already have the facilities to convert to
...ing; parking, seating, totalisator systems, concessions, in fact all
...pensive items necessary to build and maintain an operation. This
...viate most of their present financial problems, since it would
...he expense of the racing operation itself. Of course, they would
...o pay for services received from the tracks where the races origi-
...this amount would be much less than their present costs of live
...aturally, the volume would increase greatly at the tracks providing
...ices and insure their success to maintain a profitable operation. It
...rther, immediately, provide the marginal tracks the option of keep-
...doors open on a year around basis, weather no longer being a
...inate factor.

...any cases, where tracks are operating on a seasonal basis, satellite
...need not preclude their present racing dates, but rather use the
...e system on days they do not ordinarily operate. They might even
...a reciprocal agreement with another track in their area to be the track
...gin for part of the year and the recipient the rest of the year.
...rginal breeders, owners, and trainers need not be eliminated either.
...r the present system, the rapid increase in the number of racing days,
...the prospects of more of the same probable, additional numbers of dogs
...horses would be necessary. This added demand would not increase the
...sperity of the owners and breeders to a great degree. In many cases the
...posite is true. Expanding their kennels and stables would make it impossi-
...to weed-out all animals of poor quality. As in many other businesses,
...od experienced help is not available. It would not be possible to supervise
...e care of each animal as carefully as before. Added racing dates would
...sult in more starts per year for each horse and dog, but this in return often
...esults in more injuries and a shorter racing life for each animal. Longer
...acing seasons would reduce shipping costs from one track to another, but
...all-in-all, the added purses would not keep pace with the inflated cost of
...breeding, raising, and training racing stock. This is especially true at the
...smaller tracks where the quality of horses, dogs, and experienced help suf-
...fers the most. The cost of maintaining the poorer grades of dogs and horses
...usually is greater than for the better ones. The slow ones eat just as much as
...the fast ones, and often need more medical care and attention. A good
...percentage of the poorer grade animals have some physical handicaps be-
...cause of injuries, suffered during prior racing, need more professional care,
...and cannot be raced as often.

A well organized satellite betting system might decrease the number of
tracks slightly, but the increased volume of betting would provide much
higher purses per race. Owners would be able to reduce the number of
horses or dogs in their kennel or stable. They could keep the better ones,
maintain better personnel for their care, and in the long run have a better
chance to show a profit. Naturally, the breeders could be more selective in
their breeding stock, and demand a better price for their animals.

mediately is transferred to a mutuels ticket. The only contact of the customer
with the clerk, under this system, is the money transaction for the value of
the tickets. Even this figure is displayed automatically, where it can be read
by both the customer and the clerk. It is also possible to bet on more than
one race at a time. It is generally believed that this system is about as far
advanced as technology will permit for some time to come. Various cash-
sell systems are in use now, mostly at the larger tracks. Most believe it will be
used at almost all locations, large or small, sometime within a five-year time
frame. This advancement has led to some other possibilities, impossible in
the past.

BETTING BY TELEPHONE

Canada recently passed a national law that involves a telephone system
whereby a customer can call in a wager to any track in the country. First, he
must establish a credit account with the tracks involved. Winnings and
losses are then credited or debited to this account.

New York incorporates this concept in their off-track betting (OTB) system, although some of their regulations differ slightly.

Louisville Downs, a harness track in Louisville, Kentucky is pioneering a
similar system after extensive research. It is operated within the framework
of pari-mutuels legislation in Kentucky and has the blessing of the Kentucky
Harness Racing Commission. The procedures used when this new plan was
inaugurated are still being streamlined when studies show that they are
needed. Management is very happy with the results so far, and plans are
under way for expansion of the system to include twenty-four new cities in
1982.

Some of the innovations which make this system different from that being
used in Canada and by the New York OTB are that bets are being received
until actual post-time and that customers maintaining an average daily balance of $50.00 or more are being paid 5½% interest on their accounts at the
track. Live action of all races are being shown on cable TV. Information as to
entries, drivers, odds, and other pertinent information is broadcast during the
day for the benefit of the customers using this system. A customer using this
service must give his name, account number and a special code word when
calling in his bet. The current balance in his account is given at this time (a
minimum deposit of $25 is required to open a new account), and the infor-
mation regarding the bet requested entered into the computer. This is the
same computer used in the pari-mutuels system for the fans actually present
at the track. Tapes of all telephone conversations are kept to protect both the
customer and the track in case of misunderstandings resulting from these
conversations. In time, these bets will probably go directly into the computer
by voice, without the aid of operators. Japan is already using this concept.

The big advantage of this system, which has been named Call-A-Bet, is that the track, state and horsemen receive 100% of their share of money wagered in this manner, since the money goes directly into the track pools. It eliminates the cost of the "middleman" which is a factor in some of the other types of OTB wagering.

Of course, all new systems can and will be improved by trial and error and Call-A-Bet is no exception. An example is to find a way to be certain that calls are being made from within the state using the system.

This innovation is being carefully watched and analyzed by several other states. If it's popularity and increased business continues, it will probably become a reality in many other areas in the near future.

OFF TRACK BETTING (OTB)

New York and Connecticut have "off track betting" locations throughout their states. New York has more than 300 locations, their size depending on the area in which it is located. The patrons are limited to betting on tracks in their own state with the exception of some special events each year, such as the Kentucky Derby, Preakness, and other prestigious events. This, of course, enables persons in areas remote from an existing track to bet on racing, if they so desire. Off track betting on all races in New York is closed three minutes before post-time and this money included in the track totals. These places of business are open at night also, to enable their customers to bet on tracks operating at night. In 1978, these OTB offices handled $759,381,492 from four thoroughbred tracks, $385,979,353 from eight harness tracks, and $61,169,441 from the limited races they were permitted to offer from Florida, Pennsylvania, Kentucky and Maryland. A Federal Interstate OTB bill was passed in 1978 permitting one state to process wagering on racing events in another, so long as valid agreements were signed by all parties involved. Total wagers accepted from all sources at OTB in 1978 totaled more than $1,200,000,000 as opposed to $1,560,000,000 at the actual track locations in New York. Total revenue gained from OTB was over $28,000,000 as opposed to over $82,000,000 at track sites.

Connecticut had seventeen OTB locations in 1978, but their situation is somewhat different. Having no large tracks in their own state, they offer wagering on the New York facilities. Almost $115,000,000 was handled in Connecticut with a gross revenue of more than $8,000,000 for the state.

Other states have been studying the benefits of this system. The biggest drawbacks in getting legislation passed for OTB is because of disputes as to how profits should be divided between the track where the event originates, the state, OTB, and what per cent should be added to the purses of the horsemen.

TELET

A more recent innovation, satellite w... racing to accomplish the same goals... sports via their extensive coverage of the... first such facility was opened in New Hav... Named "Teletrack", it resembles a huge... type seats on the ground floor, with 200... one-half of the mezzanine, and tables for... 200 more customers in the other half. There a... those at the Astrodome and the Superdome, e... persons. There are betting lines with the new... scribed earlier, in each section, as well as in... screen is located in the front of the building, cle... each section. The action at one of the thoroug... beginning with the saddling of the horses in the pa... and the running of the race, complete with the des... announcer is televised live. The same situation e... service being initiated from a harness track in New Y... races at the Connecticut OTB locations are funneled... track". The one big difference in this operation, as opp... OTB system, is that money from persons betting in Co... pool of their own, rather than being reflected in the track... This results in different odds and pay-offs on the same ra... in Connecticut. For this reason, the one thing that is neve... sion in Connecticut, is the odds-board in New York. Payr... tracks for these services is made from the commissions wit... Connecticut pools, in the same manner as if they had their...

A large percentage of the knowledgeable people in the... with whom I have spoken, are convinced that this is definite... the immediate future. Tracks in Illinois have beamed some... Vegas on a trial basis, and negotiations are under way to make... nent practice. Colorado has already passed a satellite bill and t... projected to be in use by early 1982. The same barriers are slowi... of these systems that have plagued OTB. (A satisfactory division... between the different factions of the system.)

Opposition to satellite operations is also strong from breeders,... trainers, and owners of marginal tracks. I believe the concern of the... ticular groups is completely unfounded, if this new concept is plann... carried out in a fair and efficient manner. The bottom line for eve... connected with the pari-mutuels industry, in all categories, is volume... Those planning, as well as those already having invested in OTB, sh... also benefit. OTB locations in communities too small for satellite wager... can tie into these satellite installations in the same manner as is being do...

in Connecti... satellite bet... the more ex... would alle... eliminate... still have... nate, but... racing. N... these ser... would f... ing their... predom... In m... betting... satelli... make... of ori... M... Und... and... and... pro... op... ble... g... th... r...

Racing Commissions would be rid of their biggest problem, that of fairly allotting dates so that the marginal tracks can survive, and still grant dates that will produce the maximum revenue possible in their state. It would also greatly reduce their responsibility of enforcing the rules of racing. By ending up with a smaller number of tracks with larger handles, they could concentrate their efforts to ensure the public more formful racing.

The number of employees, especially those connected with the pari-mutuels department, would be increased to a large degree when you consider the added facilities of the satellite locations, and to an even larger degree if OTB branches were included in the system. Additional equipment and technicians would be needed from totalisator companies as well.

This system would undoubtedly work better in states where large tracks now exist, so that all the revenue could be kept at home. This would eliminate the negotiations between states, as in the example of Connecticut and New York. Pari-mutuels legislation in new states would give them an option of building a track to be the center of their satellite and OTB system, or they could go strictly with a satellite system and tie into another state with existing track facilities. Under the latter plan, the cost of construction would be reduced to a large degree and would further tend to encourage existing tracks to up-grade their operations. The satellite systems would naturally shop around to give the people of their own state the advantages that the better managed tracks provide.

In the long run, it would be the fans who would benefit most by satellite betting. Time is a big factor. Many with regular jobs could participate more often because the facilities would be more accessible. Further, the prohibitive cost of driving long distances would be eliminated. The weather factor would be reduced to a great degree. Many who do not attend now because of having to drive long distances in the rain, snow, or cold, would no longer have this problem. The more knowledgeable fans living near small tracks, where the caliber of horses, dogs, and officials is usually of poor quality, would have an opportunity to bet on entries of a higher caliber. Many who do not go to the small tracks now, cite this as their main reason. Those who bet large amounts could now do so, without reducing their pay-off prices to a great degree. Where small pools are prevalent, there is a limit as to how much a person can bet without greatly reducing his own odds.

Chapter Twenty
Bookmakers—Exotic Pools—
IRS Regulations

All of these new systems should do much to reduce the volume of money presently channeled through illegal "bookies". The two groups mentioned before, those demanding quality racing and the heavy bettors, often turn to the illegal bookmakers rather than attend the smaller tracks in their community. There are no accurate statistics to determine how much money is being handled in this manner, but those close to this situation agree that the amount is staggering. This practice is not confined to states where the pari-mutuels system is illegal, but is quite active in states already legalized. This is a no-win situation for everyone except the "bookies". It decreases the state's revenue which affects the non-bettors, as well as those who go to the tracks. It reduces the volume and possible profits for the track owners. It results in smaller purses for owners of racing animals and lower pay scales for the employees. It results in a reduction in the number of job opportunities in the industry, and actually costs the taxpayer extra money for law enforcement and the prosecution of these offenders. Unfortunately, the effort to stop this illegal activity is only a token effort in many areas of the country. Many law enforcement agencies are already overloaded with work, as are those charged with the prosecution of those arrested. Worst of all, a large percentage of the public, not only condones the activities of the "bookies", but many participate. Like it or not, it is a proven fact that large numbers of our citizens engage in gambling in one form or another. Many believe that the volume of wagers on sporting events such as football, baseball, basketball, boxing, etc., far exceeds the amounts wagered legally on racing and jai alai. I'm not prepared to argue the merits of legalizing wagering on these sports, but I do know that several states are now considering the possibility of doing so. I do question the common practice of quoting odds and point spreads in newspapers, over the radio and on television. The only purpose possible is for gambling.

If we're going under the assumption that it's illegal, why overlook and encourage it? If the practice is acceptable, why not make it legal and channel the profits into revenue, instead of lining the pockets of a few who are operating outside the law. It is hard to control this activity, especially when no one seems to want to testify against it. The practice of bookmaking is so open that clerks at a track will often reply when asked who made a large bet on a certain horse, "Oh, that was "lay-off money" from the "books". They usually know who they are, and what town they are from. Many times they are operating in the vicinity of the track, if not on the premises of the track itself. Chase them out? Sometimes this is possible, but proving what you know can be difficult, and the tracks must be on solid ground or risk the chances of a lawsuit if the charges cannot be actually proven. Many of the bets are taken verbally, and nothing can be done about it. The most frustrating, and to me the most disgusting part is when a horse owner or trainer bets with a bookie rather than through the mutuels system. Often this is the same person who constantly complains about the low purse structure. It doesn't take a lot of intelligence to figure out that every dollar wagered through the "books" reduces the size of the purse he is competing for. I don't believe it is possible to stamp out bookmaking entirely, but a satellite and/or an OTB system of one kind or another will make a huge dent in it.

EXOTIC POOLS

There is another factor, often overlooked, that would do much to divert large sums of money from the bookmaker to legitimate operations. It is a highly controversial subject, and there are arguments to be considered for and against it. That is the trend of increasing the number of exotic pools, which naturally decreases the size of the conventional win, place, and show pools. Logic will be on the side of those opposing this trend, but facts and figures seem to indicate that logic doesn't prove out in this case. The odds on the average exotic pool are much higher normally, especially on exactas or perfectas, trifectas, pick six, or comparable variations of the above. Pay offs are often huge. The advanced technology of the systems described above has permitted these pools to be added and handled in an accurate and rapid fashion. "Bookies" usually refuse action on these pools, or at least place a limit on the odds that they will pay. A bettor would be foolish to accept 100 to 1 odds from a bookie, when he might possibly receive 200-1, 300-1, or even more, if the bet were processed through the pari-mutuels system.

Advocates of keeping exotic pools to a minimum have several reasons, on the surface at least, to substantiate their belief that this trend is detrimental. It has always been argued that huge payoffs reduces the flow of the "fresh money" (the total amount brought to the track for betting purposes by all in attendance.) The secret to success, they believe, is to have more winners with less profits each race, and have this "fresh money" go through the windows several times each day. Statistics, however, doesn't seem to bear this out. There are only a hand full of tracks still clinging to this theory, and they are the ones in areas with little or no competition from tracks offering more exotic pools. Even though successful, they still don't know whether exotic pools would increase their volume or not. Most who have increased their exotic pools have not returned to the conventional ones. Volume and demand from the public have decided this issue for them. How much of this increase in volume has been siphoned from the bookies cannot be accurately measured, but it seems to me, it must be quite substantial.

Other opponents of exotic pools contend that the high payoffs are incentives to fixing races and that it will destroy racing in the long run. While there may be some isolated cases where this is true, it must be remembered that the more complicated the pool, the harder it becomes to tamper with the results. This is especially true where two or more races are involved in the same pool. With the checks and balances of modern rules, plus all the races being recorded on film, it is hard enough to fix one race, let alone two or more. Certainly the temptations will become greater, but so will the problems of successfully implementing dishonest schemes become greater. Contrary to belief, the hardest factor to control is not doing something to a dog or horse to make him win, it is in doing something to him to make him lose. Good, honest, competent officials, seem to me to be the answer, not taking away a temptation that will reduce volume and a decline in attendance.

Another item often lost in the shuffle when this subject is being argued, is the fact that exotic pools reduces the cost of operating a mutuels operation. More bets in the exotic pools are multiple, increasing the per capita wagering and results in less time being consumed to sell $100.00 worth of multiple exotic tickets than $100.00 worth of win, place and show tickets. The new cash-sell systems permit a customer to buy tickets from all pools from the same window, resulting in shorter lines and more comfort for the fans. Exotic pools payoffs are much larger on the average, and results in many, many fewer cashing transactions. It would take ten times longer to cash ten $4.00 tickets than one for $40.00. Results: fewer cashiers. This makes it possible for management to increase the pay rate for each employee and still stay within their budget for this department. The increased pay rates also results in being able to keep more competent clerks.

IRS REGULATIONS

Assuming that exotic wagering will increase volume and revenue, it would be wise to discuss what I feel to be its true drawback. It has nothing to do with the arguments most commonly used against it. It is, at the present, out of the track operator's control. This is the IRS provisions for taxing holders of winning tickets. First, let me clarify the fact that I agree that income from gambling should be taxed to the same extent as that from other forms of capital gains. But the system now being used, and attempts to adopt further measures to collect taxes from these winnings are neither productive, workable, nor fair. I do not even question IRS's intentions in their present methods. I do believe they are being counterproductive in their efforts, simply because they do not fully understand the facts as they exist. The first policy initiated was to require a person cashing a ticket paying 300-1 odds or more, to sign a federal withholding slip to that effect. The obvious unfairness of this act is that one person might have ten winning tickets paying

$599.80 for each $2.00 ticket and be exempt from signing, while another person, having one ticket paying $602.00 was required to sign. Nor were there any provisions to deduct the investment involved in finally having a $602.00 ticket to cash. The obvious happened. Holders of these tickets negotiated with persons in lower income brackets to sign these withholding forms for a percentage of the payoff price. Ten percent became such an average arrangement, that those who cashed these tickets became known, in the racing business, as "ten percenters". Illegal? Yes, because it amounted in legal terms to "Conspiracy to Defraud". Immoral? Most people didn't feel so, since they believed the regulations to be unfair in the first place, and terribly hard to prove. There were no clear cut guidelines for a person to prove his losses on other wagers that would offset the winnings he had admitted to, having signed the withholding forms. Enough pressure was brought to bear on IRS by complaints of this obvious unfairness to bring about further regulations to correct this situation. One was to tax anyone cashing $1000.00 or more on one bet. Another was to require track management to combine tickets being cashed at different locations of the track by one person, or by other members of his family, or by anyone else cashing tickets for the same person's interest. This was first, unfair to require management to assume this responsibility, and secondly, completely impossible to carry out. Whoever thought up the latter solution, had absolutely no idea of the implications, or how the pari-mutuels system works.

Ironically, the parties resisting these new regulations the most, were the casino operators and the state lottery commissions. These segments of the gambling industry are the primary competitors of the racing industry and the biggest single threat to their success. This put the racing group in a position of either joining hands with their competitors or remaining low key and suffering the consequences of these provisions. Not only was it a bad situation, but it was costly from an operational standpoint.

Aside from all of the above, the bottom line seems to me to be that the IRS, with their present regulations, are defeating the very purpose of what they are trying to accomplish. That is: to gain additional revenue. I don't need statistics to prove my point. I've been present at tracks in operation, since the first IRS regulations were implemented, and listened to observations from a vast cross section of racing fans. I am left with no doubts that these regulations have done as much, if not more, than any other single item to discourage customers from betting the exotic pools and to drive potential revenue sources back to the bookmakers. I was greatly pleased by President Reagan's remarks quoted in "Hoof Beats", the official publication of the U.S. Trotting Association—"A withholding tax on wagers is detrimental to the racing industry. This withholding tax takes out of circulation, immediately, funds which are rolled over during each night's racing." Hopefully his views will cause IRS to reconsider their present stand on this issue. Even further, we haven't even mentioned the cost of enforcing and collecting the revenues which they feel is a justifiable way to increase the revenue volume.

To sum it all up, it seems they are taking away the potential for individual states to gain more revenue from the pari-mutuels system, than IRS is gaining for the Federal Government.

Chapter Twenty-One
Lotteries, Casinos, Professional Sports

Most states are looking frantically for new sources of revenue. Lotteries, casinos, and wagering on professional and college sporting events are the areas most often considered, in addition to racing and jai alai.

Fourteen states had a lottery system in 1978, with estimated gross sales of over $2,000,000,000 annually. All fourteen of these states also had some form of legalized pari-mutuels system on either racing or jai alai, or both. It seems these lotteries did not hurt racing and jai alai to any great extent. Several more states have legalized lotteries since these statistics were compiled.

Betting on sporting events is limited to Nevada, New Jersey, and Delaware at the present time. Since Nevada's operation is tied in with casinos, it is hard to tell what impact it has had on racing and jai alai. Nevada's small population has limited pari-mutuels operations to jai alai and dog racing in the past few years. MGM closed their jai alai fronton in Reno recently, due to lack of interest. Their other fronton in Las Vegas was temporarily closed because of the hotel's fire. It was re-opened when the hotel was rebuilt. Two small horse tracks failed several years ago in Las Vegas, but the area and tourism has grown to a great extent since that time. A dog track was opened in Henderson, Nevada (a suburb of Las Vegas) recently. So far the results have been disappointing. Horse racing is scheduled to open in 1982 at the same facilities. This will further test the ability of pari-mutuels operations to compete with casinos.

Delaware's sports betting is limited to cards similar to lottery operations and is actually under the control of its lottery commission. Betting on individual pro-football games was attempted in 1976, but experienced technical problems that resulted in its being discontinued in short order. Connecticut is considering adding sports betting but is still in the planning stage.

Nevada and New Jersey are the only states now offering casino betting. Several others are looking into the possibilities for legislation along these lines. Casinos would probably be the biggest threat to the future of pari-mutuels operations, but most states run into extensive opposition to legislation of this nature and it appears tracks and frontons will not face casino competition to any great extent for some time to come.

Chapter Twenty-Two
Personal Observations

The volume of monies wagered on the three categories of horse racing, greyhounds, and jai alai has grown rapidly in the past few years. On the surface it would seem that the future of pari-mutuels wagering presents a rosy picture. But when you look more closely, this is not necessarily the case. With the never ending search for added revenues, especially of the voluntary nature, this would appear an easy and natural source. And so it could be. Unfortunately, in most cases, the industry has not kept pace with the changing times in several areas of their operations. Candidly I believe this situation not to have been caused by neglect, so much as by complacency, and by the unique framework under which the industry must function.

First of all, most of the increase in volume was caused by increased numbers of racing dates at existing tracks, rather than by adding new facilities. Per capita wagering (dollars bet per customer per racing day) is going up at a rapid pace on all types of racing and jai alai, but attendance is not. Per capita increases can be attributed largely to two factors—inflation and the additional exotic pools made possible by modern technology. Electronic improvements, added security, new types of exotic pools, and more comfortable accomodations have surely helped in the industry's expansion.

Granted, there has recently been an earnest and honest effort, by almost every faction of the industry to correct the ills that has caused attendance to come to a standstill. Hopefully, it will not be too little, too late. To be fair, a considerable share of the complacency is a product of the unique nature of the industry. But the structure of the legislation allowing pari-mutuels wagering discourages competition in most states.

I feel there are several other areas in the industry that need immediate and positive attention if the attendance problem is to be solved. Most all have to do with personal relations between employers and employees, and between both employers and employees with steady and prospective customers. Anyone who frequents race tracks or frontons with any regularity will see a very small percentage of young faces in the crowd. It's not that younger people don't like the sports involved, most plain don't understand them. This is especially true in areas where tracks draw heavily from the large cities. With the exception of jai alai, the competition is supplied by dogs and horses. The shift in population from the rural areas to larger towns and cities has limited the younger generations' contact with animals to a small pet and an occasional trip to the zoo. A much greater percentage of senior citizens and middle-aged Americans attended state and county fairs on a regular basis when they were growing up.

Often, horse races were the main attraction at these fairs. We tend to forget how short a time ago we were not such a mechanized society. To a large number of middle aged persons, horses were a part of their daily lives, when they were young. Even those who were in the cities by this time, had fathers, grandfathers, uncles, cousins, or close friends still living in the country. When they went to the country for a visit, they saw and were in contact with horses, not tractors. Even most dogs had some function other than just being a pet. They were at least expected to double as a watch dog, if not used to help herd or drive cattle or sheep. Family pictures and stories of life on the farm or in small villages kept up the interest in animals to a lesser degree for another generation of those moving to the cities. Some areas, especially in the West and Southwest had match races at bush tracks almost every week of the year, with no pari-mutuels wagering.

What does this have to do with attendance at a commercial track in 1981? Statistics will prove quite a bit. Bettors very seldom become interested in a particular form of racing. Rather people interested in horse racing or dog racing become interested in betting. I believe that a realistic educational program to get people interested in the sport itself is the first step. If they come to the track often enough as spectators and are well entertained, most will soon become good betting customers as well.

A good example would be harness racing in the midwest. Attendance at commercial harness tracks is holding up better in this area than other parts of the country. They also have lots of harness racing at county fairs with no wagering in these same states. Another example is quarter horse racing in the southwest. Bush tracks are still numerous and the commercial tracks are not suffering so much in attendance at quarterhorse tracks as in other areas of the country. An excuse often used for the fact that the percentage of young customers is growing smaller, is that in many states, minors are not permitted on track premises as spectators. And there are sound valid reasons for this. Of course they should not be allowed to wager while still a minor, any more than they should be served drinks at a bar. But it is much easier to screen the border line age group at the entrance area than at the betting windows, where demanding proof of age is time consuming and disrupts business to a great extent. Those who are obviously too young to wager can become a nuisance by their horse play when they become bored between races. Even those who behave quietly take up much needed space at some facilities. The serious bettors want to concentrate fully on their racing forms, the odds board, and other matters without being distracted, even by the well behaved children. Many parents feel that because of growing admission fees and the generally higher prices of food and drink items at a track, as compared with other recreation sources, these minors could be better entertained with the same amount of money elsewhere. Answers? I don't have them all, but I have some that might be worth considering at least.

First of all, let's start with the smaller children. What would be wrong with building separate facilities adjacent to the betting area for children, say up to twelve years of age, complete with playground equipment, qualified personnel to supervise them, a nurse, snack bars with reasonable prices and a small inexpensive grandstand where they could watch the dogs or horses parade to the post, as well as view the actual races? Too expensive? I don't think it would end up costing anything. How many customers stay away from the track because of babysitting problems? No one knows for sure, but I think the number is considerable. Besides, if the children have a good time during these visits, the track will become another option for them for recreation when they reach the legal age for betting. Some will become interested in the sport itself and betting will follow at the proper time.

One objection I've heard frequently when this possibility has been suggested, is that the facilities would end up as a cheap baby sitting operation, with the parents dropping the children off and taking their business elsewhere. Not a chance if handled properly. Parking and admissions receipts could be required proof that parents had been actual customers. Another plus is that most parents would feel more secure, knowing that their children were close by, in cases of injury or becoming ill, than if they were miles away at home with a baby sitter. It would also be less costly.

Insurance could be obtained to protect the track against any claims of injury while the children were in their care.

Constructive programs to promote interest in teenagers could also be implemented. Again, this should be geared to interest in the sport itself, rather than deal with the wagering aspect. Many operations will claim they are already doing their best in these areas. I don't believe many have even scratched the surface. Some states allow minors to attend the races, but are not allowed to bet. For the reasons listed above, in many cases the harm outweighs the good. Other states have set aside certain programs where minors are admitted. For instance, special matinees, where night racing is the norm. Again, when thrown together in the same area with the bettors, the real purpose of creating interest in the sport itself is overshadowed by their interest in attending for the purpose of wagering.

Schooling races, more common at greyhound facilities, during the pre-opening period when no betting is involved, are often open to the public, at all ages, at no charge, and is undoubtedly helpful. But this gives very limited exposure, and in most cases, the parents are more interested in getting a line on the dogs or horses for future bets, than they are to explain to the minors what the sport is all about. Guided tours by track officials to training areas and stables and kennels seems to me to be one of many better solutions. Questions could be answered correctly and honestly. Many parents' knowledge is limited as to how to wager, since they too have never been educated in what actually goes on behind the scenes or in preparing these animals for competition, or what actually is involved once the race begins. The adults could stand some education in these areas as well, rather than pass on well intended, but often incorrect information, to their children and friends.

Further tours during racing hours through different departments such as the mutuels department, the paddock, the photo finish booth, the judges stand, or whatever other area they might be interested in, would definitely help. Sure, it's disrupting to the officials in these departments, but if handled correctly, the disruption can be kept at a minimum, and in the long run, be a benefit to these officials in the security of a successful business and eventually better wages. I've noticed that those few who have had the advantage of these tours are happy to pass on what they've learned to their peers, and what they say carries more weight than if the same information comes from a track official. The uninformed fan feels these officials are speaking with bias, (which is often true.)

Many organizations are holding handicapping schools for fans during non racing hours, and this is undoubtedly helpful, but I still think it's putting the cart before the horse. The first priority, I believe, is to educate the fans about the sport itself and follow up on how to best handicap a race.

I feel another innovation that would be helpful would be to install information booths in the betting areas, complete with samples of equipment used in the particular type of racing being held at the track involved, as well as at jai alai frontons, with someone qualified to answer questions regarding these items. Training procedures could be explained, as well as the diets of the animals involved. Most tracks are now limited to information windows, manned by personnel to explain betting procedures. Helpful, but not complete. At the present time, customers get most of their information from track employees, especially the clerks at the betting and or cashing windows. Some of these employees have a general knowledge of what's going on, but often their answers are misleading, rather than helpful. There's no doubt that employees need more information about procedures around the track in departments other than their own. Often they don't even know enough about their own department to answer questions other than those pertaining to their particular job.

Crash programs to educate the public about a particular sport are usually used when a state or an area of the state is trying to legalize pari-mutuels wagering. Once legislation has passed, efforts for the most part, take a different direction. This is unfortunate, since training films, question and answer sessions etc., at locations other than the track would seem to be a partial answer to declining attendance. Booths at fairs, fraternal organizations, and civic organizations such as the Chamber of Commerce, are examples of places where this could be done.

There are other ways to encourage interest in these sports, but the examples above would seem to be helpful in another way. By putting these pari-mutuels operations under a microscope so to speak, and making the general public more knowledgeable about what's going on, it is bound to lessen the complacency that is obvious at many tracks and frontons. Racing Commissioners, track management, department heads and general employees themselves, would be forced to do a better job simply by public opinion. Let's face it. Racing and jai alai is in competition with other types of recreation for fans. The volume of wagering necessary for this industry's success will be assured if there are enough new faces in the crowd.

There are two items that need immediate attention and an honest effort toward solving, which directly involves the relationship between management and employees. It indirectly influences the growth in attendance. These items are a more equitable pay scale throughout the country, and a much larger representation of women and minorities in key jobs in all categories of the industry. Unfortuantely, racing and jai alai have been very reluctant to face this reality. I am not so naive that I can't see that the nature of this business makes a satisfactory solution to those problems more difficult than in many other industries. Discrimination in many cases is not the result of moral persuasions, but rather the result of real or imagined business implications. Most of the key spots in the racing industry are filled from personnel working their way up the ladder from within the business itself, rather than securing them from other sources. The business has no counterpart from which to draw personnel with the experience necessary to fill these key positions. The racing industry was one of the last to hire women and minorities at the lower level jobs, so it really is hard to find qualified personnel from within these groups. On the other hand, one need only to look into the crowd of customers to see the large percentage of women and minorities present. It is only natural for these minorities to be turned off by the fact that they are helping support a business in which they are not fairly represented. There is no easy solution to this dilemma, but it seems mandatory that something must be done constructively very soon, if the industry is to prosper. It is a fact that a bigger percentage of women and minorities have been hired at the lower level jobs in the past few years. Whether or not this approach will be adequate to solve this serious problem remains to be seen.

The wide range in pay scales for employees from state to state and sometimes within one state affects attendance in only one way and the degree that attendance is affected is intangible. However it's a generally accepted fact that word of mouth advertising is the best and cheapest form of advertising yet known. Happy and satisfied employees can do wonders to promote the track or fronton at which they are employed. Conversely, dissatisfied employees can negate an otherwise good advertising program.

Again we run into the unique nature of the pari-mutuels industry. As we explained in another chapter, we are faced with two types of employees. Regulars and "moonlighters". Further, we must consider the fact that many marginal operations are faced with serious budgeting problems in order to survive. The cost of living varies greatly from one area to another. Some operations are forced to employ union help, others are free to make a choice. Some operations are seasonal, some operate on a year around basis. With all these factors, it is very difficult to come up with an equitable pay scale. However, the extreme variations in pay scales seems unnecessary in many cases and are undoubtedly unfair in some. Actually, the increase in pay rates in this industry has not kept pace with most other lines of work. At some locations, it was economically impossible to do so and survive. Others who were in a position to keep pace, with no serious problems involved, have often used the rates of the marginal operations as an excuse to keep their own rates down. In my opinion, those in this category are only hurting themselves in the long run. The marginal tracks are being faced at this time with a very serious problem of keeping efficient and honest employees, in cases where pay scales are low. This problem is growing daily and in many cases is almost out of hand. New totalisator equipment which is more sophisticated and requires less personnel to operate, will undoubtedly help this situation in the mutuels departments. This department has a larger number of employees than any other, but new equipment is not available to all at this time, and the transition period will be very difficult.

Another situation facing both government and track management, is that of unemployment benefits to those working at seasonal tracks and not moving to other racing sites once these operations have completed their alloted dates. This practice is not illegal and in some cases necessary for some in this group, who make this type of work their chief or sole source of income. My concern regarding this situation is over those who apply for work at these seasonal tracks with the sole purpose of being able to receive unemployment benefits during the off season. Many in this group work very well while on the job, but others simply meet the minimum requirements to continue their employment and are not dedicated to helping the industry grow. Those in this category are partly responsible for low pay rates, since they are looking at the combined amounts of salary and unemployment benefits on a yearly income basis. Housewives, students, and retirees make up a large percentage of this group. I don't know a simple answer to this problem, but it is definitely something to be considered and some solution is needed.

The practice of issuing free passes for admission to commercial tracks, or in some cases, passes at reduced prices as an incentive to increased attendance has been one of the most controversial subjects of the racing industry for as long as I can remember. There are actually three schools of thought regarding this practice. An unlimited number of passes free to anyone who asks for them, no passes at all, or passes for the heavy bettors and influential persons only.

There is no way to accurately determine which of the three systems is best. Advocates of each line of thought is strong in his convictions that his way is best. For sake of argument of those believing in unlimited passes as opposed to those favoring none at all, the following items must be considered. For example, we'll use a standard admission price of one dollar. If the track's share of the pari-mutuels take is ten cents on the dollar, a customer must wager ten dollars before the track will break even on the pass that was given. Plus the cost of printing and distributing the pass. Plus paying the state the tax on each admission ticket whether it was free or paid for. In some cases, parking is included on the pass, which will require another $10.00 worth of bets to reach the break even point. On the plus side is the intangible amounts gained in good will, and the number of extra fans who will attend via the free pass concept, who would not otherwise be there. Also, the extra sales at food and drink concessions, plus the sales of programs and the word of mouth advertising from the extra fans attending because of the free passes. A lot also depends on whether or not an operation has a space problem. If a track or fronton is operating at capacity or near capacity with mandatory paid admissions, the added numbers present because of free passes might be a detriment. Those attending solely because of free admission ordinarily would not bet a great amount, at least not the first several times they attend. If there is ample space, it is possible that profit from steady fans developed in this manner would more than pay for the initial loss and inconvenience.

The third concept is more complicated to assess. To some fans the psychological aspect of being able to get something free that others cannot get is a big factor. I've heard many say "Why should I have to pay admission to spend my money for mutuels tickets, the main source of income to the track, and the reason I attend in the first place?" Of course, this does not apply to the group that is attending for the primary purpose of entertainment and to whom wagering is secondary. Many advocates of the limited pass idea will maintain the success of this concept depends upon making the passes hard to come by and therefore of some actual value. Also to limit these passes to "good customers" who bet lots of money. These two positive ideas immediately create two serious problems. Who is to determine the identity of the "good customers"? Are they friends of the management or racing commissioners, politicians, or successful business persons in other lines of work? Maybe the really "good customers" are those in lesser walks of life who attend regularly and say good things about the track to their friends, neighbors, and fellow employees. Where do you draw the line? And does the good will created by those receiving passes outweigh the negative reaction of those who are refused a pass for one reason or another? In regards to limiting passes to those who are "big bettors", how much is big? It all depends on the evaluation by the one putting out the passes. A big bet to some people is a small one to others. The bettors themselves have different amounts in mind when they describe themselves or others as a big or small bettor. It is a question that is impossible to answer to anyone's satisfaction.

I thought of a possible *partial* solution for tracks using the limited pass system several years ago, and presented it to various general managers. No one thought enough of the idea to give it a try, but I'm still convinced it would be helpful.

For those convinced that passes should be given to "big bettors", it seems to me that some definite figure should be determined as to what separates a "big bettor" from a small one. Once this has been settled, a customer could exchange losing mutuels tickets in that amount to designated windows in exchange for a daily pass. It would eliminate the dispute over who bets how much, and the passes would go to someone who can prove they're betting enough to warrant free admission. The biggest argument I heard against this idea was that people could pick up tickets off the floor for exchange. My contention is that the few who would do this really want a pass and has every intention of returning to the track at a later date. It would further give proof that those returning their own losing tickets give some value to a pass and would make some small effort to secure it.

In summing up the pressing problem of declining attendance, I'm sure there are remedies other than the ones described above, but a general solution to the problem seems to be; a more vigorous approach to new ideas; a more realistic and positive relationship between the different categories using the pari-mutuels system; as well as between operators within each category; a more unified set of rules and regulations nationwide; a constant vigil to see that these rules and regulations are enforced; and most of all a concentrated effort to educate the public to a much greater degree about the pari-mutuels system and the individual sports involved, so that they can decide for themselves whether or not they wish to include one or more of these sports in their recreational schedule. They must be given more attention and actual facts, if they are expected to vote in favor of future pari-mutuels legislation, a must if the industry is to survive, and prosper.

Chapter Twenty-Three
A Pari-Mutuels Glossary

ALTERED TICKETS—invalid pari-mutuels tickets with information changed in an attempt to match valid tickets for cashing.

AUCTION POOLS (calcuttas)—System used in lieu of pari-mutuels system to wager.

BACKSTRETCH—The straightaway farthest from the finish line. Often used to describe the barn area.

BANKROLL—A set sum of money used to carry on business daily at racetracks or frontons. Also used to describe money available to an individual for the sole purpose of gambling.

BERTILLION CARD—A card kept on record with identifying marks, scars, etc., used in making positive identification of an animal.

BITCH—A female dog. Applies to racing greyhounds.

BREAK—Term applied to harness horses changing to a different gait than the one specified in the particular race in which they are competing. Also the word used for the beginning of a race.

BREAKAGE—Monies in excess of actual payoffs for winning tickets. Prices calculated to nearest dime or nickle according to laws governing particular tracks or frontons.

BREAKER—A dog or horse who consistently leaves the starting box or gate rapidly at the start of a race.

BREEDERS—Persons engaged in breeding and raising racing animals.

BREEDERS AWARDS—Monies set aside from purses paid winning horses or dogs, and paid to original breeder of winning animal.

BUG—Name denoting the reduced weight allowance permitted an apprentice jockey.

BUSH TRACKS—Tracks holding horse races where the pari-mutuels system of wagering is not authorized. Any form of gambling on these races is illegal.

CANCHA—Playing area of a jai alai fronton.

CASH-SELL—Name used to describe system whereby a customer is able to purchase pari-mutuels tickets and cash valid tickets at the same window.

CATCH DRIVERS—A free lance driver who is available to drive for other owners and trainers. Race driving is his primary occupation.

CESTA—A combination glove and basket type object, strapped to the wrist of a jai alai player, used to catch and throw the ball (pelota) during a jai alai contest.

CLAIMING RACE—Races where horses are entered with the agreement to actually sell the horse to any other bonified owner or trainer for the price stipulated in the conditions of the race. Claims must be made in accordance with the rules of racing at the track where where the claim is made.

CLASSIFIED RACING—New concept of assigning grades to standardbred horses to make up races so that horses are equally matched. Similar to grading system used in making up greyhound races.

CLUBHOUSE TURN—The turn entering the backstretch from the front stretch.

COLORS—Color combinations of shirts and caps worn by the jockey in thoroughbred races. These colors represent a particular owner for all horses running in his name and are registered with the Jockey Club. The drivers of standard bred horses register the colors of their jackets and caps with the USTA and wear these colors exclusively, regardless of ownership of the horse they are driving.

COLTS—An unaltered male horse under 4 years of age.

COMMERCIAL TRACKS—Term used to designate a track using the pari-mutuels system to provide monies necessary to carry on a racing meet.

COMMISSION—Monies deducted from pari-mutuels pools to pay expenses and revenue necessary to conduct a racing meet or a jai alai operation.

CONDITION BOOK—A book containing specific conditions that must be met in order to enter a horse in future races scheduled to be run on a specified date.

CONSOLATION POOLS—Applies to pools involving two or more races. Holders of tickets having the correct selections in the races completed, but whose selection is a late scratch in the later race or races, share in a portion of the profits of that particular pool.

COOL OUT—Methods used after a race, primarily bathing and walking to gradually cool out a horse or dog. Prevents stiffness and soreness of animals after competition.

COURSING—Name given to the practice of greyhounds chasing a live rabbit.

DASH RACE—A standardbred race where the order of finish is determined by one heat only.

DEAD HEAT—A tie by two or more entries in a race.

DOG—Word used to denote a male greyhound.

DOUBLE GAITED—A standardbred horse trained for both the trotting and pacing gaits.

DRIVER—A person driving a standardbred horse in harness racing.

DROPS—Racetrack term used to describe errors in money transactions between customers and clerks, and where these errors are in favor of the clerks.

EXOTIC POOLS—Mutuels pools other than the conventional win, place, and show pools. Involves more than one entry—examples: daily double, exactas, trifectas.

FAVORITE—Entry having more dollars bet on it than any other entry in the race or game.

FILLY—A female horse under 4 years of age.

FILM PATROL—Pictures taken from various angles during the running of a race to help stewards determine infractions of the rules.

FINAL LINE—Win odds when betting has been completed for any particular race or game.

FINISHER (CLOSER)—Term used to describe dogs or horses who usually give their best effort during the later stages of a race.

FIRST TURN—The turn first entered after a race has started. Location varies due to the length of the race and size of the track.

FOUL CLAIM—A claim by a jockey, race driver, owner or trainer that their order of finish in a race was adversely affected by a rules infraction by another rider or driver in the same race. This claim is considered by the stewards and a decision rendered before a race is declared official.

FRACTIONS—Time consumed in running different portions of a race.

FREE LEGGED PACER—A standardbred pacer who races without the aid of hopples.

FRESH—An entry who has not raced in some time.

FRESH MONEY—Money brought to the track for wagering by the customers. Excludes money bet by customers from winnings earlier in the racing program.

FRIVOLOUS FOUL CLAIM—A claim of foul (described above) with absolutely no justification. Often results in a fine for the party lodging the complaint.

FRONTIS—Front wall of a cancha at jai alai frontons.

FRONTON—Name of building where jai alai is played.

FUTURITY—A race where the purse money is accrued by periodic deposits by owners in order for their horse or dog to remain elegible to compete in this particular race. Example: "All American Futurity."

GAIT—A way of stepping in a given manner. Applies to race horses as to whether trotting, pacing, or running.

GAMBLER—One who wagers on the outcome of a race, game or contest of any kind.

GELDING—A castrated male horse.

GINNY PIT—A name commonly used to describe the holding area (paddock) for greyhounds.

GREYHOUNDS—A breed of dog; the only breed used for dog racing.

HANDICAPPER—A person who projects his selections in races or games based on information of past performances of entries.

HANDICAPS—Thoroughbred races where weight carried by each horse is assigned by the racing secretary to give each entry as equal a chance as possible.

HANDLE—Term used by race tracks and frontons to designate volume of monies wagered. Applies to race, day or season totals.

HAND TICKETS—Pre-printed pari-mutuels tickets used before automated equipment was available to print tickets at the time they were purchased.

HARNESS RACING—Type of horse racing limited to standardbreds using either a trotting or pacing gait. Horses pull a two-wheeled cart called a sulky or bike and are guided by a driver riding on this conveyance.

HEAT RACING—Horse racing where the same horses compete against each other more than once. Results of the race are determined by overall order of finish in the combined heats. Used almost exclusively by standardbreds.

HOPPLES (HOBBLES)—A part of the harness used for standardbreds, namely those racing at the pacing gait. An aid to keep the pacer from breaking stride or changing gaits.

HORSE—An unaltered male horse 4 years old or older.

HORSEMAN'S BOOKKEEPER—A person who keeps an up-to-date record of each owners money during a racing meet. Credits amount earned in purses, debits deductions for jock mounts, claims, etc.

HOT BOX—Name commonly used to describe races made up of the best greyhounds available at the track where the race is being conducted.

INTERFERENCE—When one greyhound deliberately fights or interferes with another dog during the running of a race.

JAI ALAI—A game of Basque origin used in some countries for pari-mutuels wagering in the same manner as horse or dog racing.

JOCKEY—One who is licensed to ride a thoroughbred or quarter horse during an official race.

JOCK MOUNTS—Standard fees for a jockey to ride a thoroughbred or quarter horse during an official race.

LATERAL—Name used for the side wall of the cancha at a jai alai fronton.

LAPPED ON BREAK—Denotes a situation when a standardbred breaks stride during a race and the break occurs when an opponent is even with him to the extent that his nose is at least opposite the hindquarters of the breaking horse at the finish line.

LAY OFF MONEY—Money bet by a bookmaker at a track or with another bookmaker when he has accepted more bets on one particular entry than he feels is safe for his operation.

LEADOUTS—Name given a person in dog racing in charge of an entry from the time he leaves the paddock until he is placed in the starting box.

LONG RABBIT—Used to describe the situation when a lure operator in greyhound racing keeps the lure a relatively longer distance in front of the lead dog than his average counterpart.

LONG SHOT—Entry not well-regarded by the bettors in a race or game, resulting in high odds and large payoffs should he finish 1st, 2nd, or 3rd.

LURE—The mechanical device used for greyhounds to chase during the running of a dog race.

MARES—Female horse 4 years old or older.

MARGINAL TRACKS—A track whose volume of business is low enough that profits and continued operation are questionable.

MATCH RACE—A race between two dogs or horses. Held at tracks other than commercial ones, with rare exceptions. Such races are not subject to rules of racing in their particular state, when pari-mutuels betting is not used for this type of race.

MATINEES—Afternoon racing at tracks where night racing is the usual practice.

MINUS POOLS—When there are not enough profits left in a pool to pay the minimum price to holders of winning tickets, as required by law. Losses are actually made up from breakage from other pools.

MOONLIGHTERS—Track and fronton employees having steady employment in other fields and using track and fronton earnings as a supplement to their regular income.

MORNING LINE—Odds quoted prior to any actual betting by customers. A handicapper's assessment of approximately what odds an entry will be at post time, based on the bets made by the public.

MULTIPLE BETTING—The practice of a bettor backing several combinations in the same race. Pertains chiefly to exotic pools.

MUTILATED TICKETS—Pari-mutuels tickets partially destroyed, usually torn, to the extent that necessary information on the ticket for cashing is not complete.

MUZZLES—Worn by greyhounds to prevent injury to other dogs due to fighting with each other. Used during turnout periods or during an actual race.

ODDS—Number indicating amount of profit per dollar to be paid to holders of winning pari-mutuels tickets.

ODDS BOARD (PUBLIC DISPLAY BOARD)—Facilities in the infield of a track or at other locations visible to the public, to post information regarding odds, pay-offs, sometimes advertising, or any other information pertinent to the operation of tracks or frontons.

OFF TRACK—Term used for two different situations. Either when a track's surface is at less than its best potential due to rain or other weather factors or to denote business being conducted in direct relation to the track's business at a location other than the track itself.

OFF TRACK BETTING (OTB)—Legal wagering at a location other than the track where the races are being held. Must conform to the rules and regulations of the states involved.

OPEN RACE—Type of race relating to harness racing open to anyone wishing to enter this race and not limited to entries because of past performances. Usually entries are the best available at the track and often called "free-for-alls."

OUTRIDERS—Employees of track who assist and supervise jockeys and horses during post parade from the paddock to the starting gate. Responsible for catching runaways and horses who have lost their riders.

OUT TICKETS—Winning pari-mutuels tickets not presented to cashiers for payment before the close of current day's business.

OVERLAY—An entry whose odds are higher than those estimated by professional handicappers.

OVERPAY—A case where the price paid to winning ticket-holders is more than the correct price, due to computer or human error.

OVERWEIGHTS—Term used in both greyhound racing and horse racing where jockeys are involved, but has an entirely different meaning. Pertains to dogs weighing decidedly more at race time than in the past, in greyhound racing. In horse racing, the term is used when a horse will carry more weight than the minimum authorized by the set conditions of a race; dictated by the fact that the jockey being used cannot reduce his weight enough to ride at the assigned weight.

PACER—A standardbred using a pacing gait for harness racing. A pacer moves forward in a manner whereby the right front leg and the back right leg move forward simultaneously.

PADDOCK—Area of assembly for horses or dogs immediately before a race. Harness receives final adjustments in standardbred paddocks. Thoroughbreds and quarter horses are saddled and turned over to the jockeys. Final instructions are given to riders and drivers. Greyhounds are blanketed and turned over to leadout personnel. Entries in all categories receive a final identification check in this area.

PARI-MUTUELS—A system of betting, whereby the holders of winning tickets are paid in proportion to the sums they have wagered.

PARKED OUT—Term used in harness racing when a trotter or pacer is unable to race next to the inside rail due to the positions of his opponents.

PARTIDO SYSTEM—Jai alai games played by two individuals or two sets of partners only. The winner is decided when one player or one team has reached a pre-designated number of points (usually 25 to 35 points). It is not possible to use the pari-mutuels system for partido games except for win pools.

PAST PERFORMANCE—Documented records of previous efforts of horses, greyhounds, or jai alai players.

PELOTA—Ball used to play jai alai.

PER CAPITA—Average amount bet by each customer during a day's business at a racetrack or a fronton.

PHOTO FINISH—System of taking pictures of the finish of a race too close to determine the winners by the naked eye.

PIGEON—An invalid ticket paid by mistake to a customer by a cashier.

PLACING JUDGE—A racing official responsible for determining the correct order of finish of a race.

PLATER—Name often used for a blacksmith.

POST PARADE—Used to describe the field of horses or dogs going from the paddock to the starting gate or starting box.

POST TIME—Time designated to start the first race or game of the day and all races or games subsequently during that day's business.

PURSE—Prize money earned by winning horses, dogs, or jai alai players.

QUARTER HORSE—A breed of horse registered with the National Quarter Horse Association. Bred to run short distances and used to conduct quarter horse racing.

RACETRACKER—A name often used for one whose interests and income are almost totally connected with racing in one department or another.

RACING COMMISSION—An appointed body of men and women which governs and polices racing and jai alai in states where legislation has been passed to permit use of the pari-mutuels system in connection with these sports. Usually appointed by the governor of the state.

RACING DATES—Specific dates allotted to horse and dog tracks to conduct business by Racing Commissions charged with granting licenses and monitoring the conduct of these tracks in conformation with the official rules of racing in their states.

RAIL RUNNER—A horse or dog with a history of running near the inside rail of a track whenever conditions permit.

REBOTE—Back wall of a cancha at a jai alai fronton.

RECALL—Term used in harness racing when the first attempt at starting a race is nullified by the official in charge of the start because of unsatisfactory conditions. The starting procedure must be repeated until the official is satisfied that conditions are fair and even.

REPLAYS—Films of races played back for the benefit of fans and officials after the completion of a race.

RULES OF RACING—Official rules approved by the body responsible for the conduct of racing in conformance with the legislation permitting these races to be held—in most cases, a Racing Commission.

SCHOOLING RACES—Practice races held using actual racing conditions, but in which no wagering is allowed.

SCRATCH—An entry listed to compete in a race or game, but withdrawn after becoming an official entry, due to illness, injury, or other bona fide reasons.

SHORT RABBIT—Used to describe the situation when a lure operator in greyhound racing keeps the lure a relatively shorter distance in front of the lead dog than his average counterpart.

SPOOKS—Applies in rare cases to greyhounds that are extremely timid. Usually there is no logical reason for this timidity and it does not affect their racing ability to any great degree.

SPRINTER (EARLY SPEED)—Term used to describe dogs or horses who usually give their best effort during the early stages of a race.

STANDARDBREDS—Breed of horses registered by the U.S. Trotting Association. Used in races restricted to a trotting or pacing gait (harness racing).

STEWARDS—Racing officials charged with the duty of making sure races and jai alai are carried out in conformance with rules set down by the Racing Commission in the state where these contests are being held.

STEWARD'S INQUIRY—Situation where stewards suspect infractions of rules during a horse race. Race is not declared official until stewards have studied the film made of the race and have questioned the jockeys or drivers involved. If suspicions are confirmed, violators are disqualified, and a new order of finish is posted.

STOOPERS—Name given to persons looking for valid tickets discarded mistakenly by patrons at a track or fronton. This practice is prohibited by law in most states.

STRAGGLERS—Valid tickets not cashed before the next contest is held, but cashed before the day's business is completed.

STRETCH—The straightaway portion of a race track from the final turn to the finish line.

STRIKE—Term used when a greyhound deliberately interferes with another during the running of a race, and is cited by the stewards. Dog is prohibited from further competition after a designated number of "strikes" have been given.

SULKY (BIKE)—A two-wheeled conveyance carrying the driver and pulled by standardbred horses in harness racing.

TACK—Equipment used in the training and racing of horses; jockeys refer to their helmets, boots, whips, etc., as their "tack."

TACK ROOMS—Name given to rooms in the barn area of a race track in which items necessary for the training and racing of horses are kept.

TEN PERCENTERS—Name given to those signing IRS forms for actual owners of tickets paying off at odds of 300-1 or more, for a share of the pay-off, usually 10%. Practice prohibited by law.

THOROUGHBREDS—A breed of horses registered by recognized Jockey Clubs. Used for racing at a running gait.

TIP SHEETS—Selections of professional handicappers for sale to patrons desiring help in deciding which entry to wager on.

TOUTS—Persons furnishing their selections to patrons in return for a portion of the amount of money collected, should their selections win. Practice discouraged at all tracks and frontons and illegal at most.

TRACK CONDITION—Refers to condition of a track used for racing horses or greyhounds. Conditions vary due to rain or other climatic factors. Examples: fast, sloppy, muddy, heavy, etc.

TRACK KITCHENS—Restaurants located on track property, usually the barn or kennel area, to accommodate only track employees or those licensed to conduct business concerning the track.

TRAINERS—Persons in charge of conditioning horses and dogs in preparation for official races.

TRAINING BIKE—Cart used in training trotters or pacers for harness races. Differs slightly from the sulky used for official races.

TRIPLE CROWN—Term used to describe the three most prestigious stake races for three-year-old thoroughbreds in the U.S. Namely, the "Kentucky Derby", the "Preakness" and the "Belmont Stakes". In recent years, quarter horse racing has a counterpart ending with the famous "All American Futurity".

TROTTER—A standardbred using a trotting gait for harness racing. Trotters move forward in a manner whereby the right front and back left legs move forward simultaneously.

UNDERLAY—A horse or dog whose odds are lower than those estimated by professional handicappers.

UNDERPAY—A case where the price paid winning ticket holders is less than the correct price, do to computer or human error.

UPPER TURN—Designates turn entering the stretch leading to the finish line.

WEIGH IN—Term used for checking a jockey's weight before and after a race. Also used in greyhound racing when checking a dog's weight when being brought to the paddock and before leaving the paddock for the post parade.

WEIGHT LOSERS—Used to describe greyhounds having a history of losing an excessive amount of weight while in the paddock area before actual race time. Weight loss is due to nervousness.

Index